Her Write
HIS NAME

THOEMMES

ACKNOWLEDGEMENTS

The letters contained in this volume are reproduced with the kind permission of the late Alexander R. James and Alexander R. James Jr, The Houghton Library, Harvard; The Schlesinger Library, Radcliffe College; and the Trustees of the National Library of Scotland. The pictures of Alice James are reproduced with the permission of the Houghton Library, Harvard University. I am grateful for all the help I have received from the library staff at the three libraries.

I am grateful to the grants that I have received from the Research Committee of the University of Newcastle upon Tyne which enabled me to visit the three libraries cited above. I am particularly indebted to Mary Kalaugher who undertook some of the hard work of transcription. I have benefited throughout from the insight and wide range of knowledge she brought to the task. Kate Docker has been the most assiduous and patient of editors and I am deeply grateful to her for all her help. Ann Spencer has provided encouragement throughout and my life and my work has been greatly enriched by her wisdom and humour. My greatest debt is to her.

HER LIFE IN LETTERS

Alice James

Edited with a new Introduction by
Linda Anderson

THOEMMES PRESS

© Thoemmes Press 1996

Published in 1996 by
Thoemmes Press
11 Great George Street
Bristol BS1 5RR
England

ISBN 1 85506 387 5

© Introduction by Linda Anderson, 1996

British Library Cataloguing-in-Publication Data

A catalogue record of this title is available
from the British Library

Printed in England by Athenaeum Press Ltd., Newcastle-upon-Tyne

Alice James in Boston, 1873.

INTRODUCTION

THE FAMILY CIRCLE

Alice James was born on 7 August 1848, the fifth and youngest child of Henry James Sr and Mary Walsh James, and their only daughter. Her two eldest brothers achieved enduring fame: William as a philosopher and psychologist, author of *Principles of Psychology* (1890), which established him as America's foremost psychologist; and Henry as one of the most important modern novelists, a 'Shakespeare of the novel' as his biographer Leon Edel has called him.[1] Alice, as daughter, was never given the same encouragement to succeed as her brothers; yet in a family where success may have been a masculine prerogative, failure was not solely a feminine one. Alice also had two other brothers, Garth Wilkinson ('Wilky') and Robertson, who, after fighting for the Unionist cause in the Civil war, drifted unsuccessfully through their lives, unable to find their 'place'. Their attempt to put abolitionist principles into practice by buying and running a plantation in Florida where they employed freed Black men proved financially disastrous: Wilky, always insolvent, suffering from rheumatism and heart disease, died in 1883 at the age of thirty-eight; Robertson like Wilky, moved West after Florida; he worked for the railroad, tried to paint and to write and drank heavily; he seems to have spent most of his life in a state of crisis, dogged by guilt, failure and self-loathing; he died in 1910, the same year as William. In 1889, Alice wrote to her sister-in-law, Alice James, about her youngest brother: 'One must allow... something fine in Bob's attitude, (his detachment from material affairs, his fitting his needs to the supply and refusing to descend to toil and soil in

[1] Preface to Leon Edel, *Henry James: A Life* (London: Collins, 1987).

vii

the grubbing crowd) if one could only *read* about it!'[2] What could justify a life for Alice – and perhaps for all the Jameses – was not so much the living of it as the writing about it. Robertson's crises were not so different, after all, from his elder brothers: what distinguished him was his failure to 'convert' them into an intellectual or artistic record.[3]

What the younger Jameses show simply to a greater degree is the difficulty experienced by all the James children in establishing a career. Henry James Sr, having inherited enough money from his father not to have to work, dedicated his life to intellectual and spiritual inquiry, writing, lecturing and educating his growing family.[4] For the James children what their father actually 'did' was uncertain, even perplexing; he provided at best an eccentric example for them to follow. His advice to them about what they should do with their own lives was similarly obscure and 'impractical'. Between 1855 and 1860 the James family travelled about in Europe and between America and Europe, prompted by the father's 'experimental' approach to his children's education: as a result their schooling was haphazard and their lives unconventional and nomadic. Henry James Jr was to describe them in these early years as 'hotel children'.[5] What their father cared about, according to Henry, was their 'spiritual decency', something which remained vague and unattainable, but not 'our mastery of any art or craft'.[6] For Henry James Sr, particular choices of career could be seen as narrowing, as closing other possibilities for the life of the spirit. The children were expected, according to Henry James Jr, not to 'do' but 'just to be something, something unconnected with specific doing,

---

[2] Alice James to Alice H. James, 5 May 1889, Harvard, MS 1458, see p. 234.

[3] 'Convert' is a typically Jamesian term. See Henry James, 'Notes of a Son and Brother', in *Henry James: An Autobiography* (London: W. H. Allen, 1956), p. 280.

[4] Edel notes that 'there remained something rather ineffectual about him – he could lecture on art, property, on democracy, on theology, but he remained fundamentally aloof from the core of the action'. Edel, p. 10.

[5] 'A Small Boy and Others' in *Henry James: An Autobiography*, p. 19.

[6] *ibid*, p. 126.

something free and uncommitted, something finer in short than being that, whatever it was, might be.'[7] Even Henry, who triumphantly succeeded in turning his father's vague emphasis on the cultivation of the self into an aesthetic creed, could feel at times that as children they had been left in a void.

Both William and Henry, like all the James children, suffered during their lives from depression and from vague illnesses or 'obscure hurts' which were certainly partly psycho-somatic, the symptoms of a complex – and sometimes painful – family dynamic.[8] William decided to 'will' his own recovery in 1870, refusing to become the sick self which haunted him, but it was not until 1878, at the age of thirty-six, when he married and left home, that his problems finally abated.[9] Henry suffered from a series of minor ailments which he documented in detail in his letters home, as well as the 'handicap' of a bad back.[10] Jean Strouse has drawn attention to the way illness became part of the economics of the James family – literally so, since one of the recognized cures for illness within the family were restorative – and expensive – trips abroad.[11] In 1868, William wrote from Europe, deploring the slowness of his own recovery from back problems: 'I somehow feel as if I were cheating Henry of his birthright by staying here all this time.'[12] Henry, however, proved he could look after himself, having his own way of manipulating the family coffers. Accounting to his mother for his somewhat lavish expenditure whilst travelling in Europe in 1870, Henry pleaded – predictably enough – ill health: 'My

---

[7] 'Notes of a Son and Brother', p. 268.

[8] The phrase 'obscure hurt' belongs to Henry James and he used it to refer to the injury he received in 1861. See Edel, pp. 57–61.

[9] For William James's description of the crisis he underwent in 1870 and his hallucinatory memory of an epileptic patient see *Varieties of Religious Experience* (New York: Longman, Green and Company, 1902), pp. 160–61.

[10] For a discussion of whether Henry James's back problems related to his earlier 'obscure hurt' see Edel, pp. 60–61.

[11] See Jean Strouse, *Alice James: A Biography* (London: Bantam Books, 1982), pp. 121–2.

[12] Quoted in Strouse, p. 121.

being unwell has kept me constantly from attempting in any degree to rough it. I have lived at the best hotels and done things in the most comfortable way.'[13] Alice also seemed to recognize the advantages that illness could bring when, talking about future trips to New York, she confided to her friend Sara Sedgwick in 1874 that her mother 'was constantly throwing out dark and mysterious hints upon the necessity of economy' and that since she was 'in a very robust condition of health' she could not 'wriggle out there'.[14] At this particular moment Alice seems to have been unwilling to trade her health for special financial treatment.

If illness could justify trips away from the family, however, it also sustained the family interdependence, particularly the close bonds that existed between William, Henry and Alice. Jacqueline Rose has suggested that these three were constantly 'transferring' their symptoms to each other, balancing out between them their conjoined fund of weakness and strength.[15] In 1869 Henry James wrote to his father that he had 'invented a theory' that his present 'degenerescence' was 'the result of Alice and Willy getting better and locating some of their diseases on me – so as to propitiate the fates by not turning the poor homeless infirmities out of the family'.[16] Alice developed a similar theory to explain her own 'want of intelligence'. In 1867 she wrote to William that he 'must remember' that 'as she is your sister, her having so little mind may account for your having so much'.[17] Later, Alice, having made illness her 'career' and provided a home to the family infirmity, at times questioned how secure the brothers were in their success and well-being. When he heard of her impending death William wrote to her of 'the inscrutable

---

[13] Leon Edel (ed.), *Henry James: Letters*, 3 vols. (London: Macmillan, 1974), vol. 1, p. 197.

[14] Alice James to Sara Sedgwick, 25 March 1874, Harvard, MS 1430, see pp. 63–4.

[15] 'Jeffrey Masson and Alice James' in 'Sexual Difference', *Oxford Literary Review*, vol. 8 (1986), pp. 185–92, (p. 190).

[16] *Henry James: Letters*, vol. 1, pp. 157–8.

[17] Alice James to William James, 6 August 1867, Harvard, MS 1470, see p. 19.

and mysterious character of the doom of nervous weakness which has chained you down for all these years'.[18] Alice had already perceived that, in terms of the uncanny logic of the family system, she could pose a danger to her brothers if her illness could be reversed, turned back on them. There was also a serious warning contained in her seemingly flippant comment to William in 1890 that he should 'arm yourself against my dawn, which may at any moment cast you and Henry into obscurity'.[19] If Alice was imprisoned by an 'inscrutable and mysterious...weakness', it was also possible that its 'character' bore a strong family likeness.

Yet however much Alice shared with her brothers, participating in the 'experimental' trips to Europe and the intellectual and emotional intensity of family life, as a girl her life was inevitably different. As Jean Strouse points out, whilst the boys went away to various schools or were allowed to roam the streets of Geneva, London, or Paris, Alice's interests were expected to be more sedate and domestic.[20] Alice had certainly received encouragement within the context of her family to use the same language of subjecthood as her brothers, to view her own perceptions as both significant and singular. She wrote in her *Diary* in 1889, using the family philosophy to her own advantage: 'How grateful I am that I actually do see, to my own consciousness, the quarter of an inch that my eyes fall upon; truly, the subject is all that counts!'[21] 'If experience consists of impressions, it may be said impressions are experience' her novelist brother was to similarly – and famously – assert as part of his artistic manifesto.[22] Alice, however, also had another bitter lesson to learn, the highly contradictory one, that as a female subject she scarcely counted at all. 'By what process of logical

---

[18] Quoted in Strouse, p. 335.

[19] Alice James to William James, 16 March 1890, Harvard, MS 1490, see p. 256.

[20] Strouse, p. 45.

[21] Leon Edel (ed.), *The Diary of Alice James* (Harmondsworth: Penguin, 1964), p. 31.

[22] 'The Art of Fiction' by Henry James, in Leon Edel (ed.), *The House of Fiction: Essays on the Novel* by Henry James (London: Rupert Hart-Davis, 1957), p. 33.

accretion was this slight "personality", the mere shade of an intelligent but presumptuous girl to find herself endowed with the high attributes of a Subject?'[23] What for her brother Henry James could be presented dispassionately as an artistic problem was for Alice the real tragedy of her life.

For all the unconventionality of the James household, as a girl Alice was brought up in strictly conventional terms. 'To be a James and a girl...was a contradiction in terms', Jean Strouse has commented, drawing attention to the impossibility for Alice of reconciling the freedom which was part of the family rhetoric with the limited possibilities of her life.[24] It is an idea with which Henry at least would have agreed: 'In our family group girls seem scarcely to have had a chance.'[25] For Henry James Sr, women were seen as fulfilling themselves through their nurture and care of men: they were 'by nature' pure and self-sacrificing:

> The very virtue of woman, her practical sense, which leaves her indifferent to past and future alike, and keeps her the busy blessing of the present hour, disqualifies her for all didactic dignity. Learning and wisdom do not become her.... Her aim in life is...simply to love and bless man.[26]

Behind the language of idealization and the extolling of women's virtue is the notion that they are 'purely' at the disposal of men. Her destiny already determined, the woman lives without past or future, without access to history or aspiration, as a human subject.

Unfortunately for Alice her mother Mary seems to have had no difficulty moulding herself to fit Henry Sr's ideas. A successful 'Angel in the House' she was revered by all the family for her saintly, selfless devotion. In 1891, just three months before her own death, Alice, in her *Diary*, was still paying homage to her mother's memory, a memory seemingly

---

[23] Preface to *Portrait of a Lady* in R. P. Blackmur (ed.), *The Art of the Novel* (London: Charles Scribner, 1935), p. 48.

[24] Quoted in Strouse, p. xvi.

[25] *ibid.*

[26] 'Woman and the Woman's Movement', *Putnam's Monthly*, vol. 1 (March 1853), pp. 279–88, quoted in Strouse, p. 47.

intensified at the time of her mother's death when 'all personal claim on her vanished'. Since then, Alice writes, 'she has dwelt in my mind a beautiful illumined memory, the essence of divine maternity from which I was to learn great things, give all, but ask nothing'.[27] Reading between the lines, it seems significant that Alice's recognition of her mother occurs once she is no longer there to meet but, more likely, frustrate, her daughter's needs. Unconsciously Alice also raises the question, if her mother's lesson to her was to 'ask nothing' what was her mother actually required to give. Her brother Henry introduced similar doubts in his autobiography. Whilst remembering her 'complete availability' his 'only' question 'was the possibility of a selflessness so consistently and unabately active... having anything left acutely to offer'.[28] Mary's selflessness was a powerful force within the family, and seems to have produced in everyone a profound sense of indebtedness. It may also have been indistinguishable for her children, whatever they were taught to think, from absence, control or even selfishness. Lilla Cabot, who became the wife of Henry's close friend Thomas Sergent Perry ('Sargy'), and herself a visitor to the James household in her youth, adds an interesting gloss on the idealized picture of their mother which emerges in the writing of the James children: 'James's mother (even to my own perception as a child) was the very incarnation of banality and his aunt Miss Walsh who lived with them was not much better.'[29] Being 'good' for Alice meant trying to emulate her mother; trying to live up to her may also have meant, however, paring herself down, having to disavow her own intelligence and imagination. Not much wonder Alice at times 'wickedly' enjoyed her own sinfulness and retained a healthy awareness of how too much 'goodness' was bad for you. 'Original sin is my only refuge, I was born bad and I never have recovered', she joked to her friend Sara Sedgwick in 1874. Lilla Perry – who had her own unflattering opinion of the James household – is here criticized because she

---

[27] *The Diary of Alice James*, p. 221.

[28] 'Notes of a Son and Brother', p. 343.

[29] Quoted in Strouse, p. 46.

'rams her moral perfection down your throat' which for Alice is 'a little more than my imperfect digestion can stand'. It is in this same letter that Alice makes her most overt allusion to feelings of resentment towards her family. She writes longingly to Sara: 'I am strongly tempted to abandon virtue when I think of thee as a companion in vice and of the little parental encouragement which I receive.'[30] Alice had reason enough to doubt whether goodness could in fact produce its own rewards.

LOVE AND SICKNESS

Alice never married and therefore never established a home of her own in which she could, like her mother, exercise power. Although she mocks the idea that women 'ought to stay at home in a constant state of matrimonial expectation', in reality there was little encouragement for her to do anything else. 'Matrimony' she writes at the same time 'seems the only successful occupation that a woman can undertake.'[31]

Her world, as her early letters reveal, revolved relentlessly around engagements and marriage. One party she attends she deems 'not eminently successful' because of a 'scarcity of the male sex, to which on social occasions, whether we have the vote or not, we are and shall always be slaves'.[32] This scarcity was part of a general historical problem: war and the shifting of population westwards meant that by 1870 there was a huge 'surplus' of women in New England and that the number of marriages had decreased significantly.[33] As Alice accurately reflected in 1873 'matrimony is...a forlorn hope in these parts'.[34] Yet spinsterhood still constituted failure and

[30] Alice James to Sara Sedgwick, 25 March 1874, Harvard, MS 1430, p. 65.

[31] Alice James to Annie Ashburner, 12 April 1876, The National Library of Scotland, MS, p. 88.

[32] Alice James to Annie Ashburner, 14 March 1875, The National Library of Scotland, MS, see p. 80.

[33] See Strouse, p. 94: 'By 1870...the number of "extra women" in Massachusetts was up to 50,000; and by 1880 it had reached 66,000.'

[34] Alice James to Annie Ashburner, 4 May 1873, The National Library of

however much she employed wit and irony to defend herself, by the age of twenty-six Alice felt herself to have been passed over by men and perhaps, as a consequence, by life. Having heard that 'such ragged growth' as the Loverings have had 'no end of offers' she jocularly turns it into an explanation for why an 'exotic' like she 'is left unplucked upon its stem, to reach a bloom bordering, to put it delicately, on the full-blown'.[35] Two years later she is more wistful and sombre to her friend Annie Ashburner: 'Don't you love to hear of successful engagements, it always sends a thrill of joy thro' me, altho' my own turn I am afraid will never come on this side of the grave.'[36]

Alice reveals a serious attraction to only one man in her letters, the 'beautiful' and 'seductive', Mr Charley Jackson, her friend Fanny Morse's cousin. Unfortunately his affections were committed elsewhere and Alice had to concede that it would be 'altogether wild in me to nourish the faintest hope'. Meeting her rival she admitted she is 'not bad looking'. 'I refrained from looking in the glass for some time after I got home', she writes to her friend Annie. 'It's most inconvenient to be possessed of so tender and apparently undesired an organ.'[37] Yet Alice was at best equivocal about what success with men would imply. Though she is pleased when one friend acquires a 'feminine softness' through marriage that she seemed to lack before,[38] another acquaintance is satirized as 'a joy to the masculine mind for she is the embodiment of all their pet theories about women'.[39] Femininity, she suggests, means becoming secondary or subordinate, becoming a

Scotland, MS, see p. 33.

[35] Alice James to Sara Sedgwick, 16 February 1874, Harvard, MS 1429, p. 59.

[36] Alice James to Annie Ashburner 12 April 1876, The National Library of Scotland, MS, p. 89.

[37] Alice James to Annie Ashburner, 26 December 1875, The National Library of Scotland, MS, p. 83.

[38] Alice James to Annie Ashburner, 19 October 1873, The National Library of Scotland, MS, p. 41.

[39] Alice James to Sara Sedgwick, 23 September 1876, Harvard, MS 1433, p. 91.

mirror of male desire. In her own case, as she wrote to her brother William in 1886, her failure could be seen as a failure to take up this passive, 'receptive attitude' in relation to men, 'that cardinal virtue in women, the absence of which has always made me so uncharming to and so uncharmed by the male sex'.[40] Does her lack of the 'cardinal virtue' constitute weakness or strength, Alice asks; have men rejected her or has she rejected men. Alice was perhaps never sure but was at the same time unwilling to attribute totally to herself what she saw as failure and inadequacy on the part of men.

The only alternative vocation to marriage that Alice found whilst she lived in Cambridge was as one of the history tutors for Miss Ticknor's Society to Encourage Studies at Home, a correspondence course for women which, whilst not radical, did have the aim of including women of all classes in its programme. Alice was an enthusiastic advocate: 'We who have had all our lives more books than we know what to do with', she wrote to her friend Annie Ashburner, 'can't conceive of the feeling that people have who have been shut out from them always.'[41] It is, she assures her 'what I care about most just now'. Yet she was also prepared for her friends' mockery: 'You can laugh and think me as much of a humbug as you choose, you can't do more than I have myself.'[42] A letter the next year suggests that she may well have been justified in her fears about how they would respond. She writes to Annie Ashburner only half jokingly: 'I am deeply hurt at your ridicule of my professorial character I assure you it is not a thing to be laughed at some day you may be only too happy to sit at my feet.'[43] Alice clearly found it hard to take herself entirely seriously in a role which others found odd or risible. Mention of the Society dies out

---

[40] Alice James to William James, 3–7 January 1886, Harvard, MS 1474, p. 133.

[41] Alice James to Annie Ashburner, 28 February 1877, The National Library of Scotland, MS, p. 95.

[42] Alice James to Annie Ashburner, 26 December 1875, The National Library of Scotland, MS, p. 84.

[43] Alice James to Annie Ashburner, 12 April 1876, The National Library of Scotland, MS, p. 89.

in her letters shortly afterwards.

However Alice was to date one enduring change in her life from this era. It was through the Society that her friendship with Katharine Loring developed – she had met her first in 1873. By the late seventies Katharine had become Alice's more or less constant companion. In 1879 Alice extolled Katharine to her friend Sara as 'a most wonderful being' who 'has all the mere brute superiority which distinguishes man from woman combined with all the distinctive feminine virtues'.[44] To Fanny she wrote two months later: 'She is a phenomenal being and no one knows what she has been and done for me these trying months I have been through.'[45] Katharine, it seems, could be represented with bravado to friends – perhaps particularly to married friends – as being as good as a man but without any compromise to her femininity. She could also successfully compete as (with) a virtuous, all-giving mother. Alice had found a relationship in which she could be dependent without having to surrender herself to male power. Henry was to observe Alice and Katharine in England with a mixture of gratitude for Katharine's faithful care of Alice and anxiety about the intensity of an involvement which somehow also seemed to require Alice's invalidism. He wrote to Aunt Kate in 1885 that 'a devotion so perfect and generous as K. L.'s is a gift of providence' but that in any case there was 'about as much possibility of Alice's giving Katharine up as of giving her legs to be sawed off'.[46] Unconsciously Henry makes the connection he fears: had Alice already given up to Katharine the capacity to stand on her own two feet? Yet he also recognized that a 'definite understanding' had been arrived at between them which he could not but respect.[47] Their commitment to each other is corroborated by the poignant note Katharine was to write to Fanny Morse, after Alice's death, on the 1 June 1892, the

---

[44] Alice James to Sara (Sedgwick) Darwin, 9 August 1879, Harvard, MS 1435, p. 106.

[45] Alice James to Frances Morse, 7 October 1879, Radcliffe College, MS, p. 109.

[46] Henry James to Catherine Walsh, 12 May 1885, quoted in Strouse, p. 266.

[47] Henry James to Catherine Walsh, 17 May 1885, quoted in Strouse, p. 265.

anniversary of her first meeting Alice, an anniversary she
reveals that she and Alice had always kept, 'unknown to
any'.[48]

What was the nature of their relationship? William's wife,
at least, seems to have harboured the suspicion that they
were lovers.[49] This, however, is the only direct contemporary
naming of something which we can otherwise only detect
hovering between the lines of Henry's nervousness and Alice's
enthusiasm. The problem for us reading the letters now, is
neither to attribute an inappropriate – and sexualized –
meaning to what was, for the time, a 'normal' romantic
friendship,[50] nor to deny to nineteenth-century women the
possibility of any 'libidinal self-awareness'[51] – whether acted
upon or not – within the terms of this intense bonding. For
Alice, of course, the embodiment of her desires, and not only
sexual ones, remained a problem throughout her life which
she dealt with by literally making her body the problem.
Within their relationship Alice's tremulous and reluctant body
becomes as much the focus of Katharine's attention as it is of
Alice's: it becomes both the joke and the anxiety that they
share. 'The excellent and prosaic Katharine', as Alice terms
her in a letter to Sara, has an important role to fulfil on their
trip to the Adirondacks in 1879 in shielding her from the
effects of 'Nature'. 'K. ... would insist upon inserting a
hideous rubber blanket between my fair form and all the
mossy logs ... thereby putting a cruel barrier between me and
all the dear little crawlers.'[52] Later Katharine will collaborate

---

[48] Katharine Loring to Frances Morse, 1 June 1892, MS Schlesinger Library,
Radcliffe College.

[49] See Strouse, p. 220.

[50] See Lillian Faderman, *Surpassing the Love of Men: Romantic Friendship
and Love Between Women from the Renaissance to the Present* (London:
Junction Books, 1981), who argues that 'romantic' friendship was a
'normal' part of women's experience until it was pathologized and
sexualized at the turn of the century.

[51] This phrase is Terry Castle's in *The Apparitional Lesbian: Female
Homosexuality and Modern Culture* (New York: Columbia University
Press, 1993), p. 10, who argues, against Faderman, that a belief in women's
'innocence' before 1900 may be both wrong and condescending.

[52] Alice James to Sara Sedgwick, 9 August 1879, Harvard, MS 1435, p. 105.

with Alice in creating a tough, protective covering for her vulnerability: Alice, ensconced in the sickroom, becomes a stoic who transcends her body, even as it demands from them both constant acts of attention. 'Alice begs me to remember to tell you that she does not suffer all the time and I assure you that we have much joking', Katharine was to write to William, when Alice's illness was diagnosed as fatal in 1891.[53] Yet the mutual obsession with Alice's illness should not detract from the energy Katharine's presence also undoubtedly releases, a rumbustious enjoyment which pits itself against the puritanical and conventional, and which might well signal eroticism. One acquaintance, 'a Leamington spinster', becomes the subject of a mutual joke as Alice reports in her *Diary*: 'Although fifty years of age [she] embodied still, as K. said, the Wordsworthian maiden, having that wearying quality which always oozes from attenuated purity.'[54] 'Oh Lord, how thankful I am I didn't take to refined spinsterhood', Alice remarks to her sister-in law in 1890.[55] The relationship between Alice and Katharine was based, at least in part, on their shared aversion to this fate.

Alice, we could say, suffered all her life from having nothing to do. Her early letters provide a vivid record of the frustration and emptiness of her life, of her entrapment within the polite conventions of visits and sociality, which formed a kind of prolonged waiting period from which only marriage could release her. Her two major breakdowns occurred at crisis points in her life when the sense of her exclusion from life became unbearable. The first was significantly at the age of fourteen, when she was entering into womanhood. Alice returned to this time in her *Diary*, poignantly registering the gap between her hopes and the monotonous reality of the life that awaited her: 'How I recall the low grey Newport sky in that winter of 1862–3 as I used to wander about over the cliffs, my young soul struggling out of its swaddling-clothes

---

[53] Katharine Loring to William James, 30 July 1891, Harvard, MS 1492, p. 264.

[54] *The Diary of Alice James*, p. 173.

[55] Alice James to Alice H. James, 9 January 1890, Harvard, MS 1460, p. 250.

as the knowledge crystallized within me of what Life meant for me, one simple, single and before which all mystery vanished.'[56] Alice's breakdown in 1878, the same year as her brother William's marriage, and the year after the engagement and marriage of two of her closest friends, Sara Sedgwick and Annie Ashburner, seems also to have been born out of the recognition of fading hopes for herself. In this sense her current losses merely stimulated a loss – the loss of self – that had already occurred. In her *Diary* she referred to how she faced 'a ceaseless possible horror, since that hideous summer of '78'. Earlier Alice had noted her 'never-ceasing belief in and longing for action, relentlessly denied, all safety-valves shut down in the way of "the busy ineffectiveness of women"'. What is horrible is the unchanging nature of her life; in the face of a 'ceaseless' emptiness, her life feels ended before it has begun. 'The fact is', she wrote, 'I have been dead so long...that now it's only the shrivelling of an empty pea pod that has to be completed.'

What Alice did was to become ill. In a sense Alice displaced the battle against her fate into a battle within her own body: hysterical illness became the literal embodiment of the pain her female role inflicted on her, and at the same time, a way of escaping the sense of failure and frustration she endured.[57] As a hysteric she could be said to have performed her own distress in order to gain some control over it; by acting out her passivity and fragility, she also, in a tortuous way, liberated herself from them. Through an act of splitting, she could, by giving her body over to illness, engage in a never-ending struggle against it: whilst her body was prostrated by her feminine weakness, her mind and will could be alive to a masculine sense of power. In a letter to her brother William, despite her illness – and the fullness of the account she gives it – she can 'simmer with a Goethian like sense of my own

---

[56] *The Diary of Alice James*, p. 151; p. 230.

[57] See Caroll Smith-Rosenberg's 'The Hysterical Woman: Sex Roles and Role Conflict in Nineteenth-Century America' in *Disorderly Conduct* (Oxford University Press, 1985), pp. 197–216 for a discussion of the ambiguities of hysteria.

superiority'.[58] As usual with William, Alice both elicits and repudiates his sympathy at the same time.

Alice died just some three years before Freud and Breuer published their *Studies in Hysteria*. At the end of her life Alice experimented with hypnotism and seems to have received through it a tantalizing glimpse of the 'therapeutic possibilities' of the future.[59] One of the issues which Alice's eloquent accounts of her condition raises is precisely that broached by psychoanalysis – how to understand it, how to find a language which is adequate to the suffering – and joy – of the female body. For Freud and Breuer the solution to hysteria was for the patient to tell their own story; the hysteric 'suffered from reminiscences' because she had forgotten the past; she had to be released, through psychoanalytic intervention, from memory into memory, from unconscious forgetting into the order of narrative; illness became a set of symptoms to be interpreted and the hysterical body a mute witness to the story yet to be told.[60]

Alice's relentless search for a cure took her from one 'great man' to another, constantly repeating the same pattern of hopes raised only to be eventually disappointed. Alice, it seems, looked for a cure but justified (or repeated) the paradigmatic patterning of her life by resisting it. Her illness defeated her doctors and it would be hard to avoid the supposition from her letters that that was, indeed, part of the point: 'My doctor turned out as usual a fiasco an unprincipled one too', she wrote to her aunt Kate on one occasion. 'The truth was', she went on in the same letter, 'he was entirely puzzled about me and had not the manliness to say so.'[61] In her *Diary*, almost at the end of her life, she compared Katharine's

---

[58] Alice James to William James, 3–7 January 1886, Harvard, MS 1474, p. 133.

[59] *The Diary of Alice James*, p. 222.

[60] See Josef Breuer and Sigmund Freud, 'Preliminary Communication' in *Studies in Hysteria, The Pelican Freud Library* (Harmondsworth: Penguin, 1974), vol. 3, p. 58.

[61] Alice James to Catherine Walsh, 31 January 1885, Harvard, MS 1532, p. 128.

female qualities of 'watchfulness, patience and untiring resource' with 'the British Doctor' and 'the spectacle of impotent paralysis he presents'.[62] Psychoanalysis could perhaps supply keys to the transferential relationship that Alice engaged in with her doctors, the continual acting out of frustration and anger, and yet like Freud's most famous hysterical patient, Dora, Alice also seems to be contesting masculine knowledge and the way it depends upon making 'her' its object. Like Dora, Alice reflects back to her interpreters their own limits and uncertainties, transferring the 'real' paralysis to them; she suggests the way femininity exceeds or escapes male discourse by speaking, through her body, a language which the men do not understand.

Yet Alice's life hardly suggests triumph: her suffering also undoubtedly illustrates the impossibility of a subjecthood refusing or refused access to the symbolic, 'driven back to stagger alone under the monstrous mass of subjective sensations'.[63] Alice's dilemma became how to live a life which had no meaning, no structure or symbolic sanction: how to live without the 'scaffolding'[64] she required to build a home in the symbolic. Increasingly it was death she looked to not just as an end but as providing a sense of culmination to her life, a cure to uncertainty, giving shape and meaning through its finality. Having received the diagnosis of cancer in 1891, she wrote in her *Diary* that it had brought her 'enormous relief' by 'lifting us out the formless vague and setting us within the very heart of the sustaining concrete'.[65] A verifiable disease gave a 'real' explanation for her suffering whilst death instituted her within a narrative of which she could be the subject. 'Having it to look forward to for a while', Alice wrote in her *Diary*, 'seems to double the value of the event, for one becomes suddenly picturesque to oneself, and one's wavering little individuality stands out with a cameo effect'.[66] Alice,

---

[62] *The Diary of Alice James*, p. 225.

[63] *ibid.*, p. 206.

[64] *ibid.*, p. 56.

[65] *ibid.*, p. 207.

[66] *ibid.*, p. 208.

staging her own death in her *Diary*, became an actor in her own life for the first time; paradoxically her death could become the dramatic event which her life had always lacked. At last, she had perhaps even succeeded in upstaging her famous brothers:

> Within the last year he [Henry] has published *The Tragic Muse*, brought out *The American*, and written a play, *Mrs Vibert*...and his admirable comedy; combined with William's Psychology, not a bad show for one family! especially if I get myself dead, the hardest job of all.[67]

LITERARY REMAINS

Yet Alice did succeed in making her life memorable. For the last three years of her life she kept a *Diary*, unknown to anyone but Katharine and her nurse, which was privately published, thanks to Katharine's commitment and strength of will, after her death. Henry on discovering its existence found it both a surprise and an embarrassment: he opposed its publication on the grounds of his own implication in Alice's many 'indiscretions'. (His need for privacy also led him to destroy many of his own letters and papers). Yet it also prompted him, to pay tribute to his sister as both a 'character' and a writer. In 1894 he wrote to William:

> I have been immensely impressed with the thing as a revelation of a moral and personal picture. It is heroic in its individuality, its independence – its face-to-face with the universe for-and-by herself – and the beauty and eloquence with which she often expresses this, let alone the rich irony and humour, constitute (I wholly agree with you) a new claim for the family renown.

He also went on in the same letter to comment perceptively on Alice's life and illness that

> the extraordinary intensity of her will and personality really would have made the equal, the reciprocal life of a 'well' person – in the usual world – almost impossible to her – so

[67] *The Diary of Alice James*, p. 211.

that her disastrous, her tragic health was in a manner the only solution for her of the practical problem of life – as it suppressed the element of equality, reciprocity, etc.[68]

Paradoxically Alice's illness, as Henry noted, may have had something to do with survival.

The *Diary* occupied as writing a private, intermediate space: it could be said to be a rehearsal for the authorship she never publicly claimed, though may have privately coveted.[69] As a document it performs itself for an audience and seems to have contributed to Alice's creation for herself of a witty, often acerbic, public persona. Though the *Diary* does contain some intimate reflections on Alice's life and illness, in it she mostly turns outwards, commenting on public affairs – particularly the Irish question – and pondering the themes of national and cultural difference between America and England. She is also a stylist, using language in a slightly distanced way, self-consciously playing with words.[70] Latterly many thoughts and expressions pass between the *Diary* and the letters and her letters, in the last years of her life, seem to have collaborated in the same process of establishing her more authoritatively as a person and a writer.

However the letters, written throughout her life, are inevitably more discontinuous and fragmented than the *Diary*, since they were destined for many different readers, and as a consequence assume a variety of styles. They also fulfil a different function: as 'an extension of daily life'[71] they are part of a real process of exchange between family and friends and the words can have effects and consequences as perhaps no other form of writing can. In this way they provide evidence of the way, and the terms on which, Alice sought and was given 'reciprocity', the kind of relations she had with others

---

[68] Henry James, *Letters*, vol. 3, p. 481.

[69] See Strouse, p. 353.

[70] For a discussion of the *Diary* see Linda Anderson, *Woman and Autobiography in the Twentieth Century: Remembered Futures* (Hemel Hempstead: Harvester Wheatsheaf, 1996), pp. 15–41.

[71] See Mireille Bossis, 'Methodological Journeys through Correspondences' in *Yale French Studies*, no. 71 (1986), pp. 63–75, (p. 64).

and with the world. Letters are vehicles of manipulation which do not necessarily tell the 'truth' and must be read in context. They also to a degree escape the isolation of authorship since a letter always addresses but also contains the other as both destination and desire.

Alice had three main friends with whom she corresponded: Frances Morse, Sara Sedgwick and Annie Ashburner. With each she expressed herself slightly differently: though there are difficulties in attempting generalizations, on the whole we could say Alice could take risks with Annie which she could not take with Sara whilst she could express more neediness to Fanny. With all these correspondents there is a greater simplicity and emotional openness than there is in the letters to her family with whom a more complicated and conflicted dynamic is being played out.

Yet letters are also about absence and Alice's letters often take their occasion from the absence of friends on trips abroad or her own prolonged 'absence' in England in her last years. Her early letters to her friends express longing and loss and are part of an attempt to assuage distance; once in England the distance works differently: there is less regret expressed to her abandoned family, William and Aunt Kate, than the confident assumption of a space for herself and her own voice. In many ways the 'space' of the letters seems to have suited Alice: she was good at the informality and assumed spontaneity that letter writing requires. She could amuse, respond, tell stories in her letters and appear to 'speak'. However a letter also offers a natural defence against spontaneity and against the other's invasiveness and Alice's writing about her illness in her letters suggests this same ambivalence. She could offer her body in her writing but on the terms she defined; the body could become part of a tender exchange but it could also be withheld and discounted. Letters allowed Alice to commune with others whilst preserving her independence and separateness. The letters do not just provide important evidence about Alice's life; they also undoubtedly are an important part of her life.

Linda Anderson
University of Newcastle, 1996

SELECT BIBLIOGRAPHY

Anderson, Linda, 'Alice James: "The Subject is all that counts" in *Women and Autobiography in the Twentieth Century* (Hemel Hempstead: Harvester Wheatsheaf, 1996), pp. 15–41.

Boudreau, Kristin, '"A Barnum Monstrosity": Alice James and the Spectacle of Sympathy', *American Literature*, vol. 65 (1993), pp. 53–67.

Bronfen, Elizabeth, *Over Her Dead Body: Death, Femininity and the Aesthetic* (Manchester University Press, 1992), pp. 384–92.

Capello, Mary, 'Alice James: Neither Dead Nor Recovered', *American Imago*, vol. 45 (1988), pp. 127–62.

Cargill, Oscar, 'The Turn of the Screw and Alice James', *PMLA*, vol. 78 (1963), pp. 238–49.

Jacobsen, Joanne, 'Resistance and Subversion in the Letters of Alice James', *Biography*, vol. 14 (1991), pp. 366–78.

Jacobus, Mary, 'Hysterics Suffer Mainly from Reminiscence' in *Reading Woman: Essays in Feminist Criticism* (New York: Columbia University Press, 1986), pp. 249–74.

Ramussen, Barbara, 'Alice James and the Question of Women's Exile', *Renaissance and Modern Studies*, vol. 34 (1991), pp. 45–63.

Rose, Jacqueline, 'Jeffrey Masson and Alice James', *The Oxford Literary Review*, vol. 8 (1986), pp. 185–92.

Strouse, Jean, *Alice James: A Biography* (New York: Bantam Books, 1982).

Walker, Nancy, '"Wider than the Sky": Public Presence and Private Self in Dickinson, James and Woolf' in Shari Benstock (ed.), *The Private Self: Theory and Practice of Women's Autobiographical Writings* (London: Routledge, 1988), pp. 272–303.

Yeazell, Ruth Bernard, *The Death and Letters of Alice James* (Berkeley: University of California Press, 1981).

A NOTE ON THE TEXT

The bulk of Alice James's letters are amongst the James family
letters in the Houghton Library, Harvard University. I have
also included a substantial number of letters from Alice's
correspondence with Annie Ashburner, later Richards, which
is housed in the National Library of Scotland, Edinburgh.[1]
There are also a small number of letters amongst the Morse
papers which are held in the Schlesinger Library, Radcliffe
College. This edition of Alice James's letters almost doubles
the number that have so far been published and constitutes
about two thirds of her total extant correspondence. In
particular it makes available many letters which Alice wrote
before she settled in England and provides a more substantial
record of her early life.[2] The justification for publishing
letters that seem to repeat information contained in others is
to show both the continuity and variations in Alice's letter
writing and to enable the reader to consider the letters – and
indeed her whole correspondence – not just in terms of
documentation for her life – but as texts in and for themselves.
Each letter, of course, has its own addressee and it is often
interesting and significant to note what she can say to one and
not another as well as to be aware of how she says it. The
difficulty of reading her correspondence as a text is the same
as that attaining all collections of letters. There is an element
of chance about what has survived and what has not and we
cannot know what is missing. There are no letters to

---

[1] I have incorporated the individual catalogue number for each letter from
the Harvard University collection into the text. The general catalogue
number for the collection is MS Am 1094. The catalogue number for
Alice's letters in The National Library of Scotland is MS 20367.

[2] Ruth Bernard Yeazell's meticulous edition of Alice James's letters concentrated on the later part of Alice's life. See Ruth Bernard Yeazell (ed.), *The
Death and Letters of Alice James* (Berkeley: University of California Press,
1981).

Katharine Loring, for example, or to her brother Henry, arguably the two most significant people in her life.[3] Similarly there are no surviving letters from the important period of time that Alice spent abroad in 1872. The reader is also dependent on the editor's judgement as to what may or may not be important or interesting enough to include. The selection here is, it is hoped, broad enough to be representative, but all the above factors may make it hazardous to talk about Alice's correspondence as a totality.

The letters have been edited to be read as easily as possible whilst trying to preserve Alice's style. All obvious abbreviations such as wd., cd., etc, have been lengthened and & has been reproduced as 'and'. This applies throughout apart from the salutation at the end of the letter where Alice's own formulation has been reproduced. Punctuation has been added where it has been necessary for the sense. Square brackets have been used to denote an uncertainty about transcription or any doubts as to the dating of a letter. All other blanks and brackets are Alice's own. Footnotes have been kept to a minimum and I have tried where possible to recover the maiden names of Alice's married women friends and have experienced the difficulty and frustration of being able to track so many women only through the biographies of their husbands. However finding information about all Alice's friends and acquaintances, particularly the women, has not been possible and the search has provided ample demonstration of the invisibility of women's lives, an invisibility, however, which it is hoped this edition of Alice James's letters, and the record of her own and other women's lives it provides, will help to lessen.

[3] Henry observed to William after Alice died that he had received very few letters from Alice so that this absence, at least, may not be the result of Henry's need to destroy correspondence. Henry James to William James, 28 May 1894, *The Letters of Henry James*, vol. 3, p. 481.

THE AMERICAN LETTERS
1860–1884

THE AMERICAN LETTERS
1860–1884

To Henry James Sr [Harvard, MS 1467]

Sunday, 11 March 1860[1]

My dear Father

We have had two dear letters from you, and find you are the same dear old good-for-nothing home-sick papa as ever.

Willie is in a very extraordinary state of mind, composing odes to all the family. A warlike one he addressed to Aunt Kate,[2] in which the hero is her husband and dies for her, and he says, 'The idea of any one dying for her'!! And he wants mother to take them in to Mrs Thomas and Mrs Osbourn to be read, and admired by them.[3]

We have all come to the conclusion that he is fit to go to the lunatic asylum, so make haste home before such an unhappy event takes place.

We are all very well except Mrs Thomas who was not down to dinner yesterday.

We have given up our play as it is not a pretty one and is

---

[1] This is Alice James's earliest surviving letter, written when she was eleven. The James family was at this time settled in Geneva. Henry James Sr had departed for Paris and London in December, in order to study and write, leaving his family behind.

[2] Mrs Catherine Walsh (1812–1889), the younger sister of Alice's mother, Mary Walsh James, lived with or near the James family, sharing their travels and frequently called in as nurse to one or other of the children. She married Captain Charles Marshall in 1853 but it proved a 'frightful mistake' and in 1855 she resumed her life as companion to the James family.

[3] Other residents of the Hotel de l'Ecu in Geneva where the James family were staying.

too hard. Good-bye. I will try and be good and sweet till you come back, and merit the daisy curtains, and get a chance at your dear old pâté again.

Your affectionate daughter
Alice James

[All Alice's *own composition* apart from the first sentence. She wanted to be started.][4]

To Frances Morse[5]   [Harvard, MS 1496]

13 Ashburton Place, Boston

4 February 1866

My dear old Fanny

Mary delighted me this morning by coming in before church and bringing a letter from you to me.[6] We all think that you must be slightly deranged for your strange affection for your state room can be accounted for in no other way. I am so glad that you were not sick and that you had such a fine voyage. Father was very much amused to hear from you in Sackville Street, as it was the first place he went to the first time he went abroad a long while ago. It seems so strange to think how little things change there compared with here. The greatest piece of news I have to tell is that Willy James got home late Tuesday the 30th. He is looking in capital health and seems to have enjoyed himself immensely. Three of the party, Tom Ward, young Thayer[7] came home with

---

[4] This comment is in Robertson James's handwriting.

[5] Frances Rollins Morse (1850–1928), one of Alice James's most intimate friends and her main correspondent during the sixties and early seventies. They met at Miss Clapp's school in Boston. In 1866 Fanny went to Europe with her parents.

[6] Mary Morse, younger sister of Frances.

[7] Tom Ward, fellow student of William's at Harvard and one of his closest friends, brother of Bessy Ward; James Thayer, student of law at Harvard, later professor.

him. The rest do not know exactly when they are coming. It was so nice that he got home just before Mrs Henry Higginson went South so that she saw him, and heard all about her father and mother before she left. Willy seems to be very much impressed with the elegance of the manners and customs of the natives since his return. I suppose the contrast is rather great when compared to the Indians among whom he has been living for some time past. It is especially charming to get Willy back as we have lost Wilky who has gone down to Florida with a Colonel Harry Scott to raise cotton. It is rather a serious undertaking but we feel pretty sure it will succeed. Mr John Forbes is very much interested in it and has raised a great deal of money for him.[8] They are going to buy at first some three thousand acres, part of which they are going to cultivate themselves and sell the rest to other Northern men who want to go down and try the thing on a smaller scale. Their object is to make a settlement of Northern men in Florida in which way they will be doing the country a great deal of good. I only hope I am sure that they won't have a dreadfully hard time. I have been to one or two parties since you left but nothing very exciting. The Wards have been in town for the last fortnight staying at Mrs Dorr's. She had one of the Ladies Social Club's, to which she asked me, I suppose on Bessy's account. Mr Dorr and Mrs Hunt acted a charade that was rather funny, but as Mr Dwight had asked me to go to the opera to hear Fidelio with him, and as I had to go to Mrs Dorr's instead, the charade perhaps did not seem as funny to me as it might otherwise have done.[9] There is no news in particular to tell you. I still go to Miss Brown, have my German lessons and teach the dirtiest of little dirty children to sew every week just as I used to before you left.

[8] The Florida project did not in fact prove successful and they lost a lot of money. John Murray Forbes (1813–1898) was an investor and entrepreneur who financed the building of railways and roads in the West.

[9] John Dwight was a music critic. Jean Strouse comments that as Dwight was fifty-three 'Alice was probably annoyed at missing the pleasure of his distinguished company...not at missing a romantic encounter'. (p. 103)

Mary Lee just tells me that Miss Clover Hooper[10] is going to ask us to tea some night which piece of news pleases me muchly, as I shall see her charming sister for whom as you may perchance know I have a great affection. I mean, my dearest Frances, to transport my young self the first spare Saturday I have to Brookline to see your beauteous children. You cannot at all picture to yourself how much we miss you it seems so long ago that we all stood upon the wharf watching you off; I suppose though the time will pass just as it always does without one knowing it; and you will come sailing home some of these fine days, having grown into a regular young lady, and will perhaps condescend to shake hands when you first see your poor little friends. Well! Well! we will see.

I have discovered that either one's friends or oneself change I don't know which it is, at any rate one or other does. By the above remark (which I very much doubt whether you will understand) I wish to impress on your young mind that you must not change your small self in any way for [you] cannot be any nicer, any better, any sweeter, or any dearer to

Your loving friend
Alice James

My parents send their love to your Parents with a great deal to yourself. Write very often indeed!

To Frances Morse   [Harvard, MS 1497]

Boston

[3 April 1866]

My dearest Fanny

You are the best and dearest little girl in the world to write to

---

[10] Frances Morse was related to the Lee family through her mother, Harriet Jackson Lee. Mary was a cousin. Marion (Clover) Hooper (1843–1883), later became Mrs Henry Adams. Her 'charming' sister Ellen (1838–1888), married Ephraim Gurney.

me so often when you have so many other people who are so
much more deserving of your goodness. You make me so
proud that the poor family have a hard time of it, I assure
you. I have just come in from a walk. It is the most perfect
day you ever saw, but I suppose you are having just as fine
ones. Mary Lee[11] and I are in the greatest state of excitement
at the prospect of taking tea tonight with the adorable Miss
Ellen Hooper. Don't you envy us? I told you in my last letter
I think of our troubles about getting a house. We have at last
decided to take a house at Swampscott for six months, – I
think it will prove very successful for it is a very nice house
indeed and then Swampscott being so near Boston will make
it very convenient for father to go up and down to town.
People say also that houses will be much easier to get in the
Fall as every one is going to Europe and want to rent their
houses. (I seem to have tried to put in the word *house* as
often in the last dozen lines as possible. I hope that you will
excuse all such little carelessnesses.) There is nothing very
new to tell you but I suppose Mary keeps you acquainted
with all the most important events that transpire. I spent a
couple of hours last Saturday morning with Miss Ireland[12]
who is as charming as ever. I do think she is the nicest little
woman in the world! I also went in recess to school, and saw
all those dreadfully new girls. It was perfectly horrid to go in
and find Mary Tappan (who is ordinarily very charming)
sitting in your seat. Miss Clapp looked sweeter and prettier
than ever, and she cocked her little head on one side and
smiled just like a little bird as she used to do, don't you
remember? Lucy's decision about becoming a doctor is not
yet decided, so I hope it may be deferred indefinitely.[13] I
suppose you may see Ellen and Frank Washburn in France.
Poor Ellen! I hope the journey will do her good, for she was

---

[11] The Tappan family were old friends of the James family; Mary was Clover
and Ellen Hooper's cousin.

[12] Miss Ireland was Alice's teacher at Miss Clapp's school in Boston; she
afterwards became a friend.

[13] Lucy Washburn instead of becoming a doctor, later married one. In 1889
she married the physician and philanthropist, Charles Putnam.

looking so dreadfully sick before she went that I was quite worried about her.

Now my dear Fanny I have nothing more to tell except that I miss you more and more and love you more and more as the time goes on. You must be sure to keep on being good about the letters. With a great deal of love from Father and Mother to your Father and Mother and yourself. Believe me

Your loving friend
Alice James

This seems such a poor letter to send to you after your delightful ones so full of all you are doing; but you must make allowances for us poor humdrum people who stay at home and don't see any beautiful views or pictures.

Yours Alice James

To Frances Morse   [Harvard, MS 1498]

Swampscott

[7 May 1866]

My dearest old Fanny

Here we are at last settled in Swampscott for this summer and I intend to turn over a new leaf and write to my dear little girl oftener than I have done heretofore, for I think she deserves it if any one does for the virtuous way in which she writes to me, but you know my dear you were always a much better child than I. I am so glad that you are enjoying yourself so much but I hope that you won't tire your little self out. Mary writes to me that you were sick in Florence, but I suppose it was nothing very serious as you do not speak of it in your letter to me. We are very delightfully settled here in Swampscott, having a very nice house, the only objection is that we are very near the rail-road track, which makes it rather noisy but people say that one soon gets accustomed to it. The walks about are delightful and it is perfectly delightful to get into the country after having been so long in the city. I miss Mary very much for I haven't seen so much of her since you left. We have been making vain efforts to console ourselves for your departure. I expect her to spend next Sunday with us, if I can prevail upon her to come. Mother is made perfectly happy by the possession of a cow. She never has had one and it has always been her greatest desire to own one. The aforesaid cow is of course the most wonderful of its kind. It gives more and thicker milk than any cow before heard of and last but not least is named Fanny. The only objection is that we have so much milk that we have all to spend most of our time drinking it, and I am afraid that we will grow so fat that our friends will be ashamed to acknowledge us in public. I wish my dear Fanny that you were only here to grow fat with us. You ask about Wilky in your letter; he is getting on very nicely indeed, everything seems to be favourable, they have had no trouble with the 'natives', they on the contrary have been almost universally friendly to them. He always writes in the greatest spirits and seems perfectly sure of success. It is a very hard life and a very adventurous one but then it is infinitely better than plodding on in some dingy office in Slater Street. Mary is so kind as to inform me that very few young men would do it and that I ought to be very proud of him whereupon I entreat her not to preach that doctrine for I shall become insupportable to my poor friends who suffer enough on that score already. I will give Lucy your message when I see her. She told me one day that she had sent off a letter to you care of Monroe Paris. Ellen and Frank are in Nice, perhaps you may meet them. I wish I did not write such horrid stupid letters. I am perfectly ashamed to send them but I am going to be awfully good this summer, so that when you come back I shall not be afraid of seeing you. I must finish my dearest little girl as father is going in to town in a few minutes.

Your loving
Alice James

To Frances Morse   [Harvard, MS 1499]

Swampscott

[17 June 1866]

My dearest Fanny

We were delighted last night to get your mother's letter and to hear that you were better, although I had not heard that you were sick, owing I suppose to our being out of touch of Mary's reach, who has heretofore kept us posted up in all she hears from you. I am so very sorry that you have been so sick, but Miss Ireland tells me that Clare Lea said that you were living at the doctor's house, so I suppose you are in very good quarters to be sick in, which thought is very cheering. I hope that by the time you get this you will be so much better, that my sympathy and anxiety will seem very tardy and out of place. We have been very much excited lately by the unexpected arrival of the infants from Florida, the other from Burlington. Wilky came up on business and could only make us a very short visit and took Bob back with him for whom he had made an opening. It's so very nice having them there together, especially as Bob disliked the West so much and fairly revels in the Southern climate. Wilky was looking so well and seemed so encouraged about their prospects that it was delightful to see him. He has such wonderful plans for our going down South and spending next winter with them on 'our plantation'. I think it's very likely that we will take a house in Cambridge although it is not as yet at all decided. Mother has a horror of going back into one of those little bits of Boston houses again. As a large house can only be found in the country and as Cambridge combines a good many advantages of the city and the country for us we rather incline to go there. I suppose we will find it very pleasant. Now my dear I am going to tell you something pretty fine. Miss Ellen Hooper is going to ask Mary and me to spend next Sunday with her at Beverly. Did you ever hear anything quite so splendid as that?

You see Miss that although we poor folks don't go to Europe and climb mountains and see pictures and such like, we do have a little amusement as we go along. If you crow too much when you get back I shall begin and talk of my dear delightful and irresistible friend Miss Hooper. But my dear Fanny if only you come back soon you may crow all day and all night and you may tell me that I have never even seen Miss Hooper if it should give any pleasure. Your mother implied but did not say that you would be home early in the winter, if you don't make your appearance then I shall send a constable after you.

A great deal of love to yourself, and Mother's thanks and love to your mother for her pleasant letter and love also, I am, my dear little girl,

Your loving friend
Alice James

To Frances Morse   [Harvard, MS 1500]

Brookline

[22 July 1866]

My dearest Fanny

I was much rejoiced on arriving here to find your dear letters. You may perhaps not know it, but still that does not alter the fact that you are perfectly angelic. To think of your sitting down with all you have to do and writing such a long letter to me, who have treated you so badly by writing so irregularly. I shall be ashamed to see [you] when you get back.

I suppose Mary has told you that I have been spending the last week with her, and having such a nice time although the heat has been greater than I ever before experienced. Old Mr Lee is as cheery as possible, talks all the time, and is very much on the alert for fear Mary should have some admirers. I pity the poor young man who first makes the attempt of visiting the fair damsel. Has Mary told you of the fine new coat he has lately bought. It is light gray and is made in the most reversible style being a sack coat. He kept coming up the first day he had it on, asking whether we did not think it very handsome. It is really delightful to see how bright he seems to be.

Mary and I drove over to the Listers and Watsons the other afternoon and had the most beautiful drive. I think the country about here is perfectly charming. I suppose you have heard of Jenny Watson's engagement to Ned Perkins. Is it not funny, he is more than five years younger; can you possibly imagine marrying a boy so much younger than yourself? It would not be so strange if Ned Perkins was not so very immature, but he always seemed to me to be a perfect infant. Mary Lister said that she thought it was too bad that people made such a talk about it, for they had always made such a fuss about none of them being engaged that they ought to be content at least.

We get such nice letters from the boys. They are getting on so well and they do not seem to be troubled at all by the heat, in fact they say that they have had all the warmest weather in June. It is still quite undecided where we will go this winter, so we are in a pleasing state of uncertainty. We may go up Mont Blanc or we may spend the winter in Swampscott, one seems as probable as the other. I am afraid we may suffer somewhat from cold on Mont Blanc, and we might also suffer from loneliness at Swampscott so it is quite hard to decide upon which would be preferable and I am very glad that I am not the one to decide it. I am so delighted that you are so much better, if you were here I should scold you very hard for your naughty talk about keeping them back (Them meaning your Father and Mother). You are very naughty and ought to be punished as if it were your fault, it has probably been good for your Mother to have such a long rest. If you do lose the Rhine, you will only miss seeing some fields here and there on either side of a very muddy river so you need not make yourself unhappy. Mary and I try to console ourselves for your loss but I need not tell you that we do not succeed in the least. We both find that we miss you more and more as time goes on, we will both be quite desperate I am afraid before you get here so please hurry up. If mother were here she would be sure and send a few lines to your Mother, but I can send her love I am quite sure on my

own responsibility. Now my dearest Fanny with many
thanks for your delightful letter and with oceans of love.

I am your loving friend
Alice James

To Frances Morse   [Harvard, MS 1501]

Cambridge

[21 October 1866]

My dearest Fanny

Here we are you see finally settled in Cambridge entirely
against your wishes and my own somewhat, but I suppose it
will be very pleasant, for the house is a very nice one and the
situation delightful. I was so glad to receive your last letter
and to find that you expected to be home so soon although I
shall not be much the gainer I am afraid. Mary I think said
she told you of my sad fate for the winter. Is it not dreadful?
Don't you suppose you may come to New York during the
winter! I don't know what will become of me but I suppose
I will survive it, at any rate I must try to. I spent last
Thursday with Mary, and I had a very pleasant little visit.
The old gentleman was as nice as ever and the place a little
nicer. I think it is the prettiest place I ever saw. Mr Lee
wanted to give me a large plant, but as I was going into
Boston to do some shopping and then out to Cambridge in
the horse-cart I had to decline and accept a flower instead. I
saw little Mary in the cart who by the way is not so little as
she once was. She looked as pretty as ever, I think she has
the sweetest little smile, in the world. I did not see Harry
who was on the train too I suppose. Do you know the
Dingwells? If you do you will be interested in knowing that
Esther was married on Thursday to a Mr Diver and that
Lucy Dingwell is engaged to Gerrith Miller. I suppose you
have heard of Gen Barlow's engagement to Nelly Shaw. It
gives one a shiver at first does it not? Do you know General

Barlow?[14] I don't, but I have a sort of prejudice against him, it does not seem to be nice for a smart young girl like Nelly to marry a widower does it? We expect Bobby home for a visit very soon, it will be delightful to see him, and he needs a little rest after his hard work. The cotton is doing very well and they fear no difficulties now.

We have been having the most heavenly weather, for the last week and I hope you have been having as fine. This whole season has been perfect; one could not imagine a more beautiful one. We intend to get a carriage this afternoon and drive over to Mr Lee's, I want the parents to see the place so much. Mr Lee gave me such a pretty photograph of the lawn and house. Mr and Mrs Peabody are playing croquet on the grass.[15]

We have had a great many visitors since we moved and everyone seems to be very cordial and kind. We may like it so much that in the end we may buy the house, which is very nice, the rooms being very large and cheerful, although the furniture is very meagre. We see Mrs Lowell quite often which makes it very pleasant.[16]

Monday 22nd. Father has just come in to say he will post my letter by to-morrow's steamer so I must close. Believe me my dearest Fanny

Your loving friend
Alice James

P.S. Bobby arrived this morning before we were up. Mary is coming this afternoon to spend the night, it is the last visit I shall have from her probably as I am going off next week, is it not heart-breaking. You must be sure and write just as

---

[14] Francis Channing Barlow (1834–1896) became Secretary of State for New York and later Attorney General.

[15] Andrew Preston Peabody (1811–1893), Professor of Christian morals at Harvard, renowned for his kindness rather than his preaching. He was married to Catherine Whipple Roberts.

[16] Mrs James Russell Lowell was Frances Dunlop, second wife of the famous man of letters. After the death of his first wife Maria White in 1853, Lowell married his daughter's governess in 1857.

often as you can, for I shall be dreadfully lonely. Give my love to your father and mother please and to yourself.

A. J.

To William James [Harvard, MS 1469]

8 June 1867

My dearest Willy

I cannot say that I received your last letter as I was away from home when it arrived. It was read to me however by the father the moment of my return, and pronounced charming and delightful by the assembled multitude. I myself was hardly in a condition to do justice to its charms, as I had just been brought by the admirable mother in a carriage from Brookline, (where I had been staying with Fanny Morse) where she had been summoned to my bed of sickness. When I had sufficiently recovered in mind and body I asked for my letter, but was told it had been despatched to Florida. As the letter was addressed to me I thought this proceeding *cool indeed*!! The letter seems however to have given great satisfaction to the family as I hear them refer to it constantly. In future when you address letters to me you might put private on the rearside as that might perhaps secure my getting one reading of them at least. Poor father has been in a sad state for the past week, with an eruption which has broken out on one side of his head. The lid and all around the left eye became very much swollen, so much so that the eye was almost closed. The right eye was somewhat affected also. He looked very much as if he had been poisoned. The doctor says that it will probably relieve his head very much and do his health a great deal of good. The swelling has gone down this morning a great deal and he looks quite natural, but he had a pretty uncomfortable time of it for a little while. We have been having a visit of a fortnight from John La Farge who seemed to enjoy himself, although he was not particu-

larly enjoyable he was not troublesome at all to anyone.[17]
We saw the Temples for a few hours last week on their way
to Conway.[18] Poor Minny whom they had left in Newport
was to go that same night to New York with Hannah, had a
pretty hard time of it. Just as they got to Point Judith some
bolt gave way and the machinery collapsed. They were in
danger from 10 o'clock pm till 5 o'clock AM when the New
York boat came along and took them back to Newport. She
must have had a pretty frightened time of it alone with
Hannah. I only hope that she knew someone on board. Effy
Shaw is still next door looking as lovely as ever, she goes I
believe in a week. Clover Hooper I see sometimes through
the window, she comes out and spends the day often with
Effy. She still threatens to invite me to dinner but has never
been able to bring her mind to the point of doing so yet,
although from what she says she encourages me to think that
she tries very hard. The country is looking lovely just now
and Quincy Street is in its perfection. The air has been
perfectly heavy with lilacs of which there are a great many
just around us. We have had some plants put down in the
bed in front of the house so that the garden looks quite
nicely. Father spoke to the gardener the other day about
cutting the grass; he said if he could only wait till next week
it would look so much better for Class Day. The excitement
about Class Day seems to be universal. Mary Lee has been
making a long visit in Lenox with Mary Higginson at
Lilla's.[19] I have not seen her since her return but she was in
great delight with Lilla's children whom she says are
remarkably handsome. I saw Jim Higginson the other day;
he inquired after you with interest; in fact it is strange to say

---

[17] John La Farge (1835–1910) was a painter and an influential early friend
of Henry James.

[18] The Temples were cousins, related to Henry James Sr, who lived in
Newport. Minny (Mary) Temple was particularly loved by Henry, she
died of consumption in 1874, aged twenty-four. She became one of the
models for Milly Theale in *The Wings of the Dove*.

[19] Lilla Walsh, a niece of Aunt Kate's.

all your friends seemed to be interested about you. It is because they don't know the baseness of your character as I do. I hope for your sake they may never find it out.

Wednesday – Mother and I went yesterday to town to buy a sewing machine. We got a Florence which is considered the best and seems to be very simple and easy to learn to use. By the time you get back you will probably find Harry and father dressed in suits made by mother and me. *A propos* of making clothes father came in the other day with some story from the Lowells about the goodness of Mr Paige the artist who allowed his wife to make his clothes. We disputed for some time who was the most virtuous Mrs Paige for making them or Mr Paige for wearing them when Harry came in and settled the matter in his cool way, by saying that they were all very good but the clothes. The Danas from New York were here yesterday afternoon. They were on their way to Passamaquaddy Bay where they intend to spend the summer, but were overtaken by such a severe storm and were in such a miserable ship that they had to put into New London, and from there came on to Boston for a few days. They were very pleasant; Mr Dana seemed to be in excellent health and spirits, his paper is to be opened in September.[20] We get nice accounts from the boys who seem to be getting on comfortably so far; I hope they will be able to come North in the summer. Mrs Higginson has just arrived and is going to spend this summer North. With heaps of love from everybody. I am, my dearest brother

Your loving sister
Alice James

P.S. I hope that the Fraulein Smith intimacy has not increased. She must be a bold-faced jig.

---

[20] Charles Anderson Dana (1819–1897), newspaper editor who acquired and began to edit the New York *Sun* in 1867. He was married to Eunice MacDaniel.

To William James   [Harvard, MS 1470][21]

Cambridge

6 August 1867

My darling Willy

Your letter was most gratefully received the other day. The picture was excellent and quite carried us back to old times. Father has desolated me this morning by telling me about your back. How perfectly dreadful it is to think of your having to go through with all poor Harry has suffered. But how delightful it is to hear that you are already feeling better. I hide my head in shame when I think how I used to tease you when sick. Do be careful! I see you heard from Mother of Wilky being at home. He has just returned from Newport where he has been spending a few days at the Griswolds with Betty Purple. He saw all the old people, the Rokers among others; he says they both seem to cherish a warm affection for the family; he thinks that they have improved very much. Wilky is as fat and good natured as ever and seems to have more friends if possible.... Mr Ward said that he liked Harry's story exceedingly; in fact everyone seems to think it capital.[22] Wilky says that there is a perfect *furore* in Lenox among the young ladies to see the young author. But Harry with his high calm alabaster brow maintains his usual indifference to all their blandishments.

We had a little visit a short time since from Minny on her way to Conway from New Rochelle where she had been staying at the Emmetts.[23] She is not nearly as interesting as she used to be, she is so much influenced by the last person she has been with and taken a fancy to that one never knows where to find her. She is looking very pretty and her manner is certainly perfectly fascinating.

Harry and I made a visit on Mrs Charles Peirce the other

---

[21] This is only part of this extremely long letter. Written in pencil, it has proved impossible to transcribe.

[22] 'Poor Richard' had appeared in three installments in the *Atlantic Monthly*.

[23] Elly, Minny Temple's elder sister, had married her cousin, Christopher Temple Emmett.

evening.[24] Her husband was not visible but we saw one of her sisters who seemed an amiable maid but had rather a Philistine way of talking, for instance she told us that a friend of hers who just married had had the 'cheek' to sit down and write her that she should instantly marry etc., Mrs Peirce tried to suppress her anguish of anxiety when her sister was talking but only succeeded in part. Mrs P. is a nice woman, she seems very intelligent and energetic, if she would only refrain from throwing up her head and glaring at one like a wild horse on the prairies. She inquired enthusiastically and affectionately after 'Willy'. Harry's health seems very fair considering how much he is usually run down by warm weather....

You need not give us any of your theatre experiences as if we were deprived of the same delights. Did not Harry and I go to the Museum the other night and see Uncle Tom's Cabin acted with the most touching and dramatic effects? It was so touching in fact that we had to leave shortly.

You must excuse the triviality of this letter if you condescend to read it on account of the frivolity and want of intelligence of the writer. You must remember that this is not her own fault, and that as she is your sister, her having so little mind may account for your having so much. With heaps of love from every one in the family and out of it, believe me my dearest Willy

Your loving *idiotoid* sister,
Alice James

To William James   [Harvard, MS 1471]

Cambridge

13 October 1867

My dearest Willy

The photographs were received a few weeks ago and gave

---

[24] Charles S. Peirce (1839–1914), philosopher had married Harriet Melusina Fay who was herself a writer, in 1862. He divorced her in 1883, saying she had deserted him in 1876.

great delight to the family. I gave one to Mary as you
desired, and she was very much pleased to have it. I enclose
a note from her. We have been looking quite anxiously for
this last little while for a letter from you. I suppose it will be
coming along soon. Mr Holmes was here a few evenings
since and said he had heard from you from Berlin.[25] How
does Berlin compare with Dresden? Has Sargy Perry arrived
yet or are you still alone?[26] *A propos* of alone, Miss Mary
Felton anxiously asked father the other day whether you
were quite alone, when father said yes, she exclaimed, '*Oh!
what a pity*'. There is a hint for you. The little Bob left for
the south week before last. We miss him very much and
were very sorry to have him go back so soon, but he was
crazy to get back to the farm and to work which he cannot
live without. He is a most manly fellow and is quite determined to make something of the place. Wilky will probably
come north and leave him there alone, which will be a most
excellent plan, as the plantation is insufficient to occupy or
support them both, and Bob seems to be most decidedly the
one to be left. Mr Scott also intends leaving so there will be
quite a change. Tom Ward came in the other evening and
said he had heard from you. He was very pleasant, but seems
most childlike, he uses words in the most singular way.
Mother asked him how he liked your photograph, he replied
that, 'it was very astonishing but looked very genial'. What
he meant it would be hard to know. I have been invited by
the young ladies of Cambridge to join the 'Bee'. Have you
the faintest idea of what the 'Bee' consists? I imagine not. It
is a sewing society formed at the beginning of the war by the
girls and kept up now for the poor. Miss Susy Dixwell is at
the head of it and all the Cambridge young misses go, so I
shall have plenty of gossip to tell you.[27]

---

[25] Oliver Wendell Holmes Jr (1841–1934), future supreme court judge,
studied law at Harvard.

[26] Thomas Sergeant Perry (1845–1928), author and scholar, taught English
at Harvard. He was a particular friend of Henry James.

[27] Susy Dixwell was the younger sister of Fanny Dixwell who married Oliver
Wendell Holmes Jr in 1872.

Nearly everyone has got back from the country, the Nortons and Ashburners among others. Miss S. A. and A. J. Sedgwick dined with us a little while ago.[28] Miss Ashburner laughed at Arthur for sleeping so soundly, and said that the maid whom she had left in the house had told her that her only trouble had been all summer, that she had several times feared that Mr Arthur was dead. Father said that she certainly would have had no such fears if Bob had been left under her care, for he made such a noise in his sleep. 'But she would have been afraid that he was *drunk*', replies Harry, which was rather rough upon the poor little Bob who was beside him. Miss A. (who is the most astonishing and delightful old maid imaginable enjoying a joke so much, especially when you think she won't) laughed very much.

I will recount to you some jokelettes of the Harriette which will probably bore you, but which at the time they were perpetrated amused this innocent family very much. The scene is laid in the dining-room, time: dinner.

Harry to the mother. 'May I have some of those brown-rolls that were left this morning at breakfast?'

M. 'Yes, certainly, but do you wish to eat them with your soup?'

H. 'You can't certainly expect me to minutely explain what I intend to do with them.' – Laughter from the family and pause.

H. 'I was coming over the bridge this afternoon and stopped a run-away horse.' – You may easily imagine the shrieks of the family at this.

A. K. 'I hope you did not try and stop him by the bridle.'

H. 'Would you have preferred me to take hold of his legs.'

A. K. 'But you should not run after horses and stop them.'

H. 'Would you rather have me run before them'. – You must let your imagination supply the manner of this Harry, a

[28] Charles Eliot Norton (1827–1908) editor, author, and Harvard Professor of Art History had married Susan Ridley Sedgwick in 1862. Miss S. A. Sedgwick is Sara Sedgwick (1839–1908), Susan's younger sister, a close friend of Alice James and one of her chief correspondents. A. J. is Arthur Sedgwick, her brother. The Ashburners were the Sedgwicks' English aunts, Anne and Grace.

good deal of eyebrow, nostril, and shoulder affectation. I read to mother the other day out of the 'In General' column of the *Advertiser*[29] that there was a paper printed in Paris on some sort of material that could be eaten after read, consequently the contents would be well digested, whereupon mother remarks in her charming way, 'why that's very true, isn't it?'. She was also heard to say the other day that love-letters were meant for one eye, whereupon father said that he supposed that the other eye winked at them. The mother constantly makes these delightful remarks, but I forget them all. A Mr J. M. Howe called here a few evenings ago, he seems a nice man quite amusing; he said that the only remedy he knew of against fleas in Florida was 'to take one's wife down with you'. The horrid man! There is the longest list of engagements and weddings, all the world seems to be getting married. Has mother told you of May Eustis's engagement to a Mr Wister of Philadelphia. A very nice man, thirty-seven years old, very handsome and very nice manners they say. I am very glad that she is not going to marry an infant, which seems to be the fashion just now. George McLanahan is engaged to some one, I don't know the name. Louise Wilkinson is married. Mary McKim has just been married to a Mr Richard Church, and Serena Mason to somebody else,[30] also Ned Lowell engaged to a Miss Goodrich.[31] Kitty Temple's friend Mary Hane has just been married and any amount more only I can't think of them just now. Has father told you of George Cranch's death, a short time since, he died of consumption.[32] Mr Godwin and his daughter Minny were here last week having just returned from Europe.[33] Minny

---

[29] The *Advertiser* is *The Boston Daily Advertiser*.

[30] Serena Mason was a distant cousin of the Jameses, related through Henry James Sr.

[31] Edward Jackson Lowell (1845–1894), historian, married Mary Wolcott Goodrich in 1868; she died in 1874.

[32] George Cranch was the son of Christopher Pease Cranch (1813–1892) painter and minister.

[33] Parke Godwin (1816–1904) author and editor; part owner of the New York *Evening Post*.

has improved very much having grown very much more quiet
and dignified in her manners; she is also quite pretty in the
face and in the figure; being arrayed in a Paris gown who
wouldn't have a pretty figure! Mr Godwin told father that his
income from the 'Evening Post' was seventy thousand
dollars! A neat little bit, think you not? Why don't you start
a paper, and have the like? If you had any strength of mind
you would. I called with father the other day on the Fields;[34]
after awhile father and Mrs Fields began to dilate on the
vanity of riches, when Mr Fields interrupted by saying that
for his part he thought it would be very nice to have some
'aunt around whom memory does not cluster' die and leave
one a nice little sum. He said many more funny things and
told some excellent stories. I have been lately reading
somethings of De Quincey's which I found quite amusing
for awhile, but for long rather tiresome. If you ever read
novels just get 'Madame Therese' by Erkmann-Chatrian, I
read it the other day for the first time; it is the most adorable
little book;[35] I like it as well as any of the others, I think. The
country is looking superbly, and we are having the most
beautiful weather. Every one says that the trees are brighter
than they have been for a good many seasons, because we
have had so much rain that the leaves dry slowly. I spent a
week at the Clifton House with Aunt Kate before she came
home. We walked one day along the cliffs to Marble Head
and I found what I had never before suspected, that the rocks
on that shore are so fine, fully as bold as the Newport rocks
only without any surf, which makes a great difference. With
heaps of love from all believe me my Willy,

Your loving sister
Alice James

---

[34] James T. Fields (1817–1881), author and editor of the *Atlantic Monthly*,
married to Annie Adams Fields (1831–1902), who after his death became
close companion of the author Sarah Orne Jewett.

[35] Emile Erckmann (1822–1899) and Alexandre Chatrian (1826–1890)
collaborated in writing historical novels. *Madame Therese* was published
in 1863.

To Frances Morse   [Harvard, MS 1502]

Pomfret

[24 July 1869]

My dear Fanny

We were all delighted the other evening to get your letter and to learn there from you that had survived Monday's dreadful heat. Why in the world did you not tell us that you were going to the dentists and so receive a little human sympathy, to support you through the agony? I am glad though, now that it is all over that you refrained, for I think that the thought of you in the dentist's chair on that broiling afternoon would have been a little more than any of us could have stood.

I was very much pleased to hear that the picnic was such a success – Lizzie Perkins and all. Give Lucy a great deal of love, and tell her that I envy her the combination of you and Beverly which she is at present revelling in, excessively.

We have been having the loveliest weather since you left imaginable, I only wish that it might have been your lot to happen upon it, for then you might have got a faint idea of the charms of Pomfret;[36] as it was I am afraid that the heat must have been a very strong antidote, although your amiability never would allow us to suspect it.

Mother has prevailed on Mrs Hutchins to let us stay through August in the Bootts' rooms,[37] the Heads having engaged ours. The thought of going back to Cambridge and looking for rooms elsewhere was intolerable, especially as this place suits us all so well.

What a fine speech that was of the King of Prussia the other day, was it not? It can't be but that the French will be

---

[36] In June 1869 Alice, William, and their parents went to stay in a farmhouse in Pomfret, Connecticut.

[37] Francis Boott (1813–1888), an amateur musician, and his daughter Elizabeth Boott (1845–1888), who spent a lot of time in Europe, training to be an artist.

defeated.[38] Have you read Mr Godkin's articles in the past two *Nations* on the subject, they are excellent, don't you think?[39]

I have been reading 'Hard Cash', and think that it is very good, it is most certainly interesting, although not one of Reade's best – what do you mean by not liking it? But do pray read whenever you can, 'The Cloister and The Hearth' and then if you don't say that it is one of, if not *the* most beautiful book you have ever read, I shall truly despair.[40]

Lizzie and all the family desire their warmest love to you. I suppose you will shortly be on your way to the Lake. Give my love to Mary,

Ever thine,
A. James

To Frances Morse   [Harvard, MS 1503]

Pomfret

[11 August 1869]

My dearest Fanny

Your beautiful letter came last night, just as I was saying how much I hoped I should get one from you. Will you be utterly disgusted if I tell you that another plan has been proposed for our Lenox expedition? I am afraid that you will think you are treated rather unceremoniously, to say the

[38] War was declared between France and Prussia, July 1870. The diplomatic crisis of the previous year was about the Hohenzollern candidature to the throne of Spain; it was also about the balance of power in Europe and what France saw as Prussia's expansionism but for Prussia it was about national self-determination.

[39] Edwin Lawrence Godkin (1831–1902), editor of the *Nation* from its foundation in 1865.

[40] *The Cloister and The Hearth*, published 1861, is generally regarded as Reade's greatest work. *Hard Cash* was published in 1863 and is an adventure story which ends with revelations of private lunatic asylums.

least. The present idea is that October would be a very much pleasanter month to see both Lenox and the Hudson in than Sept. which is neither autumn nor summer. What do you say to this? If you agree as to the month, would the first week suit you? Let me know what you think about it, for I suppose it is about time as you mildly suggest that Lili should be at least informed of our intentions if not consulted on the subject! Your accounts of the lake are truly ravishing – what a paradise it must be! The Bootts went off Monday morning with your cousins and Mr Head who came up to spend Sunday. We miss them all greatly. It was so pleasant to see Clara and her brother. How very agreeable the latter is, he is so particularly refined and gentlemanly. An excellent thing in *man*!

We like the Heads very much, Lizzie I think is delightful. Her mother is very nice when you once know her but she is at first a little hard to get at.

Thomas Perry (Sargy) came up on Saturday to spend a week. He is making himself so far charming, he is as funny as he can be – Lizzie Head and I sit and roar, especially when he gets on the subject of hooky-cows etc. I wish you could see him when he gets in one of his gales, his face and figure lend themselves so admirably to his jokes. We stay on here from week to week and we shall stay on while the heat lasts, a truly indefinite period from all appearances. Give much love to Mary and any other members of her family who will be kind enough to accept it from

Your affectionate friend
Alice James

P.S. If October displeases you be sure to say the word.

To Frances Morse   [Harvard, MS 1505]

Monday evening, 1873

My dear Fanny

I hope you were not deeply 'offended' this afternoon by my

unmannerly departure. The car and the mud were too much for me and it was not till I saw you in the distance that I came to my senses and remembered that I had not bidden you farewell. Forgive me! I am so glad that I met you although I am afraid I gabbled more nonsense even than usual. Tell Mary that if anything can reconcile me to my sour face it will be her caring whether I like her or not. The truth is that I felt awfully blue that day as I generally do when I am with respectable people, and I suppose I looked more disagreeable than usual.

You must be all arraying yourselves for the party. I am so glad that the beloved Lucy is with you. In heaven we shall all go together where clothes and acquaintances I trust will be superfluous. Give Lucy lots of love. Good-night dear child.

Yours ever
A. J.

To Frances Morse   [Harvard, MS 1524]

Sunday, p.m. [n.d.]

My dear Fanny

It just occurs to me that, in view of your possible departure, you might find it more convenient to have your meeting of the club first. Why this very obvious view of the matter did not strike me at once can only be accounted for by the limitations of my brain.

I am so overcome with mortification at my extraordinary behaviour to Miss Putnam does she think me a NA Indian or what?

You don't know how I enjoyed seeing thee this afternoon! It seems every day more and more as if there was nothing worth living for but to love one's friends and had any one ever such friends to love as I have got?

But what a dose of my sensations I have given you within the last six hours, first hysterical and now sentimental. Be sure and say that you will have the club and remember that it doesn't make an *atom* of difference to me when we have it. I hope my little glimpse of your mother didn't tire her. It was so good to see her.

With love to all the household
Ever thine
A. J.

To Annie Ashburner[41]   [National Library of Scotland, MS]

Monday evening, 8 January 1873

My dear Nanny

I feel wonderful to tell and somewhat moved to write a letter, and methinks I could not find a worthier object to address it to than thee, having some faint memory of not having treated you very well when I first got home, but this last I am not at all sure of, it is all so vague in my mind (so don't let any statement of mine put any foolish ideas in your head). I hear through your family that you have, or are about to pull up stakes in Tours and betake yourselves to the sunny South where I trust you will find all the warmth which you may desire. We have been having a most beautiful winter so far, if it goes on to the end as it has begun we shall have nothing to envy Europe as to climate, but quite the contrary, if all the papers say about the gales and all that Harry says about the rain and the floods is true.

The latest and most thrilling event which has come to pass, is the announcement of Mr John Gray's engagement to Miss Nina Mason, which has somewhat surprised Boston and more or less amused that giddy capital. It does seem in point of sobriety of disposition rather an incongruous match, what

---

[41] Annie Ashburner (1846–1909) was a cousin of the Sedgwicks and one of Alice James' closest friends. She married Francis Gardiner Richards in 1879 and settled in England.

engagement however ever seemed anything else but incongruous? The wily John has led it seems all his friends astray, by cool calm and ruthless dissections of the lovely Nina – if John Gray can so deceive, who is one to rely upon! I suppose they will be married shortly, for there seems fortunately in this case no earthly reason for delay. Since Cambridge rose in its might and brought forth the Pickering and Sparkes combination we have subsided to our customary eventless engagementless condition. The only thing I have done lately is to go with mother to a truly tragic occasion at Mrs Washburn's, its tragic nature you will easily admit when I tell you that for the first half of the evening the males consisted of the good Master Alfred and Prof. Cooke, one or two others appeared at supper time, but they made little impression.[42] Alfred however did his best, and I never was so plied with food before in my life. He asked me a dozen times whether I would 'have tea or coffee or both', half and half I suppose was the idea.

The Bee is flourishing this winter finely and is pleasanter than usual, perhaps because I have taken to sewing violently. There are some new members to whom I can't say that I have entirely lost my heart. A Mrs Stone, sister to Bessy who talks about 'her kind girls' whatever they may be. Lilian Horsford is very nice,[43] but Ela is more than ever a horror. Julia Marcou has the advantage of being a lady, an attraction which is somewhat counteracted however by her inordinate conceit, which is truly remarkable for one of her years. I had a Bee on Friday, small but select owing to its being a very bad night, I missed thee greatly, though if you had been here the superior attractions of Mrs F. J. Child's[44] ball in honour of her cousin the distinguished journalist would have drawn

---

[42] Professor Josiah Parsons Cooke was Professor of Chemistry and Mineralogy at Harvard. His wife's nephew and niece were members of their family for many years.

[43] Lilian Horsford was President of the Bee for a while; she later married William Gilson Farlow, professor of Botany at Harvard.

[44] Frances James Child (1826–1896), Philologist and Professor of Rhetoric and Literature at Harvard was married to Elizabeth Ellery Sedgwick.

you from your humble friend but you would have been nicely disappointed Miss if you had gone, for instead of fifty guests as Madame expected she only had five or thereabouts! To think of my having written so much with never a word of our dearly beloved Nanny Kotch! All I can say about our friend is that she is more than ever like herself. I learn from William that she converses with men just as she does to us, about her *intense existence, yearning* and *her despairs* etc. – is it not extraordinary truly? Sara becomes more and more infatuated and absorbed in her, but I must say with your Aunt Grace that she is just a little wearisome to me.   Mr Trowbridge I believe is very attentive.[45]   I have made his acquaintance by the way, he came to dine the other day and was more frightened than you can well imagine, but I thought him refined and very good-looking.   I have also made the acquaintance of Mrs Anderson and Warner and somebody else I don't remember who, but some of your friends, so you see I may entirely cut you out if you don't come back soon. William in reply to my inquiry as to whether he had a message to send you, desires his most affect. regards and says that he feels very lonely in C. without you and that he had a strong desire to write to you himself last week, but it passed away without coming to a climax and he does not feel sure of any letter of his being hospitably received by you. His bluff sincerities have been known to offend in some instances. On returning to the Sedgs. ten days ago from a conversation on jealousy in town, Sara told him you had just written a letter abusive of Miss Green. This simply struck him as a curious coincidence; that is all. Miss G. is in her way one of the most remarkable young persons now living. William once more sends his regards and hopes that before long he will actually write to you. At any rate he will never forget you, which is more than can probably be said of some persons with respect to him. I hope you won't be offended by all this which I think very impertinent. Now do write soon, the southern sun ought to mature and multiply your

---

[45] John Trowbridge (b. 1843) physicist, eventually became Professor of Science at Harvard.

powers of production. Give a great deal of love to your father and mother and believe me

Ever yours
Alice James

To Frances Morse [Harvard, MS 1504]

[Monday, 1873]

My dear Fannikins

I shall keep very dark about your museum iniquity, on one condition which is, that you will come and see me once in every twentieth time that you come to Cambridge, I shan't ask for more.

Did you ever know such a pouring day? Wilky and his wife go off this afternoon. You will be glad to hear that we have excellent news from our dear little baby and its dear little mother. The baby weighed nine pounds and a quarter when it was born, which is doing pretty well for Prairie du Chien, I think, don't you? We get beautiful letters from Bob, who has had a rare experience for one so young, the more grimy and sordid his work becomes, the more spiritual grow his thoughts apparently. Do come and see us soon, I don't know what I have done to be blessed with such a friend as you are darling Fanny.

Always your devoted
Alice James

We heard from William yesterday in Florence where Harry and he had joined forces.
Monday –

To Annie Ashburner   [National Library of Scotland, MS]

Cambridge

4 May 1873

My dear Nannie

Your letter dated Tours was most gratefully received last week. I had been contemplating writing to you for some time past, as I knew myself to be in your debt, but letter writing is a joy which I have indulged in to the smallest possible extent this winter, owing to an increase of feebleness in my upper story, which though lofty, never was you know particularly distinguished for solidity. I have sent word to this effect to you, through Sara, which perhaps you may have got. I have had news of you constantly in Kirkland Street and have followed you in all your adventures and it has struck me that you have been having rather a lively time upon the whole, am I right or wrong? At any rate you have not lost anything in that way by not having been in Cambridge, there hasn't been an invitation to refuse all winter, let alone one to accept. But what a dreadful fib I am telling, I have entirely forgotten the Peabody reception where I talked for an hour and a half to your friend, Jacob, Joseph, David or whatever his name is, Haskins! As the hours rolled by our topics naturally became somewhat exhausted (I made the most of you, you may be sure) in a moment of despair I said to him, 'who is that pretty young lady in the hall', 'oh! that's my sister', 'ah and there's a divine in the doorway who may he be?' 'why! that's my father'. We then went into supper and as we went into the room I heard him whispering, 'that's my other sister, pointing to a corner, where sat a maiden whom I am very sure I should *not* have asked about. It's well they say whatever you do do thoroughly, so I can congratulate myself now upon a thorough knowledge of Joseph and his family, and feel that the evening was not so entirely misspent as I was tempted at the heat of the moment to consider. Mother (she is the partner of all my pains as well as joys) and I passed another evening at Mrs Washburn's with the thermometer at 150 in the shade, and where I had Alfred for my devoted slave; as the Governor and Prof. Cook were the only others of his sex present I think that I had rather the best of it. These have been my two social triumphs of the winter, don't you think that you have done something equal to this at Archachon? The Bee goes on as usual, I go to it as often as I can and find it very pleasant since I have taken to sewing which latter has become quite a passion with me of late. I went last Friday to Julia Marcou's, through the pouring rain, nobody else came but Marny and Carry Parsons after tea.[46] We eat in Mr Marcou's study with him in his slippers and dressing-gown and old red rug over his shoulders.[47] I wondered whether he would come to tea in this guise or not, just before it was announced he went upstairs and came in again having taken off the gown but still clinging fondly to the rug and slippers. You [see] one doesn't need to travel to have their mind enlarged. Ela is to have the next Bee, she grows hourly a greater burden and mistake, but her devotion is unquenchable. There will be no getting rid of her, save by matrimony which is a forlorn hope in these parts. Speaking of matrimony reminds me of Katy Joffey who you will be glad to hear is to be united in the bonds of wedlock on the 3rd of June. There's no escape for poor Sidney now I am afraid, he will have to face the music. They are to live in New York, Mr Smith having given them a house.

We are all convulsed at the present time with the summer nuisance, father is going to the top of Vermont and the bottom of I know not what in his anxiety for us, what we shall decide on is as yet uncertain altogether, in my next letter I shall hope to be able to tell you. You, happy creatures, are safe for that lovely England, I suppose! What do you think of the Bootts coming home the last of June? Lizzie asks in her last letter that father should engage two rooms for them in some 'cool place' – a rather cool request don't you think so? They are also desirous of a house in

---

[46] Caroline Parsons was a member of the Bee and daughter of Harvard Law Professor, Theophilus Parsons.

[47] Jules Marcou (1824–1898) geologist, was born in France and came to Cambridge to work with Louis Agassiz.

Cambridge for a year, rather an experiment after the paradisial existence which they have been leading in Rome.

I went a few weeks ago to New York, where I spent a very pleasant ten days with Aunt Kate and my cousin Mrs Perkins.[48] New York is the gayest of the gay and very entertaining for a few days but deliver me from having to live there. The journalist[49] did not come to see me, but his sisters have since soothed my vanity by telling me he was busier than usual owing to Mr Godkins' troubles. Sara I think is decidedly better than she was a month or six weeks ago but the coming month will be a great trial to her. Theodora is fat as butter and looks consequently much better than she did this time a year ago.

Will you ever forget it.[50] Your Aunt Ann talks of England again, they say, so I suppose you will have that pleasure this summer. William tells me to say that he misses you dreadfully, a remark which might be reiterated with perfect veracity by all the family. Saturday afternoons don't know what to do with themselves. Give a great deal of love to your mother and father and lots to yourself.

Believe me.
Ever yours
Alice

The word father is not intentionally blotted out I assure you!

---

[48] Helen Wycoff Perkins, first cousin of Alice James's mother and her Aunt Kate.

[49] This is probably a reference to Arthur Sedgwick, Sara's brother, who had moved to New York in 1872 to work on *The Evening Post* and Edwin Godkin's *Nation*. Two of the Godkins' children died in infancy at this time.

[50] Alice had spent from May to October 1872 travelling in Europe with Henry and Aunt Kate.

To Annie Ashburner   [National Library of Scotland, MS]

Cambridge

28 June 1873

My dear Nannie

I suppose that by the time this reaches you, you will have been established for some time in your beloved England, and have departed from *my* beloved France. I admit however that England in June is not without its attractions, and if you have been having only half as delicious weather as we have, you must have been reasonably happy.

We have been going thro' the usual Cambridge festivities the past week, Class-day commencement and now today Phi, Beta Kappa. Mr C. F. Adams has been holding forth this morning, but I was too lazy to go and hear him.[51]

The Morses all came through from Beverly on Class-day to put Mary through, I believe it is her first appearance. She looked lovely in the face, but she is possessed of such a superfluity of leg and arm and such a deficiency of manner, that she fails to make the impression she ought to. The day was hot of course, but about eleven a gale of wind sprang up, and as we have not had rain for four weeks, you may imagine the clouds of dust that enveloped the scene.

I must tell you about Katy Joffey's wedding which came off at last on Tuesday June 3rd. She was married in the Parish church at eight o'clock in the evening, by old Dr Newell, who if he had escaped from Somerville couldn't have done it worse. The church was beautifully decorated with green leaves and white lilacs, under the direction of Marny Storer and Lizzie Sparkes, assisted by Mrs Warner, Trowbridge, Meyers etc. etc. Katy and her beloved came in together and walked up the aisle as if they were carrying a coffin. Couldn't have been (dreadful thought) reluctance? Then Dr Newell began, first with a dissertation on marriage in the abstract, then a prayer then something else then another

---

[51] C. F. Adams (1835–1915), was a writer on railways and established the Board of Railroad Commissioners.

prayer and so on he warbled half the night. When it was at
last over I turned to Marny and gasped out, 'wasn't it
dreadful' to which she replied that she never had heard a
'lovelier service'. There is no accounting for taste you see. A
select portion of the company, your humble servant among
others, were off to the house, where we kissed Katy, shook
hands with Mr Smith and said something similarly foolish to
both of them. Katy looked very pretty, and Mr S. very
handsome. All the Smith family were there; they are all very
good looking people. I have been thus minute, my dear
Nannie, because I have so few things of interest to tell you.
You have heard of course of all the extraordinary engagements. Lilla Cabot's was a thunderbolt from which we have
hardly yet recovered our breath.[52] Mother and I are never to
be astonished again as long as we live, by anything that
happens. I met Sargy and her together one day on coming
out of the Hotel Boylston. S. departed and we seated
ourselves on the steps of the Hotel, and she then and there
poured out to me the affair, till I ran off desperate in the
midst. It gives me such an awful feeling of disloyalty to be
listening to confidences that one doesn't wish to hear, don't
you think so?

I got a letter this morning from Sara in Ashfield, apparently
very happy.[53] I never saw anyone so improved in health as
she is the last two months. Theodora unfortunately is quite
the reverse. The Nortons don't agree with her evidently at
all. Whether it is Charles' dogmatism or his atheism I can't
say, but it is something or other.

You must give my best love to your mother and father and
hoping to hear from you, believe me

Always your loving friend
Alice James

---

[52] Lilla Cabot had become engaged to the Jameses' friend, Thomas Sergeant
Perry.

[53] Charles Norton owned a country house in the village of Ashfield, northern
Massachusetts.

To Annie Ashburner   [National Library of Scotland, MS]

26 September 1873

My dear Nanny

I stand convicted of every crime which you may feel pleased
to heap upon me, my conduct has been of the basest I most
readily admit, especially as I have so much to tell you of all
our wonderful adventures of the summer. To begin with we
went through with more than the usual amount of anguish
and despair last spring, to know what to do with ourselves
for the fatal months of July and August, when the family
were inspired with the bright idea of betaking themselves to
the provinces. I was sent off the first of July with Aunt Kate
as an advance guard. We joined *en route* some cousins from
New York and betook ourselves to Quebec, where we passed
ten days very pleasantly at the Misses Lane's boarding house,
which has lately been made famous by Mr Howells story of
'A Chance Acquaintance', which perhaps you may have read
and perhaps not; if you have you will be interested to know
that I slept in the room in which 'Kitty' is supposed to have
dwelt, and which looks into the Ursuline convent. Whilst in
Quebec we went up the Saguenay, passing two most
delightful days. I don't know, but I have a vague idea that
you have done all this, but what I know you haven't done, is,
what we subsequently did, that is go down the Gulf of St
Lawrence, and whilst I have a drop of blood in my veins you
never shall, for its an experience to which I would hardly
condemn my worst enemy. We started from Quebec in a
boat that had previously been a blockade runner. It was
only twenty-five feet wide and there were 130 passengers on
board, all Canadians who are by nature several degrees lower
than the lowest middle-class English, and art has yet done
nothing for them. My dear, we were five days and nights on
board and I am alive to tell the tale, a fact of which I am
prouder than of anything in my adventurous career.

We landed at Pictou a little town in Nova Scotia at four
o'cl'ck of a Sunday morning, in a little sail boat, it had been
pouring pitch forks all night, but fortunately held up at that

moment. There were some twenty or thirty passengers, each trying to get ahead of the other at a certain Mrs Taylor's who was our only hope in the way of lodgings. We at last all met in Mrs T's parlour, the front door open but not a soul up to receive us. There we sat waiting our doom, with Aunt Kate who was our leader, flourishing very vigorously and audibly in the face of the others a certain telegram which she had sent and which would of course secure us rooms, when lo! a maid of all work made her appearance, saying that there was not a room to be had in the house, telegram or no telegram; then you should have seen the stampede of women in water-proofs, umbrellas and bags tearing through the desolate little town in the early dawn seeking for where to lay their heads. We finally found a spot over a gin-shop which had nothing in itself or its landlady, but necessity to recommend it, but which turned out to be on further acquaintance much better than it looked. We had with us a pleasant young Englishman, and his wife, a Dr Tredell by name, who helped to beguile the day, but such a wife! I may truly say, that never before have I seen feminine folly, till I made her acquaintance, I hope I shan't forget all about her before we meet, for my pen in quite unequal to the task of doing her justice. We went from Pictou to Prince Edward's Island which we had heard was an Earthly Paradise, but which we found a dirty desolate hole, where we lived for three nights and days over another much more odoriferous than the first gin-shop. From this sweet spot we went to Halifax and from there to St John, where I met the parents who came from Cambridge to meet us, where we stayed for four weeks enjoying the lovely cool weather and an excellent hotel, but little else the town being desolate and dreary to the last degree; but notwithstanding all our hardships your humble servant has flourished like a young bay-tree, and is now enjoying an amount of strength which she has not known for a long time. We had a good many laughs too over our troubles which I only wish you could have shared (the laughs not the troubles). I am afraid you have not had a very lively summer, but hope you will go to Florence for the winter. William sends his regards and hopes he may have the pleasure of seeing you before very long. The Ashfield summer seems to have been a success. Charles, your cousin, is less attractive I think than ever. Mother sends love to your mother and yourself and wishes very much that she could see you sometimes. With remembrances to every one believe me always

Your loving friend
Alice James

To Annie Ashburner   [National Library of Scotland, MS]

Cambridge

19 October 1873

My dear Nannie

If I remember rightly I finished my last letter rather abruptly after having given you a detailed account of our proceedings of the summer, but before I had made any inquiries about your own affairs or sympathized with what I hear from Kirkland Street, is the lonely nature of your present circumstances. I hope you keep your spirits up and manage to laugh at fate, the only way that troublesome party is to be kept in order, I have come to the conclusion. Since I wrote, Mother and I made a call on Miss Foote, who paints you all in glowing colors, but about *one* of your circle her enthusiasm knows no bounds, I wonder that one can't hear the wings flap from here, I almost fancy one can. Which one of you all do you suppose it possibly can be? No one, but your good-for-nothing self, about whom she talked in such a way as to make me feel myself to be a most presuming creature to venture to address so superior a being. But I shall do it trusting to a little exaggeration on her part. But to leave frivolity to Miss Foote and her like, have you heard of William's sudden departure for the sunny south. He left a week ago Saturday, and is in all probability at the present moment in ecstasy over the Irish coast. Father, mother and

I are left alone in our glory, which we find much more lonely than glorious, however. It will only last six months I suppose, and it seemed altogether to be the only thing for the boy to do as the work which he proposed to do in the college was altogether more than he was up to. Six months of rest and out-of-door life will set him up he hopes forever. It seems hardly wise to start on a new career with the prospect of being always a little behind hand in health. It is a terrible disappointment to him.[54]

We are having the loveliest autumn conceivable, mild and soft as possible, I am sitting writing by the open window. The trees are bright, but not as brilliant as we often have them for some reason or other. I have been ransacking the house to find another sheet of paper that resembles the one that I have been writing on and father with his usual amiability, has searched his stores (I find that he is possessed of enough to set up a large wholesale establishment so that when the next panic comes I shan't feel so anxious for our future) but in vain, and this very distant connexion with the family is the nearest approach I can make. But all the while I am forgetting to tell you of the new engagement, Miss Emily Russell's to Col. Pierson, who I should judge to be a very virtuous, awfully stupid and somewhat common individual, a combination of qualities which I trust will conduce to the lady's happiness; she has hesitated it is true before them long but that seems only in the end to add to the ardor of the flame when it is once ignited. I can't say from an outside point of view that I envy her greatly, but then again from what I know of her, I don't envy him greatly, a state of mind on my part which I sincerely trust they are ignorant of for it might cast a shade over their present bliss. Speaking of matrimony Clover Adams' match[55] seems to be successful so far and altho' she looks pale thin and ancient and has become rather silent as compared to the chatterbox she used to be, I think it has had a good effect upon her and added a charm,

---

[54] William had given up his job teaching physiology at Harvard to join Henry in Europe, in pursuit of his 'health'.

[55] Alice's friend, Marion (Clover) Hooper had married Henry Adams in June 1872.

a feminine softness which was decidedly wanting before. Of the Nortons I can't tell you much, we see them seldom. Mr Norton *never*. But one thing I can tell you of which you will be as glad as we are, that is that Sara is *not at all absorbed* by them. I had supposed that we should lose her altogether this winter but the opposite seems to be quite the case, she seems to be at Shady Hill very little and they seem to be at your Aunt's very little, all of which we daily rejoice in.[56] The dreadful horror which you know has pursued you and me and of which we have spoken under our breath is now the common topic of conversation amongst our mutual circle. I confess that last spring I qualed and quaked and I shouldn't have been surprised to have heard of it any time last summer. But somehow this autumn I have plucked up courage again, I trust not unduly. Ellen Gurney said that she had discussed the subject with Mr Godkin who with his wife share the universal terror and he said that he must allow that they had been given no grounds last summer for their apprehensions. So perhaps after all we are alarming ourselves very unnecessarily. Sara looks wonderfully well so that she can't be having anything very troublesome on her mind. Theo is in New York enjoying herself I trust. We are looking forward in about four weeks time to Wilky's arrival with his wife![57] they are to be married on the 12th Nov. Before that time we also have expectations of another arrival in the family, over which we are all in the wildest state of excitement. I hope that William will see you at some period of his travels. He is going right to Florence to meet Harry and from thence they go to Rome. Do you still think of F? Would the Corniche be better for your mother, to whom please give my love and tell her how glad we were to hear such good news of her from Miss Foote. Good-bye dear Nanny, I don't think that if you had been here this Sunday afternoon in the flesh I ——

[56] 'Shady Hill' was the home of Charles Norton. The 'dreadful horror' she refers to is the possibility that, after the death of his wife Susan Sedgwick in 1872, Charles would propose to one of her sisters, Sara, Alice's friend, or Theodora.

[57] Wilky was to marry Caroline Cary. They had two children, a boy Joseph Cary, born 1874 and a girl Alice born, 1875.

voluminously or less wisely than I have on paper. Let us hope that it may add something to the interest of my letter by giving it a more lifelike tone. With lots of love,

Always your loving
Alice James

To Annie Ashburner   [National Library of Scotland, MS]

Cambridge

[25 October 1873]

My dear Nancy

I hope Sara has not forestalled me with the thrilling intelligence of Mr Trowbridge's engagement, which has just convulsed Cambridge through all its remotest ramifications.[58] Have your family ever told you of his devotion, the summer they were all in Mt Desert together, to a beautiful widow Gray, of Chestnut Street, Boston. It seems that ever since then poor Trowbridge has been a luckless swain pining away and growing daily more and more melancholy, his anguish greatly increased by the fascination of the widow attracting numberless other youths; equally desperate with himself. But he has at last nobly won her and carried her off from them all. The first question of course that is asked is 'has she money', especially when told that among her many possessions she has a solid jewel, in the shape of a girl of fourteen summers. One's mind is greatly relieved, however, altho' one's old-fashioned morals may be somewhat perturbed, on hearing that she is 'comfortably off', whatever that may mean (T.'s standard of comfort fortunately can't be exorbitant) and that papa-in-law Gray is going to provide for the child. This is a fashion recently introduced by Mrs Moulton who in cementing the artificial tie between herself and her Bairn assisted by all the gorgeous ritual of the episcopal church as

[58] John Trowbridge was to marry Mary Louise Gray, widow of Thomas Gray.

it is to be found in Garden Street neatly severed those of nature and with, what I am sure you will think most unselfish generosity, bestowed her tender offspring upon their various amiable relatives. The ceremony attending this little operation, as fact need hardly be told, is more fitly described as obscure than gorgeous, microscopic would be the best word to characterize it. But to return to our muttons it seems to be feared that his family, that is Mr Trowbridge's, don't smile on the arrangement as his sister, the adopted one, told Florence Sparky in the horse-cars that she had never seen Mrs Gray when the former asked her if she did not think her beautiful, which as the engagement had been made public for several days was odd, to say the least. But poor things one can hardly wonder at them being disgusted, if they really are, but horse-car interviews are not always reliable. I wish I could repeat to you all that the President had to say to William on the subject, it was too funny. He was greatly excited and his whole manner was, William said, exactly as if he had as perfect a right to interfere as if it had been some arrangement in his laboratory that poor T. was planning. When he heard of the child he was quite overcome, but revived on hearing that the father was to take charge of it, and said 'that's very good, but then its very wrong', a view which I am quite inclined to myself. What are the women made of who do such things? I hope its not going to be an epidemic with widows. But it might be a good place for Charlemagne when he married his young wife and starts a fresh brood, to dispose of some half dozen of his to their various aunts who would doubtless be only too thankful to receive them.[59]

This reminds me of my last letter which I feel was a dreadful bore. I am haunted as soon as I send one to you, with a deadly fear that I have told you naught but what was in my previous one causing you to groan and curse your fate that you have got so tiresome a correspondent. But I keep forgetting all the time what I have told you and what I haven't. One thing I feel sure I have never before told you of and that is the widow Gray and another is that your last

[59] Charlemagne was Alice's nickname for Charles Norton.

letter was delightful and the proudest day of my life to be
intimately acquainted with a young woman who had tea'ed
with a real live curate. I couldn't have survived the
experience myself and consequently much prefer to have it
come through you. Your last two letters have been just like
a novel and most thrilling, almshouses, walled gardens,
parsons, curates, and all. Do frisk as much as you can and
write me all about it. I am quite jealous of Miss Jackes, do
we resemble one another at all? What is her first name? I
must tell you the most delightful tale of a Mr Rutson a shy
Englishman who was stranded from some unknown reason
on these barren shores a short time since.[60] He was the
mildest, meekest little man conceivable and happened by
some chance to spend the night unprovided with toilet
articles at the Forbes. William F. conducted him to his room
and gave him various implements and finally asked him if
there was anything more he could do for him. Mr R. said
'oh! no nothing except if he would be kind enough to give
him a new tooth-brush or *any* tooth-brush indeed and he
carefully left it behind him. But can't you see just how he
said it? Its almost as good as the Agassiz story of Aupère.[61]
Cambridge has been flooded lately with British of all classes.
The Gurneys had Lord Houghton, valet and ten parcels for a
couple of days, they then proceeded in floods of rain to
Concord to stay at the Emersons.[62] I wonder how the valet,
the parcels and Ellen got along together in the kitchen whilst
the latter was cooking the dinner. The last importation is a
Dr Appleton editor of the *Academy* who is puzzled to know
who Fanny Kemble is and is quite sure she isn't an English
woman or he would have heard of her.[63] So you see that if
we have not curates of late we have a few jokes as we go
along. Father and mother have betaken themselves to the

[60] Albert Rutson was Henry James's 'neighbour' in London and figures
briefly in letters and in his autobiography, *The Middle Years*.

[61] Jean Louis Rodolphe Agassiz (1807–1873), born in Switzerland,
renowned zoologist and geologist.

[62] Ralph Waldo Emerson. Ellen (1839–1909) was Emerson's daughter.

[63] Fanny Kemble (1809–1893), actress and writer, was a close friend of
Henry James.

West last week to make the acquaintance of their nieces and nephews, I mean my nieces and nephews and their grand-children. Aunt Kate, William, and I are consequently at home alone in our glory. I am the house-keeper, and a very good one too although the cook told me she wished Mrs James would come home soon, but this was only owing to my having a tea-party on Sunday night when she wanted to go out.

We have been having a little visit from Lucy Washburn who looks older and sadder poor child but is sweet and cheerful as ever. She told me that they were living without a servant, Martha and she doing the work. Mrs William is also with them, but I believe they have divided the establishment and make two households, a wise plan. I have scribbled till I am quite tired and you must be too, so good-night with love to all and believe me

Always your affectionate
A. J.

To Annie Ashburner   [National Library of Scotland, MS]

2 November 1873

My dear Nannie

I hope you won't be too much alarmed at the frequency of my epistles of late, but I suppose that if I wrote every other day I should still get messages of reproach through Sara, which to say nothing of their untruthful nature are discouraging in their effect. But I shall keep on suffering with all the rest of the world with whom virtue is the guiding principle! I don't know what I have to tell save a thrilling event in the family annals, in the erection of a lamp-post, for which we have waited and petitioned the common-council for anxiously and long and saw yesterday, with breathless interest, put up. You may easily imagine our impatience for the shades of night to fall, and our disgust when the moment came and they didn't fall at all, but the moon rose up with a brilliancy never before imagined in one's wildest dreams and never a lamp was lighted that blessed night in the whole of Cambridge. This afternoon looks equally unpromising, there's not a cloud to be seen and the moon I suppose is making all her preparation with the greatest satisfaction to pop up at the earliest possible moment. Isn't it provoking! I went up this morning to Kirkland St. but found them all flown, to their devotions let us hope.[64] On my way back I met Lizzie Boott and we started off on a walk and got as far as the botanical gardens where we collapsed on one of the green-house steps and baked ourselves in the sun for an hour and a most delicious process we found it. We are having such weather as no mortal ever saw before or as I am afraid we shall never see again, our autumn always so fine is this year far surpassing itself. Lizzie has been off staying in Waltham for a week or two. She told me some gossip, nothing much worth repeating, unless the following example of the degeneracy of Boston fashion you may find shocking, if not agreeable or valuable. The ladies give extensively champagne parties, suppers etc., and in some cases are found to partake somewhat too largely of this agreeable mixture and consequently comport themselves in a way hardly becoming a lady of taste. Mrs Gordon Dexter whether more than once or supported by some other fair ones I know not mounted on the table and danced about holding up her petticoats as high as you please. Is this the manners you meet with at Tunbridge I am afraid that when you get back you will be quite behind the age, there's no knowing what we may have got to then!

I don't think I told you of our going down to breakfast one day at St John and finding Mrs Sparks and family arrived. We became intimate for the first time with the former and our vague plan of departure for the next day became in the course of a few hours fixed as fate. Was there ever such a horror? Her children are marvels of patience and virtue I think, and as for the noble Pickering what can we do to testify our admiration of his courage. The only possible

[64] Kirkland St. was the home of the Sedgwicks.

explanation must be that he is in love with Lizzie as few men
are with women. They are to be married it seems to be
generally hoped in the spring. Mrs S. expressed herself with
such admiration of you all, especially your mother whom
she considers one of the rarest persons – 'a person, Mrs
James, whose taste you can always be sure of, you will find
that her taste always agrees with your own'. I could hardly
refrain from asking her if it extended, this congeniality to
collars, for if I remember rightly it seemed to me that it took
a different form in your mother's case from what it does in
Mrs S. But don't let's say another word about her, she seems
to me to be an unholy object. After I had been home a few
weeks from the provinces, I skipped down with Lizzie B. to
Beverly to spend a few days with the Morses. We had a very
nice time. I saw no one save Mr Charles Jackson, by whom
my affections would instantly have been captivated had not
I been told that his were already engaged with Miss Fanny
Appleton, not openly I believe as yet but in aspiration.[65] Isn't
he lovely and hasn't he got the nicest face and the sweetest
smile you ever saw? I hope I shan't see him again or I am
afraid the illusion will be dispelled. I renewed my acquaintance with Dr James Putnam popularly known as Jim. He
has grown an inch or more physically and Europe has added
to his many inevitable Jackson virtues a charm and attraction
which they possessed not, so that he is a very pleasing object
now. The contrary process seems to have taken place unfortunately with his brother Charles, if one can judge by merely
passing him in the street, which perhaps you may say is a
superficial method of forming one's conclusions.[66] It's
characteristic at any rate! On reading over my letter I am
somewhat struck with its disjointed nature no two sentences
apparently belonging to the other giving a jerky character to

[65] Charles Cabot Jackson, the cousin of Alice's friend Frances Morse, studied
law and then became a banker. He married Frances Elizabeth Appleton
in 1876. They had five children.

[66] Dr James Jackson Putnam (1846–1918), neurologist, researcher on
nervous diseases. He believed the physician should be a 'healer of the
mind as well as the body'. His brother Charles Pickering Putnam
(1844–1914) was a physician and philanthropist.

the whole, but you who know in what flowing numbers I can write if only I choose will forgive me, for should I tear this up you won't get another I am afraid you ungrateful creature for some time. Write soon and tell me that you keep your spirits up and that life has some joys if not all we should wish. Every one sends love to all and believe me my dear Nannie

Always your loving
Alice James

To Annie Ashburner   [National Library of Scotland, MS]

Cambridge

[30 November 1873]

My dear Nannie

You may have noticed a slight interruption the last week or two in my hitherto *rigorously* regular correspondence, which may be explained by a period of unusual excitement in the usually monotonous annals of the James family caused by the admission into its circle of two new members, one of each sex. To begin with the smallest but most thrilling, I must tell you that on the 18th of Nov. (the anniversary of its parents wedding-day) a minute object of the masculine gender presented itself for admission into this troubled sphere in a little western town hundreds and hundreds of miles away from its enthusiastic but distracted relations.[67] Considering its tender age it was a most substantial party, weighing at the time of its birth nine pounds and five ounces. We get most beautiful letters from its fond papa, who says that it eats and sleeps all day and cries for conversation and exercise all night, which must be somewhat inconvenient, but does not detract apparently from its charms in the parental eyes. You must excuse this long description, but remember I am an

---

[67] Robertson James's wife Mary Holton had given birth to a boy, Edward Holton James.

Aunt! for the first time.

Mr and Mrs Wilky! left us a fortnight ago tomorrow, having only given us a week of their company. Wilky has such hosts of friends, that a great deal of their time was taken up with them. He is very much enamoured apparently, and his wife is a very gentle quiet ladylike person, reserved and not easily got acquainted with in such a short time. Whilst they were here the Jameses distinguished themselves by giving a ball, which might have been worse I suppose. The next week the Bootts gave a little fight and last night the Childs ditto in honor of Miss Rosalie [Butter]. To-night we are expecting them all here, so you see Cambridge is gradually waking up to a sense of its responsibilities. But what a monumental creature is Rosalie, fine, but to be enjoyed and admired at a distance.

I went on Friday to the Bee at Marney's, whom I like more and more all the time. I have cut you out entirely with one of your admirers Miss Lilian Horsford, such kissing and hugging and general gushing as goes on between us, you never saw. She is an excellent girl but sadly wanting in the power of perceiving that her affections are not as vehemently responded to as she imagines, an amiable weakness however! Emily Atkinson's death about which you have of course heard, was a dreadful shock to all the girls. Her poor young husband has a desolate future to look forward to. The saddest part of it all is that he was not here, he could only come once and preferred to wait and take them home. The baby is a fine one and is to be taken care of by Mrs Holdridge, the mother. It is a sad, sad story. But a sadder story still is this horrible wreck of the Ville du Havre. It's the most horrible thing of the sort that has happened since the Arctic I suppose. There were only three lives saved then I believe. I knew those dear Hunter girls very well in Newport and went to school with them for several years, little imagining that such a fate was in store for them. They are cousins of Nanny Kotch which brings it all home most forcibly to her. The world seems to be very full of trouble just now. You have heard of course of the Washburn's loss of prosperity thro' their brother William's speculations.

Yesterday I heard that Frank was dangerously ill and his poor wife on the verge of her confinement. Mrs William owing to reduced finances is passing the winter with Lucy, Martha and their mother in a small house in West Cedar St. Don't you think that poor Lucy is having her share of trouble. She is just as sweet as ever. I saw your friend Mr Trowbridge last night at the Childs, he is worse than ever I think for his bovine capacities.

Give my love to your parents and believe me,

Always your loving
A. James

Mother has just come in having met Don Carlos and Theo. I think she is more endangered than Sara, which would be bad but not so bad as what we feared, she not being of such fine clay as Sara.

To Annie Ashburner   [National Library of Scotland, MS]

Cambridge

21 December 1873

My dear Nannie,

Your letter of Nov. 19th was duly received and gave as much pleasure as your letters always do. I am beginning to agree with Miss Foote that you are really growing in grace as you condescend to acknowledge that I have written to you once or twice! I am sorry though that you can give no definite account of your plans. I had hoped that Italy would be your destination. William is at present in Rome, he sent for your address in order to put himself in communication with you, hoping that his path might cross yours at some point. I suppose you will hear from him before long.

The principal interest with us has been for the past week Prof. Agassiz's illness and death. It is a great shock to his friends of course, but what a blessing that he did not live on half paralysed as there was a fear at one moment that he might. Have you come across the Feltons in any of your wanderings? Julia they say is much better, poor thing. Mr Agassiz's death I imagine will be a great sorrow to them. I saw Lisa the other day, she seems to be happy enough, but what a dreary sort of life she must lead. But I don't know why one should throw away their sympathy upon people whom I suppose would be very much astonished if they knew how generously one lavished it upon them.

Lizzie Boott and I went in the other day to see the Tappans who are away down Beacon St. in the Bangs' house. We went at lunch-time as Lizzie was going afterwards to the symphony concert and as she had been especially told by the T's to come at that hour. We went in and sent up our names, when a message was brought down to say that Mrs Tappan begged to be excused as they were dressing to go to the concert! What do you think of that for manners, to say nothing of friendliness? The concert was not to begin for an hour and a half, don't you think that those poor girls are to be pitied with such a mother. She has taken all their friends from them one by one. There have been no balls lately I think in Cambridge. I believe I told you about the one at Lizzie Bootts where I talked for an hour or more with Mr Frank Loring. (Charley Atkinson's Loring).[68] I think he is simply nauseating, his sentimentality is incredible, I was particularly disgusted as the beautiful Mr Charles Jackson was there with whom I had only a word owing to Mr L's gushing nature. It's perhaps well for the charms of Mr J. might have been more than I could resist; for it would be melancholy to throw away one's affections hopelessly from the start. His hair is what I find now my greatest snare, but I must say its beauty is somewhat counterbalanced by the tone of his voice which you may remember is not particularly musical in its quality. I am bidden this evening to tea at the Kotches to meet Miss Louise Minot – but alas! I cannot go having promised to dine at the Gurneys with Sara. Aren't

---

[68] Frank Loring was a Boston publisher. William's friend Charles Atkinson was in love with a Miss Loring, presumably a relation of Frank's.

Miss Minot and Nancy K. a curious combination? Nothing more is heard of Prof. Fisher, I don't think that Nancy would have him if she could get him, but why I should think so I don't know, having no sort of right to any opinion on the subject. Your 'Cousin Charles' has been distinguishing himself lately by telling Ellen Gurney that Venice in its glory was the highest form of civilization conceivable to the human mind and that it was such a pity that people at the present time should not wear swords and go about keeping them bright. Imagine *Don Carlos* himself with one! He is also talking in a way that is perfectly foolish about America, its such nonsense that one would be ashamed to think of it a second time, if you didn't feel badly on account of the girls, or rather Theo who drinks it all in, and as Mr Boott says it's too bad 'as he has taken heaven away from her to take this world too'. Theodora however from some mysterious reason or other has brightened up the last few weeks in the most astonishing way. Our fears about Sara are gradually dying out entirely. She is as bright and well apparently as ever and is a delight to all the world. She does not seem at all absorbed by the Nortons or the children and we don't feel as if we had lost her at all. I expect to go to New York in January when I trust the journalist will be more civil than he was the last time. I do wish I could tell you such a funny time that I had with your Aunt Grace about him the other day. I hope I shan't have forgotten it all before you come home. Write soon again and give me good news of your plans. With much love to all.

Always yours
Alice James

To Sara Sedgwick   [Harvard, MS 1428]

1 February 1874

My dear Sarakins

I am going to please myself this morning and I trust not seriously displease you by sending you a few lines, which if you are merely just – a base, masculine, habit of mind, you may take as an answer to the letter with which you were so good as to cheer my exile, but knowing that you are nothing if not generous, I shall live in the hope of better things. I trust that New York is amusing you as much as it did me, and that in spite of the ash-barrels, old shoes, hoop-skirts and all the other various objects of art and virtue which so richly decorate them, you find the streets sufficiently entertaining. Aren't the women lovely creatures? I wonder if you are ever torn by pangs of envy and cry aloud as I did, 'why am I not made as one of these!' or rather why are not my gowns, for my features I have long since ceased to question as the work of an inscrutable wisdom, but I can't get reconciled to the peculiarities of my clothes, so that when I see a maiden arrayed as I am not, I am greatly visited by hankerings, hankerings which I am sure no woman's breast is quite a stranger to, be she Miss Abby May herself.[69]

Cambridge my dear, is in one of its convulsive fits of gaiety, for no known reason save despair at your departure manifesting itself in hollow mirth. Last night was a ball at the Bootts, which went off very pleasantly. We had songs from Mr Szimelinyi (in an arsenic green cravat) Mr Boott and Lizzy. I had a talk with Dr Haagen[70] if talk it can be called, this is a specimen; 'You knew Dr Freund, he has *lost* three children!' 'Impossible' cried I, 'yes' said he, and consulted his wife in German, who turned to me and said 'oh! yes, they had four children in three years!' and thus our souls communed for half an hour in sweet accord. Baron von Ostensacken was presented to me and I greeted him affably as Mr Ostens: (I couldn't for the life of me remember the end of his name) which insult he revenged by turning his back upon me after only one or two remarks, which may have

---

[69] Abigail Williams May (1829–1893), had published a pamphlet called *Dress* and was an advocate of dress reform.

[70] Dr Hermann August Haagen (1817–1893), entomologist had come to Cambridge from Germany at the invitation of Louis Aggasiz to develop an entomology department at Cambridge. He refused an invitation to return to Berlin to take charge of great collections there.

been baronial, but was certainly not gentlemanly. I don't believe he is any more of a baron than the clerk at Tiffany's, his nose looks at any rate as if it had come very recently into the family (the baronetcy not the nose). You will be glad to hear that we have had excellent news of the boys, William's fever was of the slightest. Please give my kind regards to Mrs and Mr Godkin, come back soon yourself and believe me as ever

Your loving friend
Alice James

P.S. I open my letter to protest against your staying away two or three weeks more as Theodora, who has just been in says that you contemplate doing. We will have none of that Miss, just you come home after a respectable fortnight, that is quite long enough for a modest woman to stay away from home, so we shall expect you tomorrow week at the latest.

I meant to tell you in my letter, that I had heard that Sargy and Lilla are to be married in a month or two and to live on no one knows what, they themselves less than any one I fancy.

Sargy's philosophy can hardly be of the fashionable positive school exclusively or he would never run the risk of assuming the entire responsibility of Lilla's solid proportions in addition to his own six feet of muscle, on such slender expectations as a summer to be passed in the sylvan shades of Park Sq. in Dr Cabot's house, which is the only tangible provision for the future with which they seem to be provided. Isn't it wild? I wonder what they'll make of matrimony between them. They seem to be such an impossible couple. Lizzie Sparkes told me yesterday that she was to be *guillotined* the first week in March! Mind about the coming home or you'll not find us which perhaps won't terrify you greatly however.

To Annie Ashburner   [National Library of Scotland, MS]

Cambridge

14 February 1874

My dear Nancy

I suppose you may have heard through Kirkland St. of my visit to New York, which went off very successfully more so than usual from some reason or other, probably because of the *robusteous* health which I have been indulging in so extensively of late, and which allowed me to be amused and not simply fatigued by the vast metropolis and its singular ways. It's a very entertaining spot, more so speaking humanly, not *architecturally*, even than London or Paris. I should think that a foreigner of the male species would be completely captivated on his first walk up Fifth Avenue and Broadway by the feminine specimens of loveliness which abound on all sides. The streets fairly swarm with them and although their faces may not individually be more beautiful than their New England sisters, their toilets are certainly more successful and exhibit their charms to the fullest advantage. I made no new and thrilling acquaintances but indulged in the usual succession of cousinly interviews, the length of which succession you will have some idea of when I tell you that in one family there are nine children in the next eight, and so on down to one! So you see even if I were greatly bent on it, I wouldn't have much time for cultivating relations other than those of the closest consanguinity. *A propos* of consanguinity, your consanguinity behaved itself most unhandsomely, never came to see me although I met it in the street one day and received a most flourishing bow, which I considered at the moment rather an insult. I haven't heard of any excuse for his conduct in the decease of any of his *collaborateurs* children, unless perhaps one of Mr Garrisons offspring may have taken upon itself that moment to leave this troubled sphere. If such was the case I should think that my visits would make them superstitious and that they might easily be induced to offer me a stipend to suspend them, at any rate till the offspring had passed from the susceptible years of childhood. I regretted especially that he should have behaved so on Sara's account as I think she was very much mortified, but won't dare to tell him so, which strikes me as a strange sort of affection and most unjust and really in the end unkind to him. This is the only trait which I don't admire and can't at all understand in our beloved Sara, but I believe that they assure us that there are spots even in the sun! I was very much startled the other day by Miss Grace asking mother whether she had heard any gossip about Theo. She put it however in so strange a form, whether Theo's manners were considered too affectionate with a certain party, that our minds were at once relieved. Who could have put such an idea into her head I can't imagine. Mother then told her all that had passed among us on the subject, which I think was a great relief to your aunt, as she has had no one for so long with whom to unburden herself. A few weeks ago we were all very much excited about it, but of late there seems to have been no new developments, so that our feelings which have been divided between hopes and fears have calmed down considerably. This is the whole history; Theodora's countenance I am sorry to say has for some time past not worn a cheerful and happy expression, such as one would wish to see in the face of a maiden, suddenly a transformation took place, she looked a different creature, with no change apparently in her circumstances save *constant* twilight strolls with you know who, and a perfect absorption in the children. For a week or two we thought of little else, but lately matters have settled down. At first one was naturally shocked as it is not an ideal alliance for a young woman, but in looking at matters all round I think better of it. Theo. is not a person to be happy as an old maid or to make others happy, and she is not likely in her present circumstances to have many chances, so that in that view it's not so bad, but for Heaven's sake don't repeat any of this for I should be shocked beyond measure if they should ever hear of it, as its just as likely as not that it will all fizzle out. Have you heard of William Sparks engagement to a Miss Mason of Taunton, Thomas Kotch's engagement to his cousin Helen Kotch, five years older than he, an invalid to boot, also the sudden sad news of Frank Atkinson's death in California, isn't it hard for the poor family? Charley looks like a ghost. Sargy Perry is to be married in April, I asked Marny on what, she replied, 'faith, hope and probably charity'. Mustn't Lilla be irresistible? Lizzy Sparks is to be *guillotined* she told me the 1st of March, so you see we are not going to sleep in these regions. I heard at the last Bee, which met here by the way, that the Miss Loverings[71] had more offers than any young women in C. which quite solves the mystery which has been so long troubling me, of why they were so scarce in Quincy St. don't you think its quite satisfactory? Marny has the most Boston arrangement with Mr Warner.[72] What do you suppose they do? Why, they read Constitutional History and meet once a week to discuss it! Doesn't it savour of the soil, if it had been anything but Constitutional one could conceive of it, but thus are the youths and maidens made in these latitudes! I have just been interrupted by a call from Lillian Horsford who is going away on a visit. I am to be president of the 'Bee' in her absence, don't you think I am getting on. Give much love to your parents and believe me as always,

Your loving friend
Alice James

To Sara Sedgwick   [Harvard, MS 1429]

Cambridge

16 February 1874

My dear Sara

Why, oh! why, don't you come? We're perishing without

---

[71] The Loverings were the daughters of Joseph Lovering (1813–1892), Professor of Mathematics at Harvard and his wife Sarah Gray Hawes.

[72] Margaret Storer was to marry the lawyer Joseph Banges Warner (1848–1923) in 1876. Joseph Warner was later to be the executor of Alice's will.

you! You are the most wretched fibster, that I have met in a long time. Didn't you promise that you were not going to stay more than a fortnight, and here it's months that you have been gone! If you don't come soon I shall in desperation elope with the handsome butcher-boy, with whom I have an interview every morning for the purpose of telling him that Mrs J. does *not* wish anything. He must think that we are a curious race, living on our own fat, unless he knows that madam only has him come for looks and galavants herself to market every morning. He is very good-looking and is filled with emotion whenever he sees one, so you had better fly to the rescue. Your letter came and caused deep joy, it was like your excellent self to send it to such a miserable sinner from amidst all your superior and *millionairy* friends. What does a millionaire look like? You must tell me all about them when you get home.

I had a letter from Bessy Ward two days ago announcing her engagement to a Saxon Baron Ernest von Schönberg. I think that if I condescended to a title I should draw the line at a duke. Aren't you sick of these flimsy Barons who are always on hand to be converted into husbands? How much more respectable a good solid shoemaker would sound, even better than a butcher boy! The Ward family are very much pleased I hear, so I suppose they imagine he is a somebody. Bessy says that it has been very hard for her to give up America and that she 'smiles through her tears', which is a very good occupation for the present, as long as she doesn't in the future weep through her smiles. There is nothing new. I took tea last night at the Bootts to meet the Ned Lowells, but only Mr Ned appeared. He is an unattractive youth possessed of concentrated Boston qualities, with a sad resemblance about the back of the neck to Harry. He paid Mr Howells a very great compliment, by insisting in a frenzied manner that *Arbuton* could not possibly have behaved otherwise than he did and introduced the Boston ladies, for the piazza on which they were was only three feet wide![73] Poor creature! if he takes novels so hard, what does he make

---

[73] This is a reference to W. D. Howells' story *A Chance Acquaintance*, published in 1873.

of history, to say nothing of his wife's flirtations. Your dear friend Mr Anderson popped in to call on Lizzy; he sat on the edge of the sofa tight and compact, like a neat little parcel drawn up at Metcalfs and talked for about ten minutes, and almost in the middle of a sentence, popped out again. He treated me with his usual contempt. What is the opposite to *elective affinities*! Whatever it is, he is one and I'm the other![74] *A propos* of elective affinities I have been reading Merimée's letters, a dozen of which are much better than three hundred, notwithstanding their excellence of style, they are awfully monotonous, treating of his personal relations alone with the fair unknown, of whether she will take a walk with him or whether she won't, usually she won't.[75] It is hard to imagine how a man could write year after year to an intelligent woman, letters which were not simply love-letters, about such trifles. But such are men! French ones especially I imagine, from my vast acquaintance with them, I judge. But what a string of nonsense I have treated you to, when I began I only meant to show you the base, blackness of your conduct, but my usual intemperance has as ever disgraced. Come, oh! come or you will have another dose! What do you suppose I heard the other day? nothing less than those dreadful Loverings had had no end of offers! It was insulting, but satisfactory as explaining the mystery of why the article had been so scarce in Quincy St., for if such ragged growth as the Miss L's are what's courted, it's no wonder that a rare exotic like – modesty forbids my saying who – is left unplucked upon its stem, to reach a bloom bordering, to put it delicately, on the full-blown. But to come to business, A. K. says she thinks the chocolate an imposition, if you think the same pray leave it behind, as its no sort of consequence. I fancied it would be a small parcel or I should never have suggested your bringing it. My paper is all gone and you must be glad. Every one sends love and prayers that

---

[74] Alice is referring to Goethe's novel, *Elective Affinities*, published in 1808.

[75] Prosper Merimée's *Lettres à une inconnue* were published in 1873.

you will soon make your appearance. Believe me,

Ever yours
Alice James

To Annie Ashburner   [National Library of Scotland, MS]

Cambridge

8 March 1874

My dear Nanny

This is the most beautiful Sunday afternoon imaginable. I
have been sitting by my open window for the last couple of
hours amusing myself with the adventures of Mme de Staal-
Delaunay as told by herself in her memoirs. I wish that I
could retell them to you in a more concise, but not less
charming manner than her own, but mayhap you have read
them, in which case you wouldn't certainly thank me for my
trouble and would much prefer bits of my own biography,
and consider my pen more adapted to relating the adventures
of a maiden of the nineteenth century than those of one of the
eighteenth who was shut up for months in the Bastille, a fate
however which she seems to have enjoyed considerably.[76]
But, now let me think what I can tell you out of my late
thrilling experiences that will be more interesting and exciting
than imprisonment in the Bastille! Whiste! I went out to
luncheon twice last week! A good beginning you must
confess. One morning I was innocently sitting with my book
after breakfast, when down pops like a thunder-clap an
invitation to lunch the next day at Shady Hill! Imagine my
tremulous excitement! Although I had determined to go to
town that day I instantly decided that it never would do for
me so to neglect my social position as to refuse such an

[76] Marguerite-Jeanne Corelier de Launay, Baronne de Staal (1684–1750),
intellectual and writer, was implicated in a plot against the Regent and
imprisoned in the Bastille. Her *Mémoires* were published after her death
in 1755.

invitation! So behold me trudging up the avenue in the drivingest of snow-storms, to find Lizzy Boott, the only other guest, awaiting. It was gently broken to us that the master of the house had been suddenly called off to New York, his sorrow at missing us was only of course surpassed by our despair. The combination of the departure and despair produced a very pleasant visit for Lizzy and me however. The women of the family are certainly delightful.[77] Since Charlemagne has been away, they invited father and mother to dine one day and several other people, no one went but the Gurneys, and Ellen said that she had all the time the strangest feeling that they had been asked whilst the cat was away. I believe he finds intercourse with the natives very distressing to his exquisite and Europeanized soul. His sisters had better not insult the natives by proclaiming it quite so loud, lest the latter should grow wrathy! My second luncheon was at Lizzy Bootts where I met a very select circle, consisting of Mrs Gurney, Adams, Whiteside (Eleanor Shattuck) and Greely Curtis and the Misses Marion Jackson, Rose Lamb, Lilly Cleolland and *self*! They were all extremely pleasant, I took a great fancy to Rose Lamb, do you know her? What should I get the other day, but an invitation to lunch from Miss Mary Loring, whom I met one day for half an hour in a railway carriage going from somewhere to Strasbourg and have never laid eyes on since, although I have basked in the presence of her irresistible brother Frank several times. She evidently thought that I would jump at her proposition which I didn't however and respectfully declined the honor. This is the end of my gayeties which I am afraid I have made seem even less brilliant than they actually were. We have been jogging on since in the same old way. Sara came back from New York in not very good spirits for some reason or other. I don't think that going away from home agrees with her, Lizzy Sparks is to be married tomorrow, I suppose you got some of the *two thousand* cards which I hear were sent. Don't you think that was a heavy price to pay for Mr P? I

[77] Charles Norton's sisters Jane Norton (1824–1877) and Grace Norton (1834–1926). Grace was a close friend and correspondent of Henry James.

leave open my letter to tell you how it goes off. They had a reception a short time since for Miss Mason and Grace Hop— told me that Mrs Sparks was ill so she received in a pea-green flowered chintz dressing-gown! Maria Peabody says it was foulard but I stick to the chintz as more natural. I don't know whether Florence has turned up yet or not.[78] However badly her mother may have behaved, F. is revenging it with interest on Lizzy. She has apparently done nothing to help her in her wedding preparations. It is a most extraordinary case and I should think that L. would feel it greatly. It wayeth dark and I want to leave the rest of my paper for the wedding, so fare thee well! I hope the Miss James of eighty whom I hear of, hasn't driven her humble namesake entirely from your affections –

10 March. Lizzy's knot was tied yesterday as tight as the numberless prayers and meanderings of the Drs Peabody and Newell could tie it. She looked as fine as a gorgeous gown of white silk with a train yards long could make her. Mr Pickering looked *awfully*, if looks prove anything one would say that he hadn't many years to enjoy his connubial felicity.[79] Mrs S. was grand in black silk and a great extent of widow's cap in all directions. Florence looked remarkably well in a beautiful embroidered muslin over pink silk. But the crowning glory of the occasion was Beatrice who waddled down the aisle in gray silk on a gentleman's arm as placidly as if she had been in Quincy St., with a great bouquet in her hand. Mrs S. they say struck an attitude, by the pulpit after Lizzy had walked away and gazed after her in the distance. Her poor son had the greatest difficulty in getting her down the aisle. She went at such a tragedy queen's pace. The reception was very small I believe. But ain't I glad it wasn't I! So is undoubtedly Mr Pickering! Mr Trowbridge was chief usher, he looked distressed in mind. Write soon, love to your father and mother and believe me,

Ever yours

---

[78] Florence Sparks, Lizzy's sister.

[79] Edward Charles Pickering (1848–1919), Professor of Physics at MIT.

Alice James

Do you recognize the enclosed Verses?

My dear Annie – Your letter of 19th came yesterday and I add a line of acknowledgement to my letter which has been waiting impatiently since the first of the week for my photo. Your excitement about Theodora seems to be natural, but not exactly necessary at present from all appearances. Theodora continues to improve greatly in spirits but that is all that there is to be said about it. If you were here I don't think that you would feel at all as badly about it for *Theodora* as you seem to do from your present point of observation. I understand it perfectly and should feel in the same way if I hadn't seen Theo. the last years. I wish you were here that we might talk it all over together. To put things down in black and white seems to make them so much more serious. But don't worry yourself unnecessarily, nothing will come for the present I imagine at any rate, so only be glad that Theodora has revived somewhat. I heard this morning that the Kotches expect a visit from Mr and Mrs Plunketchild, nurse, maid, and valet!! Mr P. is the son of an Irish Earl, your peerage will tell you which. Don't you think the little wooden house on Kirkland St. will be stretched to bursting? I hope it has been recently shingled! When you pick up your Earl's son I'll take you all in but the valet. In his place I will provide the distinguished services of Mr Simon or if the Earl's son should prefer him Mr Marshal if he is still alive at that period.

To Sara Sedgwick   [Harvard, MS 1430]

Cambridge

[25 March 1874]

My dear Sara

My joy at receiving your letter this morning was somewhat

tempered by my having so little deserved it. But I shall not bother you with excuses for the very good reason that I have none to give. Original sin is my only refuge, I was born bad and I never have recovered.

But to return to your letter. I was delighted to hear from you but sorry that you were not having that eventful career in search of which you deserted these classic shades. I had hoped from certain references of your Aunt Grace's to luncheons and dinners that you were as hilarious as possible. Is not the New York easy, good-humoured, unsophisticated gabble a relief after our tormented culture? Why don't you pitch in and throw it all overboard and become like unto them? It's the best thing you can do for yourself as long as you are too inferior a being to be a manageress of the S. H. society.[80] *A propos* to the society, my social position in Boston which as you probably have observed, had but the feeblest tenure of existence especially this winter having bravely sustained life upon the slender nutriment to be extracted from *dec*lining *one* Beacon St. invitation, is now forever assured. I have not only been invited but have *assisted* at one of Miss Leihnor's kettle drums tenderly conveyed thither by Fanny Morse who, if I had been a sucking babe could not have more carefully guarded me from the boisterous winds of heaven than she did from the cold neglect of the world. I have always heard that sick parasites worried their way into society by their connection with various *societies*. It only proves the superiority of the S. H. to all other organizations, that no matter how abject your poverty if you are only a parasite it will hold out a friendly hand to you in the very face of a phalanx of patricians. And a solid lot of them there were last Saturday in Park St. and a stupid time of it did we all have together!

Poverty reminds me of my visit to New York, or rather of my non-visit. You must not mention this on your return in Quincy St. A vague rumour reached number 20 a few days

---

[80] S. H. is a reference to the Society to Encourage Studies at Home, a correspondence school for women, started by Anna Eliot Ticknor in 1873. Anna Ticknor lived in her parents' mansion on 9 Park Street, Boston. Alice was persuaded to become a 'manageress' by her friend Fanny Morse.

ago. A package of dynamite suddenly introduced into the midst would have produced a less shattering effect on the family circle – parent and child torn literally limb from limb. You may think it ridiculous, but it's true nevertheless. If I go to New York I shall have to buy some weeds, which in these rural districts I can do very well without. Mother is constantly throwing out dark and mysterious hints upon the necessity of economy and how I am economizing! (is it spelt with an s or a z?) I am in a very robust condition of health so that I cannot wriggle out there, but I am strongly tempted to abandon virtue when I think of thee as a companion in vice and of the little parental encouragement which I receive. But I shall be rewarded, I have quite determined elsewhere.

I agree with you with a painful intensity about Mr H's story. I could hardly read the last number. I am so sorry that he has written it. I met on Wednesday at a little fight given by Mrs Putnam for Ellen Emerson. I couldn't say a word to him about it, it's uncomfortable to meet him.

There has nothing new come to pass since you left. I have been making all the visits I can before the spring days come, a time contrary to the rest of the world, not joyful to me. Among others I made one upon Lilla Perry, who for a long period I have been struggling to like, but it is a struggle that I can no longer keep up I was thoroughly routed horse and foot the last time. When she confined her wonder and admiration to her intellectual achievements I could stand her, but now that she rams her moral perfections down your throat its a little more than my imperfect digestion can stand. Sargy always had the capacities of a cormorant, so he is able to swallow her whole, not having to think about her as she is going down must make it much easier. He looks worn-thin poor fellow. I am dreadfully afraid that he is very anxious about their future. They live in the smallest of conceivable houses, and altogether its awfully dreary, and she the dreariest part of it. I hug my own ignorance if all her learning can do no more for her!

Our dear Gurneys I am afraid plunged into a dreadful storm. How they must have longed for Faycreadeather St. and how we shall long for them. The Bootts gone now we shall be deserted next winter. With love from all and kind remembrances or something that's proper of that sort to your brother. Believe me

Ever your affectly
A. J.

To Annie Ashburner   [National Library of Scotland, MS]

Cambridge

9 June 1874

My dear Nancy

I am going to try and write you a respectable letter, being quite filled with mortification when I remember the shabby nature of those which I have recently sent you. I have been so glad to hear from Kirkland St. of your late gayeties. Dissenting bachelors must be irresistible. When you write you must tell me all about it and about some one in particular. I was also pleased to hear that you had seen the Dixeys, and liked the mother. You must have been disappointed if you expected to find Ellen changed. She only waked up for a brief moment, whilst she was announcing her engagement, when she seemed transformed. It was soon over and she relapsed into the same old story. What did you think of Richard? Is not she a strange creature for him to have chosen!

Have you heard of my recent adventures? I shall suppose that you have not and tell you all about them. Some four weeks ago my fond parents imagined that their delicate flower was pining for a change of air, so I was despatched to New York, to pick up my courier Mrs Walek, who not knowing her business thoroughly well, kept me waiting whilst she made her preparations, for a week. When we finally started we went to Philadelphia where we passed a day very pleasantly and from there proceeded through, what

I have always heard was very beautiful, the coal-region of Pennsylvania to the seductive town of Elmira. The coal-region is hideous and we had a wretched night at E., but all our troubles vanished when we reached Niagara the next day at noon, that being the end and aim of our careerings, which must have seemed rather vague hitherto. I suppose you have been there, but I am going to gush about it just as if you hadn't. We stayed four days and the last was the most beautiful of all. Did you ever know such an exquisite spot, notwithstanding all the brides and grooms, and the Sallies, Nellies, Minnies and Carries written over every available spot? We used to spend all our days in gazing at the beautiful thing and I wonder now what kept me from gracefully leaping over the railing and floating down into the beautiful soft mist below. But I must stop or you will regret that I neglected the little feat. We stopped on our way home for a day in Albany with some cousins of ours. The Misses Gourlays, four old maids, who live together in poverty, ill-health and the most pious cheerfulness. They killed me with admiration and amazement. How do people manage to behave so well, it's discouraging to one who is alone distinguished for her ill behaviour under the most felicitous circumstances. The last two words remind me of a letter which I got a couple of days ago from Nanny Kotch. She is at Heidelberg in a German family eating raw fish, cold sausage and beer and flirting and breaking the hearts of the natives, I imagine from the hilarious tone of the epistle. She is the most amusing creature. How any human being can have lived in the world for twenty-eight years and have learnt so little about it as it really is, is a great mystery to me. She is just the creature for a romantic German to fall in love with, I only hope she won't reciprocate the little attention. She is too sweet and clean for such a calamity to befall her.

A propos of falling in love there is a young Englishman recently imported of the name of Benson of whom everyone is supposed to be enamoured. I took tea with him on Sunday night at the Gurneys, he has certainly a most sweet face but one feels all the while as if he ought to be a woman which is fatal I think to *la belle passion*. And then my dear, he possesses a tenor which every one admires to distraction, and which bored me to death, as he sings nothing but the most extreme German songs. I am pursued wherever I go by music, and I am getting very sick of it. It does very well in its place, a very small one it should be by-the-by, but when one goes out to be talked to, to say nothing of occasionally putting in a word one's self, to have this perpetual singing sprung upon me is a swindle I think. I hope you won't be too much disgusted with me, as I hear you have recently been to a musical party at your cousins. That's a different thing, for then you start out fair and square and make up your mind to put it through, and you are not taken unawares as you are on a social occasion.

I wish I had some thrilling event to communicate to make the rest worth sending, but Cambridge is in the most stagnant condition lately. There is nothing new in Kirkland St. Charlemagne keeps up his attentions to Theodora of whom I see very little. Sara is lovelier than ever I think. She goes off soon to Gorham where I am afraid she has rather a poor prospect for enjoyment. You know of course of Mr Godkin's being established in the Eliot or rather Richardson house. He seems to like it very much and he bears up in the most remarkable manner. Mrs Richardson and her children are going to pass the summer with him which will be a great thing for him. Aunt Kate and I are going off the first of July to Ripton where we were last summer, preferring to bear the ills we have there than to fly to those we know not of. A letter has just this minute come in from my brother Wilky's wife sending a photograph of the baby. It's lovely and the boy altho' his name is Joseph must be quite a little beauty. Is it not hard that we should have two babies in the family neither of whom have we seen? William is just starting off however to get a sight of them. He is going West tomorrow morning to spend a month in visiting his relations and his native land. I trust he won't broil to death. You may thank your stars that I interfered in time and saved you from the photo which he meant to send you. Do write soon, though I deserve it so little both as quantity and quality. With love to all your circle.

As ever
your affectionate friend
Alice James

To Frances Morse   [Harvard, MS 1506]

[Wednesday, 1874]

My dear Fannykins

I don't know whether you have heard of my return or not, –
I am going to pretend that you have not and announce the
thrilling event and so have an excuse for sending you a few
lines.

We had four lovely days at Niagara. The weather was
perfect and is there anywhere under the sun anything so
beautiful as the falls? The more one gazes the more exquisite
they grow, don't they? Didn't you almost die to lie down and
just be scooped over into the foam? What a pity it is, that it
should be so far off and can belong so little to one's existence,
it must make one better to have such an object constantly in
one's life. But I have been quite consoled for this bothersome
world by a little sight of Sara the other day. When I got
home and reflected that you and she were both in it and that
you both condescended to look upon me in a friendly manner
I came to the conclusion that I couldn't be so abjectly base as
I seem to be to myself. Pray don't abandon me in disgust for
my only hope of salvation will be gone.

Theodora says that you are coming to Class-day. Won't
one of you come here. I suppose it is hopeless to hope for
Mary too as she is promised to the Ashburners as usual.
Don't you like this weather and isn't the country exquisite?
Drop me a line and say that you don't hate me. Give my love
to all the family that will accept of it – and believe me my
dearest Fanny

Always your loving
A. J.

To Frances Morse [Harvard, MS 1507]

Bread-Loaf Inn
Ripton

21 July 1874

My dear Fanny

What a worrying sort of a week you must of all had of it. I only hope that you were quietly at Beverly and not in the midst of the hubbub at Saratoga all that time. We are so far off and get so little news that I feel as if I had hardly heard anything about it. Is it true that Sall disgraced herself as they say she did? Do write and tell me all about it. I suppose you are all content as Sall didn't beat it? But how glad you must be that it is all over. I should think that the suspense would have been dreadful.

Now for the Bread-Loaf.[81] We have been here past three weeks today and are all thing considered very well satisfied. The house is very comfortable the air delicious and the country about has many beauties. I have had some delightful rides, the roads which are much too rough for driving are just the thing for horse-back. I only wish I had a congenial soul beside me, my companion hitherto having been confined to Mr Battell and a youth from Brooklyn who calls me *maam*! In August however I expect to have the gallant Edwin to escort me. I wish you could see the sunsets, they are perfectly gorgeous. The hills slope down on either side making a hollow in the middle of which on a clear day rises one of the Adirondack flank behind which the sun sets, it looks exactly as if it had been arranged on purpose to produce the best effect. The forests are extremely handsome from a distance

[81] Alice had gone with Aunt Kate to the Breadloaf Inn, at Ripton, Vermont.

but are too dense in quality for agreeable investigation at present, at any rate. The constant showers which I believe you have had too have kept everything deliciously green haven't they!

I want muchly to hear from you, do write soon. The one blot upon our happiness is the absence of anyone to speak to of an interesting nature. The people are all excellent harmless stupid creatures, with only one person who is positively disagreeable, but they are deadly tiresome. The boasted talent hasn't yet given any signs of life. But from Lizzy's and Sara's accounts I don't believe that they are much better off, and then these heavenly rides console one for every other woe. Mr Batten has two or three excellent horses a most unusual thing in the country I believe. Tell Mary that I wish she were here that we might go off together some of these beautiful afternoons.

Our landlord is a curious specimen. His family it seems are very respectable people, gentlemen and ladies, but he unfortunately doesn't take after them in that particular. He is as good as he can be, but so peculiar. All the people about the place though are delightful, the best sort of Yankees. I never saw the race before in such perfection, uncorrupted and I trust uncorruptible. The stable man is a devoted admirer of Don Quixote and the waitresses are all called Mrs and Miss. Mrs Trussell who is our faithful friend came up to me the other day at breakfast and looked into my face with her sweet eyes and said 'you don't feel very well to-day, do you' and then tenderly stroked my hair back. I could have kissed her then and there, in the presence of the whole dining-room. She looked so sweet. It is a perfect pleasure to have such sort of people to wait on me. You ought to have seen John the aforesaid stable-man refusing a fee to-day, his superior smile as he shook his head and declined the insult was rich.

I have just been reading over my letter and feel ashamed to send you such a shabby scrawl so stupid and half the words left out, but it is too late to begin again, so I shall inflict it on you in hopes that it may have one virtue, that of bringing forth one from you for which I pine. I send a great deal of love to your mother and Mary and whatever is proper to the gentlemen of the family.

Ever your loving
A. J.

To Annie Ashburner   [National Library of Scotland, MS]

20 Quincy Street
Cambridge

11 October 1874

My dear Nancy

I have at last returned, I hope for good, from my wanderings, having got back [the] day before yesterday from Brattlebro,[82] whither Aunt Kate and I went to pass a week with the Bootts. We had heard that there were very good saddle-horses to be had there, so we thought, Lizzy and I, that it would be pleasant to verify the statement. We found that it had some foundation in fact, but as, owing to fatigue, weather and a strict observance of the Sabbath, I was unable to take more than four or five rides together, the first two or three being devoted to inducing the wretched stable-keeper to give me a decent horse and an endurable saddle, and the last two or three to developing a spirit sufficiently superior to such trifles as legs scraped to the bone and the consciousness of looking like an animated meal-bag to the jeering natives of the village, the equestrian side of our expedition was not surrounded by the glory with which my fancy had fondly clothed it. Brattlebro itself, however, was charming and we made acquaintance with some of the people who were quite characters in their way. First and foremost I came near having an offer! One old gentleman who came to see us one evening, asked one of the ladies the next day whether she thought Miss James would have him. Imagine the flutter-ation within my bosom! At last I was to have the privilege of

---

[82] Brattlebro had a famous water-cure sanatorium, as well as horses.

declining matrimony and of escaping the mortification of descending to the grave a spinster, not from choice of the sweet lot, but from dire necessity. But, alas! no such fate for me, the man was a wretch, it being his habit to destroy the peace of any maiden who might come along, by this airy little remark. My fate, which if he had spoken I should look upon as rapturous, is as humdrum and hopeless as ever.

We also consorted with some friends of the Bootts, the Wells, who trace their descent from the English kings before Jesus Christ. Mr Boott questioning Anglican BC royalty received for answer, 'oh! you know those old northern creatures, Fergus, Thor, etc.' Now I don't believe Devonshire aristocracy can beat that! certainly you don't find it in lodgings.

I was delighted to find that you were in Devon, for if there is an earthly paradise there it is, in my opinion. Not lodged in Ifracombe, however, but in Lynton, which if you haven't been to, I shan't speak to you when you get back. Such a spot! One can hardly believe it's true at first. I have been out taking a little walk this afternoon. I went first to see the Nortons and then to the Sedgwicks. Theodora I found alone. Sara has gone off to Naushon. I am sorry that Theo. shouldn't have had an invitation too, she has been so shut up all summer and has behaved so beautifully about it that she deserves some amusement. But Sara is much the greater favourite of the two, and I am afraid it will always be so. There does not seem to be any cause for immediate anxiety from Charlemagne, I don't think anything is going on at present.

I wish I had something new and exciting to tell you the only thing of interest for us has been the birth of nephew no. two! Wilky's wife presented us with this addition last week.[83] Everything is very prosperous so far. I am so glad that it is a boy and not a miserable girl brought into existence.

Harry's return has been another source of pleasure to us, but we shan't keep him long, he already talks of spending the

---

[83] See note 57 above.

winter in New York or Washington.[84]

Theodora told me that they had not very good news from your mother that she had some trouble in her foot. I hope it is all over by this time. Write soon and tell me your winter plans. I have made the most virtuous ones for myself on the score of letter writing to the world in general and to your fair self in particular. So expect to be bored. Tea awaits me so good-night with much love to all.

Ever yours
Alice James

To Annie Ashburner   [National Library of Scotland, MS]

20 Quincy Street, Cambridge

21 November 1874

My dear Nancy

Your letter from Bath came a few days ago and gave me much satisfaction. I am very glad that you are thinking of London for the winter, I should think that after one got used to it, it would be a most interesting spot. I was never there long enough to be anything but oppressed and depressed by its size and by the great seething multitude which it contains, but that, as one grows familiar with it passes off, after awhile I suppose. Do you remember that day, that Aunt Kate, Harry, and I lunched with you and after luncheon walked round to the Nortons. I don't think that I was ever more impressed with the size of the place than by seeing this great quarter the existence of which I had never heard before, with its interminable rows of houses all packed with human beings. Do you expect to be in that region again?

---

[84] Henry James had returned to Cambridge from Europe where he had been travelling and writing for two years. He spent winter in New York, putting together his first three books and launching his literary career. In 1875 he returned to Europe.

We are all anxiously waiting to hear what you say to Sara about going over to see you. I should think you would enjoy seeing her, but I am selfish enough to hope that you will discourage the enterprise. It seems a great undertaking for her at this season of the year, but I believe she is a pretty fair sailor. I should think that you yourself would joyfully hail the proposition. I shall envy you dreadfully the possession of the lovely creature. I hope that if she goes it will do her good, she seems dreadfully sad lately. I am afraid that it is that [dreadfully scored out] (I must change my adjective having twice already made use of the above elegant one) *horrid* man who is preying upon her. I have little doubt (remember that all this is *strictly private*) that last winter he either offered himself or made known to her his intentions on the subject. I only wish you were here that we could talk it all over together, it's so hard to write about such things, putting them down in black and white is rather alarming. But I can't but think that whilst Sara was in New York something dreadful happened. She looked when she came back as if she had seen a ghost, as Ellen Gurney says. She was gone several weeks and the very day she came back Charles suddenly skipped off himself without waiting to see her, which was rather curious considering she had been gone so long and that he was such a beloved brother. From that time, I have heard from good authority that all demonstrations, which she used to indulge in so largely, toward him have ceased. And then the ways of the Norton women towards her have changed greatly. Whether they are angry that she won't marry Charles, or whether they think that she is endeavouring to entrap him the dear only knows, but whichever it is it seems hard that they should visit their vengeance on her, poor innocent victim. Oh! I should enjoy strangling him! But I think that Sara will hold out. Ellen Gurney has a horrible impression of his persistency and strength of will, when he once determined on anything. Poor Sara may be used up in the fight but at present at any rate I imagine she holds the idea in horror. One never can tell what a human being may do, however no matter how well one may seem to know them, so any-day the thunder-bolt may fall, but I am in no immediate fear. I don't know why I have written you all this, I am afraid I shall startle you unnecessarily, don't imagine that anything new or definite has taken place, but only that my mind is very full of it and I know that nothing could interest you more.

The James race has at last risen in its might determined to do what it has been endeavouring to do for eight years, that is give a *Cambridge* party. Next week is the appointed time, so that unless you hear of the sudden decease of any of the family you may imagine us towards Wednesday or Thursday in the throes of anguish; but I forget you won't get this till it's all over, but your sympathy after the event will be equally if not more necessary than before, remorse being a more deadly affliction than anxiety. Would that you were here to adorn the occasion! I saw your friend Mrs Peabody the other day. We confabulated about you and came to the conclusion that you were a pretty nice crittur upon the whole. She is a pleasant comfortable little party isn't she? I haven't yet heard her husband hold forth, everyone is delighted with his preaching I believe. With love to all your circle. I am

Ever yours
Alice James

To Annie Ashburner   [National Library of Scotland, MS]

Cambridge

13 February 1875

My dear Nancy

Your last letter was most gratefully received and would have been long ago answered were I not the most abandoned of sinners, a fact which you have doubtless long ago discovered. I am glad that you are established so comfortably in London and that you are enjoying it. I saw Miss Grace this morning at Mr Bocker's lecture, whither we go every Saturday for an hour to cultivate our little minds (not to great affect I am afraid in my case) and she told me that you were seeing something of Mr Cunningham and Sarah Forbes. How do you find the latter? She has always seemed more like an imp to me than anything else, but I am told that as you know her better something of the human appears. Is this so, or are you still in the early stages? Alice's engagement seems to be satisfactory and wonder of wonders think of Ellen Tappan's![85] Sara has told you of course all about it, and how secretly she has behaved, just like a great innocent babe, going about telling everyone herself in the most unconscious naive manner, so that one could weep over her. I only hope that the dear child has fallen into tender hands. Every one that knows him likes him very much and say that Ellen has been most fortunate. It's very funny, but I am told that he is an ardent episcopalian so Ellen will be a member of the church before you know it. It's the best part of the whole thing, she was always meant to lead a pious existence and now she will get a chance poor child. Between ourselves, though, can you conceive what the youth wanted her for? You may say money, but after all she hasn't got enough in her own right to make it worth while and her mother may live half a century. She has only between six and seven thousand a sum not to be despised for a spinster but hardly enough to make an inducement to matrimony with such an extravagant unpractical creature as Ellen. So my dear there must be a little love in the business, and what is there in her to attract a man who has been flirting about for several years past with the fast set of women, most of them clever, Mrs Bell and that set I mean. She is a most excellent girl and I have no doubt that if she only breaks loose entirely from her mother's tyranny then she will develop wonderfully, but my dear, consider that he has leased her for life! Isn't it awful, horrible, and incomprehensible. So think well before you bring your mind to it. When you see the horrid muddle some people make of it, it's enough to make all sensible spinsters congratulate themselves. The especial muddle which I have in my mind at the moment is the William Hunt menage which has been the

[85] Ellen Tappan had become engaged to a Mr Dixey.

talk of the town.[86] They are separated they say for good
now, and I should think that they might hold their tongues
about it. I believe he does behave pretty well but she prates
to all the world on the lovely subject. Don't you think that
if you had once had a man for a husband that no matter how
he treated you, you would keep it to yourself as much as it
was practicable? Ellen Gurney was so funny the other day,
she was repeating some one's having intimated that the
matrimonial state was rather a complicated one and subject
to more or less rubs of one sort or another, when she said
suddenly, 'can you conceive what she meant? I can't I'm
sure', whereupon I burst out laughing and told her that she
must not take her blissful condition with her beloved
Whitman as a sample of marriages generally.[87] She is
certainly the most *married* and the most happy woman I
know. It has wonderfully improved her, she grows all the
time more and more delightful. I seem to have laid myself
out on the marriage question rather extensively, you mustn't
be alarmed for I have no plans for myself just yet, but it is a
topic always interesting you know to the spinster mind. We
had a call this morning from young Mrs George Shaw who
has just come to Boston. She was a Miss Motre of
Philadelphia, her mother was a friend of father's. She is a
nice girl and quite handsome. I wonder if she has the least
idea of what is thought of her husband in these parts, I hope
not. I haven't seen anything of your friend Mrs Peabody
since I called, she has had a sad time with her husband poor
little woman. I believe he is much better now. They are all
well in Kirkland St. I am to take tea there to-morrow night
to meet Lucy Washburn, why, oh! why, not you too! That
joy will come some of these days I trust. I was so sorry for
your disappointment about Sara it must have been a great
one. She seems to be quite bright at present I don't know of

[86] William Morris Hunt (1824–1879), painter, pupil of Thomas Couture,
who had settled in Boston in 1864. In 1855 he had married Louisa
Dumeresq Perkins.

[87] Ephraim Whitman Gurney (1829–1866), educator, taught classics and
philosophy then became Harvard professor in History in 1869.

any new complications with the Nortons. Charles I believe is devoted to Theodora, I suppose because he can't get hold of Sara. It seems to agree very well with Theo. she is as stout and rosy and cheerful as possible.

I don't believe that I have written to you since the ball which was most successful. Every-one said they enjoyed it and they seemed to. There were much fewer middle-aged spinsters in black-silk than I had feared there would be, and more men also than we feared. Since the great event I went off to New York for three weeks and enjoyed myself greatly. It's an entertaining spot always and this time more than ever so. William is there now for a week's holiday. Harry is there for the winter so that our family is reduced to the slenderest proportions. I have since I began this been interrupted by a call from Charley Atkinson, who sends something to you in the way of regards and wishes me to add the word '*Fire*' whatever that may mean, he thinks you will understand it. He looks quite well but they say he is pining for Miss Loring, isn't it sad? This is the most foolish of all the foolish letters which I have inflicted on you but I am too stupid to send you anything better, so here goes. With love to you.

Your affectionate friend
A. J.

———————————————

To Annie Ashburner   [National Library of Scotland, MS]

Cambridge

14 March 1875

My dear Nancy

I had hardly sent off my last letter when I received yours enclosing the photograph. I felt I assure you duly reproached for my long negligence, but I was notwithstanding glad to hear from you and thankful for the letter but most

unthankful for the picture, which I think simply detestable.
You look as if you were about sixty in the first place and in
the second as if —— [her blank], but there is no use trying to
express my sentiments on the subject, do send me another, as
soon as you can so that I can destroy this wretched libel. I
may as well now as later explain the mystery of the enclosed.
If your memory is good you may remember that the original
is of rather an original nature, so you won't be much
surprised when I tell you that the day your letter came and as
soon as he saw your photograph he went and got one of his
own beautiful self and brought it to me saying that I must be
most particular to send it to you in my next letter. I asked
whether you had expressed any desire to have it, whether he
thought you had meant yours for him or whether he had the
slightest grounds for thinking that you would consider him
very forth-putting, as they say in these parts, young man.
To all of which observations he answered 'no but I wish it
sent'. So here it is and don't make me responsible for it.

I have been having quite a gay time lately, Cambridge has
been entertaining Ellen Tappan and Mr Dixey. They dined
with us last week, and after dinner we went to a little party
at your aunts, yesterday evening Lizzy Boott had a little party
for them and tonight we are going to dine at the Gurneys to
meet them, so you see there is no danger of our not seeing
enough of them or they of us. Mr Dixey I am horribly disappointed in. He is about the lightest weight that I have ever
had the pleasure of knowing. He seems like nothing but a
little society creature and rather a snobbish one too. I
imagine he is very amiable and good and he has a certain
physical refinement, but I should say that that was all. What
he wants of Ellen is more than ever mysterious. Oh! he is so
flimsy, *so flimsy*, whether he seems more so because we know
so few *party*-men, I don't know, but he is certainly a triumph
of the kind.

The party last night at Lizzy's was not eminently successful
owing to rather a scarcity of the the male sex, to which on
social occasions, whether we have the vote or not, we are and
shall always be slaves. I talked most of the evening to Mrs
Child, Ellen Tappan and young Eliot Lee, one of Bessy Lee's

wild butcher boys of brothers. Mr Charley Atkinson was
there, he asked as usual with interest after you, what a pity it
is that he always thinks it necessary to talk nothing but
nonsense at parties, it's dreadfully tiresome after a while.
The poor fellow looks thin and pale, I wonder whether it is
still Miss Loring. Why is it that love affairs appeal so much
less in real life to one's sympathy than they do in the silliest
novel, even in a double-column Harper's reprint? Lizzy had
fortunately refrained from inviting the odious Mr Frank
Loring whose sentimental goody compliments are a little
more than I can stand. But she had there a funny little man,
a Mr Bancroft, do you know him? He had been talking for a
long time to Fanny Morse, during a respite I went up and
spoke to her, when suddenly Mr Bancroft appeared behind a
large cake-basket which he offered first to Fanny and I,
supposing he meant to do the same to me, bowed my head
and said, 'no thank you' whereupon he became much
convulsed and said 'oh! good-evening, Miss James', and then
turned and fled with the cake-basket never again to reappear,
whether he was so frightened at having called me Miss James
without having been introduced or whether he thought that
I was a bold-faced jig and needed snubbing I can't tell, but
the effect was most peculiar, especially as he is a friend of
Harry's and was invited to the ball, accepted the invitation
and never came. It is a queer world and people behave in the
strangest way. The absurd little William Apthorp who has
been introduced to me more than once comported himself as
usual last night, looking everywhere but at me; as Mrs Child
says they seem to think that if you bow to them across the
room that you are trying to hook them into talking to you.
They have got about as much manners and civilization as
gorillas. I hope you don't think that I am in a very ill-
tempered condition but they all provoke me dreadfully, for it
is so easy to be gracious and courteous and it makes life run
so much more smoothly, and there are so many, many
corners to turn.

But I must go on with my list of gayeties, I think I have
exhausted those of the past however and have only
prospective ones to tell you of, and the only one worth

speaking of is a dinner-party at the Morses, where I shall see the beautiful Mr Charley Jackson, for whom I still cherish an unhappy and perfectly hopeless passion, he being still equally hopeless and passionate about Miss Fanny Appleton. Things are all wrong aren't they? Do they go as badly in England as they do in this beloved land I think that I am most decidedly written out and had better bring this feeble production to as speedy a close as possible. To think of what a contrast it is to a Norton effusion, full of good grammar, spelling, and writing, but my writing has been and will always be the bane of my life. There is no news in Kirkland St. Give much love to all and believe me

Always affectionately yours
Alice James

To Annie Ashburner   [National Library of Scotland, MS]

26 December 1875

My dear Nancy

I suppose that by the time that this reaches you all your Christmas festivities will have been almost forgotten. But if I am too late with a 'Merry Christmas', I can surely wish you a 'Happy New Year'. I only wish that I might have some hope of seeing you before the new year has worn itself into an old one, but I had even a faint hope I am afraid that it would prove so very delusive a one I fancy I am better off as I am, without any. I got your last letter with much pleasure, also the *Academy* for which please thank your father with my love. We were very glad to see the notice of Harry, its altogether the best that he has had in any English paper.[88]

What sort of Christmas have you had? It could not have been quieter than ours. But we have had one good present in the shape of a little niece born on the 24th making the fourth

---

[88] A favourable review by H. G. Woods of Henry James's *Transatlantic Sketches* in *The Academy* in October.

grandchild.[89] When I last wrote I think that father and mother were gone West, perhaps Sara has told you about our having had to send for them home on account of Aunt Kate's sickness. The day I wrote to you was the first of it, I had little notion how sick she was, thinking it was nothing more than an influenza. She has got well over it now and is almost as strong as ever. I went with her to New York about a month ago, and stayed a few days and did my winter's shopping. I shall make more of a visit later I suppose. It is too bad that Theodora's plans should be so unsettled. I wish that they had some one to ask them every now and then to make a visit. I should think that staying in a boarding house with a brother would be far from interesting. The journalist I believe has finally arrived, they have been expecting him for several days. William and I were invited to dine with him on Thursday last, but we were disappointed and I had to console myself with Mr Godkin and Mr Charley Jackson, the former as uproarious and the latter as beautiful and seductive as usual. My passion grows, it's fortunate I see him rarely for I am told that it would be altogether wild in me to nourish the faintest hope, Miss Appleton still reigning supreme over his affections. I saw her the other day at the Morses. She does not attract me in the least, but I am forced to confess that she is not bad-looking, its painful, but true. I refrained from looking in the glass for some time after I got home. It's most inconvenient to be possessed of so tender and apparently undesired an organ as mine. It was seriously threatened again the other night at Ellen Gurneys dinner-table, and it was only through immense self-control and the knowledge of his married condition to which I couldn't shut my eyes for a minute, but what they would open upon his stout washer-womanly wife who sat like a great sun-flower opposite me, that I preserved any tolerable equanimity. Perhaps you will be surprised when you hear that my charmer was Mr Moorfield Story.[90] I used to know him slightly long ago but

---

[89] Her niece, Alice. See note 57 above.

[90] Moorfield Story (1845–1929), lawyer and writer. He had a law practice in Boston and supported the rights of Black and Native Americans. In 1870 he married Gertrude Cutts.

never then understood my advantages, perhaps if I had I might have sat in the place of the sun-flower! Now what under the sun did he want to go off to Washington for that creature! It's a mystery of mysteries! But he is an adorable creature at any rate. But to return to my sense – Have you ever heard of Miss Ticknor's society for studies at home? If you haven't the enclosed circular will enlighten you, and you will be edified I trust by hearing that I have become one of the Managers.[91] The society has grown so much the last year that they have been obliged to add managers, and Fanny Morse who has had to do with it from the beginning came out the other day and said that I must be one of them, so after violently declining I finally meekly succumbed. I am with Miss Katharine Loring and have charge of the historical young women.[92] I think I shall enjoy it and I know it will do me lots of good. Don't you want to become one of my students? I will write you the wisest of letters about any period of the world you choose. You can laugh and think me as much of a humbug as you choose, you can't do so more than I have myself. My work has not fully begun till the first of January when I shall have about twenty letters pouring in from all parts of the union. Some of them are very entertaining and some very poor, but the best of the joke is that in June the students come to Boston, those that are able, and one has to go and be introduced at a yearly meeting, don't you think they will be impressed when they see me and Sally Russell. You must treat me mercifully when you write on the subject. I told Sara the other day in fear and trembling.

Did you hear through Kirkland St. of Mrs Greenough's receptions? Well Mrs J. has been inspired to have some too, so she is going to be at home on Thursday evenings in January, I wish you would look in upon us on one evening at least. I hope they will be successful, I am sure. If they are I suppose we shall have to have them every year. They are to

[91] See note 80 above.

[92] Katharine Peabody Loring (1849–1943) was to become Alice's closest friend and companion. Her father was a lawyer, her mother died when she was twenty. She lived at Prides Crossing in Beverly Farms with two younger brothers and a younger sister Louisa.

be very informal and sociable. I have it quite on my mind to tell you that I have seen Miss Louise Minot several times lately and have got to like her very much better than I did at first, one gets used to her absurdities. I have also become a bosom friend of Lillian Horsford at whom we used both to rail, she is a most excellent creature. I am dying to know who the mysterious man is whom you allude to in your last, the ex-lover of Sara. Do tell me. I am so glad to send this to London I like much better to think of you there than in the country notwithstanding the fogs and the smoke. Have you as good lodgings as last winter. Write soon and believe me

Always
Your loving
A. J.

To Sara Sedgwick   [Harvard, MS 1432]

[8 December 1875]

My dear Sara

As mother and I are sitting alone this evening, father having gone into Boston to read his lecture on Carlyle to a select audience of, I hope, admirers, methinks it would be sweet to send thee a few lines, my beloved Sara! Before I go any further however, I insist on one thing, and that is that you don't trouble yourself to write an answer, for strange as it may seem and badly as I know it sounds, I should be greatly displeased to hear from you, for all my immediate anxieties about you being satisfied by the admirable Theodora, I should be very much distressed to give you cause for any greater exhaustion than what will inevitably ensue from receiving this. Cambridge has been visited by no atmospheric or social convulsion since you left; we have been going on in the same old way, trying to do without you gracefully and cheerfully, but not very successfully, I must confess. I

went to a very stupid 'Bee' last night and on Tuesday evening
we went in to one of Thomas's concerts, about which there
was much to admire, too much in fact, for we were all
exhausted by its length. Theodora and Miss Lowell[93]
favoured us on Thursday at dinner, the latter somewhat too
rigid and established for a maiden of her slender stock of
summers. Yesterday morning the sun being more than
usually balmy, I was invited by William to take a drive in a
buggy. We made quite a circuit seeing many objects of
interest by the way. Tufts College, the Poor-house and
countless railway stations, risking our lives on any number of
rail-way crossings till the miserable sun by insisting on
staying under a cloud drove us shivering home at last. But
there is after all, one must allow, a certain charm about our
native land-scape, its broad and vacant expanse suggesting so
many possibilities to the aspiring mind, everything is yet to be
done. There is none of the oppression which comes from
contemplating the awful perfection of English beauty, where
there is nothing more to do, everything that could be done
having been done centuries ago. We got a letter yesterday
from Harry, who is still in Paris having lived under an
umbrella for the last fortnight. He had dined with the
Emersons at the Lowells hotel where they were staying and
said that it was a great sensation to see Ellen at a Parisian
table d'hôte.[94] What a sad business this seems to be of the
Bowleses.[95] I heard yesterday that poor Mrs Andrew had lost
largely by them. The world seems to be topsy-turvy just
now; it makes one feel very unrespectable not to be involved
in any of the fashionable catastrophes, our turn may come
though before we know it. All the family, that is mother,
father and William send their best love to you and hope that

---

[93] Mabel Lowell, daughter of James Russell Lowell and his first wife Maria
White.

[94] Ellen Emerson, see note 62 above.

[95] A reference to Samuel Bowles (1826–1878), influential editor of the
Springfield Republican. His younger brother, Benjamin Franklin Bowles,
was dismissed as head of finance, and died in Paris in 1876. Samuel
Bowles, himself suffering from declining health, was in Europe 1874–5.

you won't leave us pining too long. I should be very glad if you would remember me to Mrs Bristed, whom I can hardly flatter myself remembers me, but I recollect very well the Christmas week I spent with her at the Wards years and years ago. With deepest affection dearest Sara.

Ever your A. J.

To Annie Ashburner   [National Library of Scotland, MS]

20 Quincy St.
Cambridge

12 April 1876

My dear Nancy

It seems to me that it is an age since we communed one with the other. How does it strike thee? I am getting to feel as if you had turned into a regular British maiden and to fear that you are growing to despise your humble American friend. If such be the case, pray oh! pray never let me know, for it would afflict me deeply, my sentiments for thee, being unalterable! How strange it will be after all these years to meet and have a regular talk once more, such as we were wont to indulge in on those Sunday afternoons when you used to come and sit with me whilst I lay on the bed. I do not pine for the lyings on the bed, but I must say that an occasional confabulation would be refreshing to the soul. I have just been having one of an hour and half with Lizzy Boott who as you may have heard is off once more in a month for Europe. We shall miss them greatly, Mr B. especially, who keeps one in a continual state of irritation either of pleasure or displeasure one hardly knows which predominates. He is more of a child than most infants of six, but then he is very nice too. He is so handsome and frank and honest that one can't but forgive him all his absurdities till the next time he provokes you, when you make up your

mind that you will never speak to him again. Lizzy hopes to
study with Couture in Paris.[96] I wish that her work would
come to more than it does. She gives so much time to it and
it seems so the main interest in life for her that I am afraid
that as years go on and it comes to nothing more decidedly
good that she will be disappointed. Feminine art as long as
it remains a resource is very good but when it is an end it's
rather a broken reed. Matrimony seems the only successful
occupation that a woman can undertake. This reminds me of
the most idiotic conversation I had the other evening with
Miss Jane Norton with whom I dined at Mr Godkin's. She
said that she thought all these Boston women instead of
devoting themselves to painting, clubs, societies etc. ought to
stay at home in a constant state of matrimonial expectation.
They were all so happy together that men said to themselves
oh! she's so happy we won't marry her! Which was a new
view that men were attracted by depressed and gloomy
females, and also that they generally married them from
compassion. She also abused their habit of wearing water-
proofs – her own gown as she was speaking was of so
hideous a description that I should have been only too
thankful if I had only had a water proof to cover her up
with. Whether it was all palaver to please Mr G. I do not
know but whatever it was it was awfully foolish. Don't you
think its despicable for women to run each other down
before men? I always have thought it the shabbiest sort of
sycophancy. But to turn to a pleasanter subject I have just
got the most enthusiastic letter from Fanny Morse
announcing Bessy Lee's engagement to Dr Fred Shattuck.[97]
There has been lots of talk about her and Ned Lowell, who
there seems to be little doubt wanted to marry her. The
Frank Lee's started the business and now she has had a great
triumph in taking them entirely by surprise. They, or none of

---

[96] Thomas Couture (1815–1879), French painter of portraits and historical
subjects.

[97] Frederick Cheever Shattuck (1847–1929), physician. He had settled in
Boston to practise in 1875, having worked and researched in London,
Paris, and Vienna.

her family expecting it. It seems that eight years ago when Bessy was abroad with Mrs Edward Perkins, Mrs P. when in England wanted to go into retreat and she left Bessy with Mrs Shattuck and her daughter and Dr Fred who were there at the same time. The impression was then made upon the youth who has been constant ever since, but not in circumstances to declare himself. The moment has now come and all the world seems delighted. She is too pretty and attractive a creature to be unmarried and beside she would have no meaning as an old maid. Don't you love to hear of successful engagements, it always sends a thrill of joy thro' me, altho' my own turn I am afraid will never come on this side of the grave. I am deeply hurt at your ridicule of my professorial character I assure you it is not a thing to be laughed at, some day you may be only too happy to sit at my feet. Theo. dined here yesterday. Her visit to New York has worked a marvellous transformation she is cheerful as she used to be before Charlemagne exhausted all her vitality. I only wish she might permanently keep house for the journalist I think she would be quite happy if she could and then I think NY a much healthier atmosphere for her than this. For she is not an intellectual being and it does not agree with any one to try to be what they are not. All fears from Charles with regard to her are quite over we all think, I am only sorry that I should have communicated them to you. Sara is still in NY we miss her awfully. What joy it would be to have her engaged wouldn't it. This is a horribly shabby letter but if I don't send it I know not when I can write again so here goes.

Ever yours
A. James

To Annie Ashburner   [National Library of Scotland, MS]

[21 June 1876]

My dear Nancy

Many thanks for your note. We were for a few days very

anxious about father, but all that is over I am thankful to say – at least for the present, but when a man of his age has had one such attack one cannot but feel insecurity for the future. One immense blessing is that he does not feel nervous about a return of the trouble himself.

I was truly sorry to hear from Sara that you had a little uneasiness about your father, I trust that it was only a passing indisposition and that he is quite himself again.

It was very strange to think that you and the Gurneys and Bootts were all lunching together in London. How do the dear Gurneys seem out of Cambridge? I cannot imagine them out of their own setting. I hope that nothing was said or done on the occasion to offend Frankie who is the most delightful but uncomfortable infant of sixty conceivable. And to think that he is the father of that placid Lizzy! I enjoyed your account of Warner extremely and still advise you to go in for him. I should go in for any one I could get hold of, but I am less fortunate than you, my only prey are widowers and I have not reached that stage yet, I want to have a little hand at bachelors first. I hope you will excuse this shabby note but it is a regular dog day and my brain is more than usually stupefied. Father sends his best love and is much gratified by the kind messages which you sent him.

With lots of love
Believe me, As Ever
Yours affectly
A. J.

To Sara Sedgwick   [Harvard, MS 1433]

23 September 1876

My dear Sara

Having delayed writing to you so much longer than I meant to when I sent you those few hurried lines a fortnight ago, I thought that in the direct of excitements I would delay my letter a few days longer and tell you about the Warner-Storers wedding, but perhaps after all, the groom being from the Port, you won't care to hear about it – but it will be a good discipline for you.[98] But first, – I must say how delighted I am to hear that you are somewhat better and are about to exchange Mrs Cook's individual vegetables for Mrs Hooper's communistic board, to speak of naught but carnal gains.

I have given up all idea of going away as it seems altogether unnecessary for I am so well that to be any better would be quite superfluous, unless Miss Lichnor is to be more than usually erratic; (Fanny Morse says she feels as if we were the tail of a comet) she made a good beginning by summoning us all to Park St. on Thursday, to decide upon absolutely nothing. The ladies whom she had sent for to New York fortunately not arriving, she would think nothing of asking them to come from Timbuctoo. Mary Morse had said the day before on seeing the house all shut up, that she was quite capable of coming up on Thursday morning and opening the house and having the meetings, we laughed the idea to scorn, but it proved to be even so, and more, for when I got there at twelve, she told me that she had left Newport at seven and had had one meeting at eleven and now ours at twelve! She must be a joy to the masculine mind for she is the embodiment of all their pet theories about women. But me fears that you are sick of her and that you will think that I have got her on the brain, remember the paucity of our existence and be merciful.

Now for the wedding – well at a quarter before eight on Wednesday evening I sailed in solitary grandeur (William being ill in bed) to the mansion in Garden St., the door of my coach thrown open and I assisted to alight by two police men (fortunately not mounted) and saved thereby from some doubtless infinite, if unimaginable peril emanating from the brain of that red and white rotundity Mr William Storer; the pressure of so many Port-chucks suggesting to that feeble organ the possibility of a row. Dr Newell married them very inoffensively for him. The house was charmingly decorated

---

[98] See note 72 above.

with flowers and leaves, the handiwork of some half-a-dozen male friends of the bride, some of whom were ex-aspirers to the maiden, truly noble of them to thus adorn so beautifully the triumph of Joseph B. The company was large and I need hardly say peculiar, when I tell you that Concord was largely represented. Miss Peabody and the Kangaroo her nephew,[99] who nobly comes to our defence in the last Nation and that corpse of a Mrs Emerson, naturally home of the pattern.[100] All the Emersons were present, Edith Forbes more offensively complacent than ever, with a gown which she had attempted to have made low-necked but her courage gave out, an immorality which she might have spared herself considering the present fashion.[101] But the being who of all others interested, that is in appearances, was Mr Forbes who is a most striking and curious looking creature, but you have doubtless seen him. He has thirteen children, I believe and three very pretty daughters were there. We stayed till about ten o'clock and then came away congratulating ourselves on our single-blessedness.

William has been ill since he came home from the mountains on Saturday, but I hope that before many days he will be himself again, it is too bad that he should have such a drawback just as his work begins.[102] We hear though of sickness on all sides.

[99] Elizabeth Palmer Peabody (1804–1894), educator and author, member of the 'Transcendental Club'. The 'kangaroo' was presumably one of the sons of her sister Mary who had married the educator Horace Mann (1796–1859) and who after her husband's death moved back to Concord.

[100] Mrs Emerson had starved herself in her youth believing 'food was poison and that what she did not eat did her more good than what she ate'. (Strouse, p. 72)

[101] Edith Emerson, daughter of Ralph Waldo Emerson, had married William Hathaway Forbes, later president of Bell Telephone Co. His father John Murray Forbes was a business man who had a summer home in Naushon, Buzzard's Bay, where he entertained generously.

[102] William was appointed assistant professor of physiology at Harvard in 1876. Henry wrote to William in April: 'Guard yourself on your return to health, against expecting to be without fatigue. When it comes one regards it as belonging to one's old invalidism, but often it is quite normal and one would have had it if one had never been ill.' *Henry James Letters*, vol. 2, p. 43, 25 April 1876.

I had a letter this morning from a new student, who has as William says the spirit of a Crusader. She has been most anxious to improve herself but owing to the discouragement she has received on all occasions she has feared that she would be nothing but 'a cipher in the world's history'. She is truly pathetic and lovely and I am sure I shall enjoy her greatly. I had the most amusing call on the Haagens yesterday. The dear Dr surpassing himself. He has been called to Berlin 'the greatest honour my country could have paid me, [my former successors were then most distinguished early in Germany]. My former successor an intimate friend of mine has gone etc. etc.' He is too delightful and I trust they won't go. They hesitate in material terms being better off here. I hope they won't go he will be a great loss socially and scientifically. The family all send a great deal of love. Father is doing famously. Pray remember me most kindly to Mrs and Miss Hooper. Don't bother yourself to answer this letter if you are not in the mood.

Always affectionately yours
A. J.

To Annie Ashburner   [National Library of Scotland, MS]

Cambridge

28 February 1877

My dear Nancy

I was delighted to get your last letter and to hear that you had seen the young Henry. A day or two after yours came one came from him telling how much he had enjoyed seeing you and how friendly and pleasant you had all been.[103] I cannot

---

[103] Henry James had written to his mother that the Ashburners 'live in a remote, depressing quarter, and seem not without domestic dreariness. They were very friendly, and seemed to cling to me for society. I got the impression of their living in such deadly tranquillity that my coming was really a social event for them'. *Henry James Letters*, vol. 2, p. 93, 31 January 1877.

tell you how strange it seems to me to hear of your being homesick for these barren shores. I should be ashamed to have you know how I long for some of that picturesqueness and beauty on the face of nature, in which you are perpetually wallowing.

I am frightened sometimes when I suddenly become conscious of how constantly I dwell in the memory of that summer I spent abroad.[104] I suppose, however, that you will say to Lizzy Boott, that man liveth for people and not things, and that you are not pining for the rocks, boards and wooden shanties that so plentifully bestrew this blessed land. But for its delectable natives, who, to be sure, are excellent creatures, but then there are not more than half-a-dozen whom it would cost one much of a pang never to see again but then, again, you will say, that these half-a-dozen make up life and that without them beautiful scenery nourisheth not the soul. But is there not some one young woman with whom you can commune? What and where are the maidens, to whom I hear constant reference made in Kirkland St., as very attractive, whose names I know not, but think they are nieces of Miss Travers? Are they not to be consorted with? Or mayhap is my Nancy difficult to suit? Would you like to know what would fulfil, at the present moment, my highest ideal of earthly happiness? – Nothing more than to be driving thro' the streets of London town, with thee by my side, in a hansom-cab! Now, this consummation of bliss, with the exception of one trifling element, is constantly attainable by you – so why, oh! why, are you not happy? It can't be possible that the absence of the few molecules, which go to make up the person of your humble servant, should poison all your joy. I am too modest to think that! Talking of friends I have had it on my mind to tell you several times how much I am getting to like your ancient crony Mrs Cora Peabody. I have seen her at the Bee lately and have had long talks with her. You know we always have a fruitful and most harmonious theme in thee – commingling our sorrow for your absence, our hopes of your return and our joy in

[104] The summer of 1872. See note 50 above.

your virtues. I have never met her husband, but I think she seems to be thoroughly married to him. He shines through much of her talk. They have both behaved very nicely to a friend of ours, who has lately had a very disagreeable experience thro' a busy-body of mischief-maker. As the mischief was *a propos* of Mr P. he took pains to relieve the mind of our innocent friend and did it very nicely as did also his wife. All this I need hardly say is, of course, strictly private.

I wish you had some work to do that amused you half as much as my society work does me. I suppose it seems to you like an awful humbug, but it is not half so much so as it seems, and I in attempting to teach history am not half the fool I look. You may laugh as much as you please, but I am nevertheless speaking the truth. In the first place we attempt very little, and the little we do attempt we entirely accomplish, that is so far as our own part of the business goes. You see it can do very little harm to a poor uneducated maiden in the wilds of California, Kansas, Missouri, Michigan, Kentucky, Florida, Iowa and Illinois (I have students in all those states) who has never seen but half-a-dozen books in her life, to get a letter once a month from a semi-educated being in Boston who recommends and sends her good books to read and who has a very beneficial effect upon her spelling.* We who have had all our lives more books than we know what to do with can't conceive of the feeling that people have for them who have been shut out from them always. They look upon them as something sacred apparently, and some of the letters I get are most touching, girls who write to say that they have longed always for just such help and never hoped to get it, and the difficulties that they will overcome to join the society are incredible. Now this is the sort of being that we want to help and that we do help, so I do not see that there can possibly be any harm in it, if we are willing to take the trouble, and it is a good deal, I have to write between thirty and forty letters in every month, but I have nought else of importance to do. Perhaps you may wonder at my sudden onslaught upon your innocent self, but I feared it must seem very silly to you, and as it is what I

care about most just now, I did not want you to judge it
without a hearing. My paper is gone, so fare thee well and
write often.

Ever your loving
A. J.

*Mind I don't say grammar, so you needn't laugh at my hers
and theirs being somewhat mixed.

To Sara Sedgwick   [Harvard, MS 1434]

Cambridge

[20 September 1877]

My dear Sara

We have been all delighted after a period of suspense, to find
that you are not going to give us the slip for the winter,
conduct which would have been as base as well could be,
after all your fine professions of homesickness, etc. We are
rather anxious, however, if the truth must be told, about
your return, Miss Grace having recently plunged us into the
depths, by predicting extreme anguish on your part.
Assuring us that you were living with, as well as on 'la crème
de la crème'. She was busily reinforcing herself with brandy
peaches to let the inner woman down as easily as possible,
but what intellectual confectionery could we hope to lay in,
in six weeks, to throw a momentary glamour over our
bareness? We have been relieved tho', since, by a letter from
Harry making some reflections upon Mrs Dix, as a type
which makes us feel less like skimmed milk. But this is
wicked both to you and Harry, who would chop off my head
if he knew, forcing you into the same critical relations with
regard to the salt upon the verge of which I have so often
tottered after a sojourn, you know where. I was glad
yesterday to see Theodora who has returned from a whole
week of trial as rosy and rotund as she departed, and with

loud proclamations of enjoyment. I am convinced that it is only a spirit of opposition to us, and to brand us with dishonour. I have just been interrupted by a little call from Nancy, who has at last finished her round of visits and is going to condescend to us here in Cambridge for a while. You have no idea how she has brightened up since I saw her first in Newport, when it truly seemed as if she had been 'sat upon' by the whole of Great Britain for the past five years. Mount Desert has, however, worked a transformation and she is as lively and amusing as she used to be. Her deafness seems a dreadful pity, though slight now, I suppose, it must inevitably increase. From all she says I should judge that she is happier now living in England than she would be here and that we have mainly ourselves to pity in the loss.

So you have betaken yourself, madam, to Yarmouth to find a spouse after the manner of your great grandmother. It seems a strange matrimonial fishing-ground, herring having hitherto been my only association with those waters. Good luck to you, however! May he only not carry with him too strong a reminder of whence you hooked him. If they bite in numbers, bear in mind* the lone card spinster you have left behind. But aren't you frightened tho', at the mortality that has overtaken these since your departure. Cambridge is utterly demoralized, and those of us who have been always most-resigned and modest are in momentary expectation of presidents, widowers, lawyers, professors we know not what, dropping at our feet. If it goes on much longer all the virtuous little courses of history, art, charitable institutions etc., from which we have sought and derived so much consolation for our loneliness, will be utterly abandoned and many of us, I am afraid left disconsolate having sacrificed our 'resources'. Miss Farley was married yesterday and the six millions invited to Miss Choate the day before, such was the mob assembled at the latter festivity that the bride had to leave the house by the back door.

Of course you have heard from Kirkland St. the lamentations over Mr Godkins going to New York. Apart from the loss that he will be socially, I am very glad of the change on his account. Cambridge always seemed to be an unnatural place for him to be in permanently. In the first freshness of his grief I suppose, it was the best thing altogether for him. Miss Jane Norton must have done everything that any one could do to help him over it. But she has gone and now man-like he is beginning to take an interest in life once more and surely New York is a much wider field for him.[105] What strange things men are. Women never, I suppose, can understand them, and certainly they can never understand women. President Eliot's engagement has thrown a calcium light on the nature of man, on their capacity for renewing their existence. He has surely greatly lost in dignity by it, not that he shouldn't have married again, poor man, if he wanted to, but that he should have been able to fall in love again so completely as to have chosen a person so unsuitable as Grace for the position.[106] He is much excited, transported as if he were twenty, they say. The young woman herself doesn't seem nearly as much so. I fancy she feels her response belittles painfully. Father sends his love especially he says. He is pretty well, the summer in Newport was successful as summers go, but it worked no miracle for any of us. We are delighted at hearing of your going, but mind you we won't allow any staying all winter. Harry tells me he is going to send a hat by you. Be sure and not bring it if in any way a trouble. I shall never forgive you if you do. Well, lots of love,

Ever thine,
A. J.

* [A blot.] This melancholy revelation I have just made on turning over my sheet. You won't make me write it over will you.

---

[105] Godkin's wife had died in 1875, after the death of three children in infancy. Godkin had moved to Cambridge for two years; in 1877 he returned to New York.

[106] Charles William Eliot (1834–1926), President of Harvard, influential educator. His first wife, Ellen Derby Peabody had died in 1869. In 1877 he married Grace Mellen Hopkinson.

To Annie Ashburner   [National Library of Scotland, MS]

[n.d.]

My dear Nancy

Many thanks for your prompt and satisfactory epistle with
all its thrilling details. But why, oh! why, when you told so
much, did you tell so little? Especially about Mr Darwin, of
whom you say nothing, save that he is bald and elderly in
appearance, two highly interesting facts, I admit, but you
know that simultaneously with the news of Sara's
engagement came the news of his baldness and advancing
years, the latter industriously circulated, if you remember, by
the friend on the hill.[107] Now if you had only added, whether
he was tall or thin, short or fat, blonde or brunette, as the
transcript says, I should have blessed you forever. Sara's
dress must have been very pretty, the scrap of silk was a
most delightful thought. But I am distressed about the
presents, does the solitary bracelet represent the generosity of
the race of Darwin? Tell me all the others the next time you
write and don't forget me. Also just transcribe one little
remark made by William, no matter how insignificant, so
that I may feel for a minute that he is a living human being.
I suppose that you will soon be going to Basset to stay at the
'establishment' do write to me whilst there.[108] But I am
afraid that you are tired with all my curiosity. We were all
delighted that you had such a good voyage, and what storms
you just escaped! It must make you shiver when you think of
how near you came to them. The Kirkland St. household are
all well, we see them constantly of course, and they always
seem cheerful and happy, whether it is all heroism they alone
can say, but it looks like nature and proves them to be
excellent actresses if it is all assumed. Letters are thin daily
bread, and they have a provoking way of making themselves
waited for, in this stormy weather. There is nothing new in

[107] Sara married a banker, William Erasmus Darwin, son of the famous
naturalist, in November. Henry wrote that 'she struck me as very happy
and comfortable, and I should have great confidence in Darwin and his
prosaic virtues'.

[108] The Darwins' home was at Basset in Southampton.

our own household, we are all well, father especially so, better than he has been at all since his attack a year and a half ago. I have my letters each month and they keep me very busy for a fortnight, and I go to the Bee occasionally, tonight I am going to the theatre with William and so we jog on, and I suppose we are happy, at any rate we are not very miserable. We are having by the way lovely weather, mild as possible and as we are almost at Christmas the winter will seem a very short one, although we are so bereft of our friends. How is Theodora and how does she amuse herself? I heard that she was not rapturous about brother William, by which I was depressed for a minute, but I consoled myself very soon, by remembering that rapture was not her way and that Sir Philip Sidney himself would doubtless have met with but mild approval at her hands. She would have been afraid of compromising herself by showing what she calls 'Boston enthusiasm'. Give her my love notwithstanding and tell her that I mean to write to her whenever she writes to me. She has so many letters to write that one more won't make the least difference. (Private.) Do you know if a violent correspondence is kept up with Charlemagne? Mrs Child told the funniest story last night, she said that Mrs Norton had told her that Charles had received a letter from an English lady, a friend of the Darwins as well, saying that it would be highly probable that the widower Frank D. might fancy the youngest Miss Sedgwick! Wasn't C. a funny person to pick out for the suggestion. Mrs Child is completely puzzled about what it can all mean. She says he hardly goes to the house at all since the fair maid's departure. But I am tired as you must be. With love to all your circle.

As ever
yours affectionately
A. J.

To Annie Ashburner   [National Library of Scotland, MS]

Cambridge

14 November 1877

My dearest Nanny

I was thoroughly delighted yesterday to get your letter containing such good news. But *news* it was not, as you very truly say, for I have been a most interested follower of the little romance all winter and you may easily imagine, consequently how greatly rejoiced I was a few days since when your Aunt Grace came in to tell me that the affair was all settled.[109]

I have always had a weakness for having my friends married but I must confess that I began to feel rather hopeless about you buried among all those wretched John Bulls. I am therefore proportionately grateful to Mr Richards for showing himself to be a man of so much discrimination and I congratulate you most warmly dear Nancy upon having secured the affection of a man so highly esteemed as Mr Richards seems to be by all who know him.

I had a very enthusiastic account of your new home in Maine from Katharine Loring who made a visit there last spring.

I am sorry that you are not to come right home after the marriage, but of course it would be a dreadful season of the year. I hope that poor Mr Richards is a good sailor, for if he is not he is paying a very heavy price for you, Madam. I wish I could write you a respectable letter but I can only send this note now, which is very inadequate to bear all the deep interest I feel for you and the hearty wishes I have that all your present hopes of happiness may be more than realized in the future. Mother and Father send their warmest love and congratulations. I enclose a little note from William.

Always your loving
Alice James

[109] Annie had announced her engagement to Francis Gardiner Richards of Gardiner, Maine. They were married in London in February 1878. When he died in 1884 Annie settled in England.

To Frances Morse   [Harvard, MS 1508]

Cambridge

25 November 1878

How can I thank you, my dearest Fanny, for all your goodness to me this summer? – It seems absurdly presumptuous in this little sheet to think that it is competent to navigate the seas burdened with such a weight of gratitude as it must carry.[110] Your letters have been most delightful and I do not know what I have done to deserve them in such bountiful measure when your time must be so constantly filled up, pray never write when it is a tax. I am afraid that you may think that it is all very well if I had only said it some months ago, but it is only within a short time that I have begun to write letters and I find that I have to pay my debts much more slowly than I want to, for my friends have all been so kind that they have greatly accumulated during my long idleness.

I am very glad to hear that Mary is able to go about a little in Paris, I have been so sorry that she should have been so shut up through the summer and losing so many of the beautiful sights that you were all enjoying. But how much I envy her! – convalescence in Europe seems such an easy process, where there are so many helps on every hand. When one can only take a passive part in life, the bare, crude, blankness of nature here with nothing to call one out of one's self preys upon the soul, and makes the process of getting well a task and not a pleasure. But I hope that this does not sound like a lament over my own circumstances, for, I assure you, I am no longer an object of compassion. I shall have to admit, however, that I was pretty wretched through the summer and gave my poor family an immense amount of trouble, but for the last couple of months I have been learning to behave myself better and better all the time. My physical sufferings would have given me no concern, but my

---

[110] Alice had suffered a breakdown in April 1878 and seems to have considered suicide. In her *Diary* in 1892 Alice looked back to 'that hideous summer of '78 when I went down to the deep sea, its dark water closed over me and I knew neither hope nor peace'. (p. 230)

patience, courage, and self-control all seemed to leave me like a flash and I was left high and dry. For a young woman who not only likes to manage herself but the rest of the world too, such a moral prostration taxed my common sense a good deal. But, I suppose I needed the lesson greatly and I only hope that it will bear some of the fruits that it ought.

Why, my dear Fanny, have you never congratulated me upon the great joy that has been brought into life by William's marriage?[111] A happiness which grows day by day as we get to know our dear Alice better. How William can have been so fortunate a man, we cannot any of us understand, and he himself less than the rest of us. She is a truly lovely being so sweet and gentle and then with so much intelligence besides. I do not believe there ever was a marriage that gave so much satisfaction as this, to one side of a house at any rate. It was entered into by both of them so seriously and deliberately that I cannot but feel that the years will justify them. They have rooms very near us in Harvard St. – so that they are constantly with us and a little call upon them makes a delightful stroll at dusk.

A propos of marriages of a happy description, I have so often wanted to tell you, of how much I am getting to like Margaret Warner. I have seen a great deal of her this autumn, as she is very fond of driving and is always a willing companion. Her intelligence and sense make her more and more estimable the better you know her, and then she is so very entertaining. Her cheerfulness and happy way of taking life, must make her an invaluable mate for a solemn being like Mr Warner.[112]

We were all more than pleased with Mr Darwin, and think that Sara has had most uncommon good-luck in her matrimonial venture. Her visit, however, was a great disappointment for she looked so wretchedly forlorn and unhappy

---

[111] William had announced his engagement to Alice Howe Gibbens in May 1878; Alice was 'too ill' to attend the wedding in July. Fanny presumably guessed that Alice's illness was somehow connected to William's marriage.

[112] The former Margaret Storer. See note 72 above.

at first that one did not know what to make of it. I suppose the truth is that we have taken Sara's troubles too hard in the past and they were always physical and not moral. But I cannot take up the burden again, and lament with the others over the 'dulness of Sara's neighborhood', for I cannot, just now, at any rate, forgive her for not being able to make some enthusiastic expression about her delightful husband, for how is existence possible unless we resolutely make the most of all our blessings. I am afraid that this may sound very brutal to you but it was such a disappointment to find that she was not doing her best. But how wrong it is to judge other people by our own foolish little standard. That is what you don't do. Pray give a great deal of love to your Father, Mother, and Mary. I hope it won't have to be so long again before I write to you.

As always
Your loving
A. J.

To Sara (Sedgwick) Darwin   [Harvard, MS 1435]

Cambridge

9 August 1879

My dear Sara

I have two very agreeable letters to acknowledge and thank you for. For not having done so before I have no excuse to offer save that natural depravity with which you have been so long familiar. I have been very glad to hear from time to time that you are feeling somewhat stronger, a strength which I trust will continue to increase uninterruptedly, for ill-health though not an exceptional or tragic fate inevitably brings a certain monotony into the lives of its victims which makes them rather sceptical of the much talked of and apparently much believed-in joy of mere existence. But your life now is

so full of new joys and interests that an occasional headache or a little graceful languor is merely a decent tribute
which you ought willingly to pay to your mortal state and
single sisters.

If all that the newspapers say is true the summer has not
gone as pleasantly with you as with us, for with the exception
of two or three hot spells the weather has been deliciously
cool and the frequent showers have kept the grass and trees
as green as possible.

The first of July I made a bold push and started off with
Katharine Loring for the Adirondacks to try William's
panacea for all earthly ills – the Putnam shanty.[113] We had
meant to spend a month but I found that the air did not suit
me at all so we left at the end of a fortnight, having found
that the bosom of nature was just about as much of a
humbug as I always knew it was. You will never find me
being taken in again by any of her snobbish votaries who are
half of them only too craven to say how squalid it all is. We
made a very thorough trial for between ourselves the shanty
lacks nothing in the way of discomfort and is no doubt after
camping the worst thing. We stumbled gracefully over the
stones in the brook and K. bathed therein, but I assure you
that for purposes of cutaneous refreshment a tub in the hand
is worthy fifty brooks in the bush. We perched ourselves on
the sharpest stones we could find and religiously spent
endless hours in listening to the babbling water, the gentle
hum of the mosquito, giving j'oy [sic] untold to the sportive
midge who found me quite the loveliest production
civilization had as yet sent to him. The beauty of the sylvan
scenes was sadly marred by the excellent but prosaic
Katharine who would insist upon inserting a hideous rubber
blanket between my fair form and all the mossy logs upon
which I wished to extend it, thereby putting a cruel barrier
between me and all the dear little crawlers I had come so far
to feel and who would no doubt have found me as delectable

---

[113] The Putnam Shanty was a log cabin near Lake Placid jointly owned by
William, Charles and James Putnam and a physiologist friend Henry
Bowditch. William had spent his honeymoon there.

and succulent a feast as did their winged brethren. We had the shanty fortunately all to ourselves and the only romance in the situation was at night when we sat by our bonfire, the woods all round us and no one else within a mile, save some lively cows who in the middle of the night with that unreasonableness characteristic of their sex would charge the shanty with their horns driving K. to her revolver and me under the bed. But this joy was soon denied to us for a male protector presented himself in the person of the virtuous Dr Charles Putnam who stayed a few days. He ate and consorted with us through the day but when the deeper shades of night fell he with great and unexpected propriety betook himself to the other house. It just occurs to me that perhaps those new friends of yours in Basset, for whom you have so easily abandoned the old, might be shocked to hear of two virgins of thirty summers living alone in the woods with a bachelor, but I think if they were to see the piety of his mouth, his virtuous spectacles and the general maiden-aunt like turn of his figure the veriest prig of them all would fall back abashed. Our food was sent to us from the other house under the auspices of 'Si Ware, the gentleman-cook, and a hired girl', which shows you that the same inequality between the sexes exists in the wilderness as that which disgraces the effete civilizations to which you so passionately cling. We were not so well off as we should have been had we had Hat Shaw the factotum of last year to look after us. She was a delightful creature. She had a sister who much to her disgust had aspirations after 'culture' and having been through the High School wanted to go to the Normal School. Hat got Katharine L. to examine and discourage her for she said that it made no sort of difference after you were married whether you were a 'lady-graduate' or not. The girl turned out to be a semi-idiot and has since sought refuge in matrimony – like yourself.

I wish you could know Katharine Loring, she is a most wonderful being. She has all the mere brute superiority which distinguishes man from woman combined with all the distinctive feminine virtues. There is nothing she cannot do from hewing wood and drawing water to driving run-away horses and educating all the women in North America.

But how mercilessly I am running all about my own affairs without telling you anything about any one else, but you know at this season we are very much divorced from the rest of the world, so that I have absolutely no news to give you. I had a very kind invitation from Nanny the other day to make a visit. I was sorry to miss her when she was in town. I am delighted to hear that she has got back her old life and spirits and that she is no longer the pale shadow of her former self that she was when she was here last.

William and his family are off to the White Mountains. Alice is very well and the infant is a dear little man[114] though I am sorry to say he is entering life through a good many stomachic tribulations, but those will pass in a few months I suppose.

If Miss Ashburner is with you pray give her my love and to Mr Darwin my kindest regards. I only wish that I were going to have the pleasure of making his acquaintance this autumn, for I feel as if I had got a very indistinct glimpse of him through the maze of wretched feelings in which I was sunk last autumn. Father and Mother join me in a great deal of love to yourself dear Sara and believe me

Always yours very affectly
Alice James

To Frances Morse   [Radcliffe College, MS]

Cambridge

7 October 1879

My dear Fanny

I had a dream the other night at once amusing and distressing in which your Mother came into the room and said, with

---

[114] William and Alice's first son, Henry, was born 18 May 1879.

wrath and indignation in her face and voice, that you must not write to me again until I had answered your letters, that my conduct was past forgiveness, which shows you that I am haunted with remorse by night as well as by day for the evil of my ways. But notwithstanding that appearances are so much against me I am deeply grateful for your letters which always give so much pleasure though I have one fault to find with them, that you devote yourself too exclusively to what you are seeing and say nothing of what you are feeling and being. If you would apply your admirable literary skill to a few physiological and psychological details your letters would be perfect. I should also like to have a little light thrown upon your plans which in my mind are still shrouded in mystery for you seem to be taking it very coolly for granted that we are all going to give our consent to your staying away indefinitely. You will please to remember that when you went away, this autumn was to be the extent of your tether.

Your last letter reached me at Cotuit whither I had gone to spend ten days with the ever faithful Katharine, and a delightful ten days they were, we should greatly have liked to have made them twenty but K. had an engagement which obliged us to leave. It was doubly pleasant to hear from you in such a charming spot and to have such good news of dear Lucy and Lizzy, the latter of whom we learn from Mr Boott you must have since seen in Munich. What is Duveneck doing for her?[115]

I have found on getting home from Cotuit a volume addressed in your hand-writing by an author to me unknown. Many thanks for it though I have not been able yet to read it, but I suppose it must be something you have been enjoying and that I have a treat before me. And now I have something else to thank you for and that is the very pretty little sacque you sent the baby. Alice was going to write you a letter of thanks but I, knowing she was unfit, told her that I would tell you how pleased and grateful she was,

---

[115] Lizzie Boott had become engaged to her painting teacher Frank Duveneck (1848–1919) who had started a school of painting in Munich in 1878. They eventually married in 1886.

but I would not have her know how tardy I had been in giving you her very grateful message. The sacque was characteristically pretty and the little man has already found it serviceable. Alice got up rather slowly from her illness and is still not as strong as she ought to be for the baby has given her rather an anxious summer owing to the unsatisfactory state of his little stomach which gives him much tribulation. The last few weeks he has picked up very much and seems much better. He is a dear little soul and we have a delightful visit from him every day, the day seems quite lost if we don't see him. We have no domestic news, we are all well, Father unusually so. I am growing stronger all the time though I cannot do much or walk much yet. I was a good deal knocked up the first of summer by a crazy expedition to the Adirondacs, a place only fit for the most robust in health to whom perpetual tramping is possible, but the last place for a degenerate being like me who needs to spend most of her time in padded seclusion. I am very glad however that I went and have been consoled for all disappointments by the revelation of Katharine Lorings virtues whose depths I had thought I had sounded long ago but found that I had only stirred the surface thereof. She is a phenomenal being and no one knows what she has been and done for me these trying months I have been through.

Our great interest of course is in watching the European news. The spectacle of poor England's ignominy is truly a melancholy one it seems almost as if her sun might have set. Did you see the question of the French paper asking whether Miss Braddon and Ouida were not to be in the next Cabinet?[116]

Have you read such a pretty story 'Cousins' by the author of 'Mr Smith'?[117] If you have not I should think that it would be a delightful book to read aloud. The little brain that I ever had has all run utterly to waste the last two years, as I spend my time reading the trashiest of novels. I hope when the cool

---

[116] Britain's invasion of Afghanistan. The irony is directed at the fact that the Prime Minister, Disraeli, was also a novelist.

[117] The popular novels *Cousins* and *Mr Smith* were both written by Mrs Lucy Bethia Walford (1845–1915).

weather comes to be able to make a reformation but I doubt my success.

Pray give a great deal of love to all your circle, and remember that though I do not write I think of you all the time.

Believe me my dearest Fanny
Always your loving
A. J.

To Frances Morse   [Harvard, MS 1509]

Boston

11 September 1882

My dear Fanny

I told you the other day that I had got your sweet note, but it did not seem an appropriate moment to add that it had for me a melancholy side in that it revealed what a burden I had been upon your friendly spirit all summer.[118] Pray do not let this be so for I assure you I have not more to do than I can manage – now that the moves are all over and this little box is pretty much in order the paddling of the domestic canoe through the placid waters of Mt Vernon St. will be child's play.[119]

The last seven months have brought such changes in so many ways and to me so many new responsibilities that I feel at times that I may not be equal to them, but I find I am from day to day and try to keep in mind as much as possible the invaluable thought that one has only to live one day at a time and that all the vague terrors of the future vanish as the future at every moment becomes the present. I used to think

[118] Alice's mother, Mary Walsh, had contracted bronchial asthma and died suddenly in January 1882.

[119] Alice and her father had moved from Quincy Street to a smaller house at 131 Mount Vernon Street on Beacon Hill, Boston.

that I loved my dear Mother and knew her burdens, but I find I only knew half of them, and that in losing her I am only nearer to her than I ever was before; it is such a happy thought that her dear, tired body is at rest and that the blessed memory of her beautiful spirit will never grow dim. Remember dearest Fanny that if I ever want anything that you can do, I never should hesitate for a minute to ask your help. So do not let me prey upon your mind.

Always your loving
A. J.

To Henry James   [Harvard, MS 1466]

20 December 1882

My darling Harry

Darling Father's weary longings were all happily ended on Monday at 3pm. The last words on his lips being 'There is my Mary!' For the last two hours he had said perpetually 'my Mary'. He had no suffering but we were devoutly thankful when the rest came to him, he so longed to go, the last thing he said before he lost consciousness was, 'I am going with great joy'.

The end of life had come for him and he went and I am sure you will feel as thankful as I do that the weary burden of life is over for him. I have no terrors for the future for I know I shall have strength to meet all that is in store for me, with a heart-full of love and counting the minutes till you get here.

Always your devoted A.

The funeral is to be tomorrow Thursday 20th at 11am. There seemed no use in waiting for you the uncertainty was so great.[120]

---

[120] In November Henry James Sr began to decline rapidly, refusing food. He died on 19 December 1882. The date of the funeral was Thursday, 21st. Alice has here made a mistake.

To Alice Howe Gibbens James   [Harvard, MS 1451]

February 1884

My dear Alice

A thousand congratulations upon your happy deliverance. The young man seems to have shown the most happy alacrity in entering life, I hope it is a prophecy that he means to take and make life easy.[121]

I am sorry that he has chosen the inferior sex, though I suppose it is less on one's conscience to have brought forth an oppressor rather than one of the oppressed, and you won't have to look forward to evenings spent in Lyceum Hall trembling lest he should not be engaged for the German or left dangling at supper time.

I shall not come out to see you until I hear from your good mother that it is well for me to do so, as I have no confidence in the discretion of the 'bundle of fleas'.

With a great deal of love
As ever yours
A.

To Frances Morse   [Harvard, MS 1525]

[n. d.]

My dear Fanny

I just want to send you a few lines, for no purpose except to tell you how glad I was to see you the other day and how much I wish I could see you oftener – in short that I love you very much. I hope you won't mind my telling you so, I know you would not if you knew how true it was. I feel myself to be a more respectable human being when I consider that I

---

[121] William and Alice's third son, Herman, was born 31 January 1884.

have you for a friend, and I have you, haven't I, notwithstanding all my sins. You seemed so sweet the other day that
my heart has been full of you ever since. I am scribbling this
in the most improper way on my knee in the midst of doing
up my hair for the night – so that I mustn't write another line
but wish a God bless you, wish you good night my darling
Fanny.

Yours always
Alice James

Sunday evening: Do all you can for poor Theo. who has
thro' herself and her outward circumstances a hard battle to
fight. I never till lately understood how hard it must be to
have no father or mother to help one out of the wood in
which we are all floundering.

To Frances Morse   [Harvard, MS 1526]

[Spring, 1884]

My dear Fanny

You must not measure my satisfaction in getting your letter
by my delay in answering it. I was more glad than I can tell
you, with this stump, to have news of you in this alien,
odious spot. How any one can live here and lead a virtuous
and reputable life amidst the Jews, the tawdry, flimsy houses
and the ash-barrels seems hard to understand, but I suppose
there is some domestic existence somewhere. That blessed
hamlet, Boston, seems like a shrine of all the virtues.

I am very glad upon other than moral and aesthetic
grounds that I came, the place would be a failure indeed if it
could not do something for one's base, physical necessities!
The first ten days I was here I felt a wonderful change quite
as if I had been transformed, and I came to the conclusion
that I was the lowest organism with absolutely no insides but
a stomach, if that were in order the universe might crumble

and I should be found dancing a jig on top of the heap. This state of things has not continued, however and the last ten days I have had every reason, either on account of the atrocious weather or the misconduct of the doctor, to consider myself as belonging to the highest form of created thing; which means nothing more tragic that that I have had a long indigestion, owing to my having been obliged to walk too much when I first came, I suppose. The doctor[122] is as kind and easy to get on with as he can be and the only thing I have to complain of is that 'Rome was not built in a day'; as I have known this fact for a month or two I was foolish to allow my hopes to rise through the specious representations of a non-Puritan temperament, to put it mildly. I am beginning to sympathize with the lady who died and found Heaven delightful 'only it was not Boston'. I am delighted with your suggestion of telling me something about your work.[123] Your silence on the subject has always made me feel very much left out in the cold as if I were not worthy to be taken in to your confidence. I have delightful quarters and Mary's virtues increase every day. I expect to come home a pauper,[124] and hope that you will bend all your energies to helping Lizzie with the concert she is going to get up for me when I return, which blessed moment I am all in the dark about, not for a fortnight, at least. There is a lady upstairs who talks about the 'nerve tone' of negroes being so delightful! Write me just a word if you can dearest Fanny. I miss your dear face more than you suspect.

Love to the Parents
Yours A.

---

[122] The doctor was William Basil Neftel (1830–1906), a Russian born emigré who treated his – mostly female – patients with electrotherapy in the belief that hysteria was the result of electrical currents in the body that had gone wrong.

[123] Fanny worked with the Associated Charities of Boston which had been set up in 1879. It was a non-sectarian organization which attempted to co-ordinate other relief work.

[124] Neftel was reported to be very expensive and charged up to $100 for a consultation.

To Sara (Sedgwick) Darwin   [Harvard, MS 1436]

131 Mount Vernon Street

5 May 1884

My dear Sara

I have left your kind letter of January '83! so long unanswered that it may seem as if I had forgotten your existence, but I am sure that your benevolent mind has not allowed you to harbour any such thought. I have been so ill for the last year and a half that I have done nothing in the way of letters excepting what was absolutely necessary and that is why I have not thanked you for the sympathy and affection you expressed after dear Father's death. We were so glad to have him go and that he was not kept in weariness and desolation any longer after Mother's death that we could give no thought to our own loss. It has fallen most heavily of course upon me, but I am gradually getting used to my loneliness and I find as every one else does that no burden is given that one cannot fit one's self to, after the necessary hewing and hacking. I have every consolation in having so many kind friends and brothers, Boston surpasses itself, you know, when trouble comes. I am having a more than usually strong sense of its excellence now as I have just got back from two months spent in that wilderness of Jews and ash-barrels, New York, where I am willing to allow that there may be a sporadic instance, here and there, of domestic virtue, but absolutely no civic ones. Boston looks like Nuremberg architecturally and like – Bassett shall we say? – morally and socially. I ought not to be too hard upon New York, however, for my visit did me a great deal of good. I went to test the skill of a Russian electrician, a Dr Neftel, of whom I had heard great things and who certainly either in spite or because of his quackish quality has done me a great deal of good in many ways. I was charmed at first with the slavic flavour of our intercourse but I soon found myself sighing for unadulterated Jackson.[125] To associate with and

----

[125] A reference to James Jackson (1777–1867), the Boston physician.

to have to take seriously a creature with the moral substance of a monkey becomes degrading after awhile, no matter how one may have been seduced by his 'shines' at the first going off.   His electricity however has the starching properties of the longest Puritan descent, and I wish very much that you might try it some of these days.   I am sorry to hear that you are still bothered with your head, it has not been all climate with you and the British absence of 'snap' is not all that you want.   I see on re-reading your letter that you speak of my going to England to live.   Two friends called to see me the other day to say good-bye, they having seen in some newspaper that I was on the eve of going.   I have no intention of doing so myself at any rate for a year or more to come.[126]
I have been anxious to solve the problem first as to whether I could not make a home for myself here and to my great satisfaction I find that I can.   Some of these days I shall be bothering you for information about ways and means in England and the feeling that you are there, dear Sara, will strengthen my hands very much to undertake what might otherwise seem a very forlorn venture.   Pray give my kindest regards to Mr Darwin and believe me.

Always very affectly yours
Alice J.

---

[126] Alice in fact embarked for England on 1 November 1884, never to return.

THE ENGLISH LETTERS
1884–1891

THE ENGLISH LETTERS
1884–1891

To Catharine Walsh,
William James, etc.

[Harvard, MS 1531]

40 Clarges St
Picadilly W.

22 November 1884

Dear Aunt, brothers, and sister

I am sorry that so many days have passed without my
writing, but you have heard that I have not 'passed away' yet,
from Katharine and Harry. We had for the season a very fair
voyage, tossing most of the time but only one storm. The
most comfortable stateroom and ship I ever was on for
though the ports were only open twice there were absolutely
no smells. Excellent service, a stewardess worthy of her
name, Devine, and a devoted and innocuous doctor who
unmurmuringly obeyed all Kath's behests. Our miseries
began however immediately for by 10a.m. the morn we
started we were both in our berths sweetly carolling. K.
revived somewhat at the end of a couple of days and afterwards made the best voyage she ever did, which she
attributes to the fact of her having had one of William's
blisters suspended to a wisp of hair four inches from her
head for 48 hours. I was not, I am sorry to say, so fortunate
for after the sea-sickness subsided all the winds of the
firmament took possession of that omnivorous Organ of
mine and I was rent by perpetual and violent indigestion
which is only now gradually subsiding. Even sea-sick
Katharine was, of course, equal to the occasion and only
gave out once when throwing herself into her berth she called

out to Mattie Whitney[1] (a perfect sailor) 'do come and hang
on to Alice's head', and there was such an incubating fervour
in her voice that that amiable young woman's embryonic
protestations were brought to life and she came and hung,
instead of letting the poor thing lollup off. But it is all a
horror of the past and though I swore I should not return for
30 years and then only as a corpse to enrich the soil having
done so little for the history of my native land, I am now
ready to go in six months. Through the agency of Mrs
Stanley Clarke, Harry brought an excellent maid with him to
Liverpool.[2] Her banged and bugled definiteness is in
amusing contrast to that soft mass of formless virtue Mary,
she is an excellent servant and as kind and devoted as she can
be and her conversation constant and comic. She has been
my one study as my observation has been limited to four
walls except during my journey from Liverpool, the most of
which took place after dark. I sadly find on looking out of
the window that all sense of novelty and excitement has worn
off, it all seems as if I had been here yesterday. I have a pleas-
antish little parlour with a tomb-like closet for a bedroom
attached in which one cannot see to read two feet from the
window 'on a very fine day' but I feel as if I had been there all
my life and it is just the place to spend the day in bed with a
head-ache. I enjoy the dusky darkness greatly it is like living
in a tunnel. I shall hope to go out a bit next week in a bath-
chair in the Park which is only five minutes off. One or two
people have called but I have not been well enough to see
them, my only social excitement has been Bob's friend Mrs
Van Rensselaer who has been in London the last year much
sought by the aristocracy![3] Harry says that she is nothing but
a little round ball that has rolled about in the dust all its life

---

[1] Mattie Whitney was an American friend of Katharine Loring's sister
Louisa.

[2] Mrs Stanley Clarke was Mary Rose, daughter of Sir John Rose
(1820–1888), a financier who was married to Charlotte, a daughter of
Robert Temple, and thus distantly related to the Jameses.

[3] Mrs Philip Livingstone van Rensselaer was an American expatriate who
Henry James also knew, having met her in Rome.

– if half her tales of the turpitude of her present associates are true she is in the dustiest place she ever was in before. I have heard of more horrors from her, from Harry, from Campbell, and the newspapers than I ever heard in all the rest of my life put together.[4] It makes one cry out for the burnished purity of Mt Vernon St. – The last week there have been five or six families of high degree figuring in the Police Court, for libels, assaults, divorces, and murders, a more horrible state of society one cannot imagine.

I am looking for Katharine and Mattie Whitney this afternoon who are coming to town to see the sights for a week. I shall stay on here as long as I am comfortable and until I get decidedly stronger. Sara has asked me to stay on the 10th through Christmas but I am too flabby yet to engage myself. I shall go later.

Mrs Lowell asked me to the Thanksgiving dinner, but she won't get anything so precious.[5] I am much obliged to the aunt for her letter, but why did you let Charlotte King loose upon me, I have had two notes already from her inviting me to stay in Versailles, it is all owing to William.[6] I shall write again soon. With lots of love.

Yours as ever
A. J.

P.S. Campbell considers it included in her functions to administer moral support and consolation for the feebleness of my body, her latest is – 'you are indeed very delicate, Miss, and it is hard to be so ill, but then you ought to be thankful that there is nothing repulsive about you and you have no skin disease, as long as I have no skin disease and my body is whole I feel that I ought not to complain of anything!' Forward to Cambridge. Give best love to Cousin Helen.

---

[4] Campbell is the maid referred to previously.

[5] See note 16, *The American Letters.*

[6] Charlotte King was a cousin, on her mother's side.

To Alice H. James   [Harvard, MS 1452]

London

8 December 1884

Dear Alice

I was delighted to get your letter a few days ago and to hear of the great land purchase. It is of course *terra incognita* to me, but a settlement anywhere with a family on one's hands seems like the first necessity of life. I am glad that you say it was a bargain and that you have some trees already started. I suppose John Gray sold to you cheap as a bait to future purchasers. Perhaps its being more or less countryish will simplify the summer question. I have nothing new or interesting to tell you. Katharine and Miss Whitney were here for a fortnight, and though they were out literally from morning to night it was a great pleasure to have occasional glimpses of them. Although the thermometer has only been about 30° the cold has been intense owing to its damp quality, by constant stoking day and night my little apartments have been kept habitable. Kath. says it is warmer here than Bournemouth, with unremitting care she could only get Louisa's room up to 65°.[7] They say you feel the cold out much less than in the house. The only new person I have seen is Mrs Stanley Clarke who very kindly came one afternoon when I was well enough to see her. I had often heard of her charms, but I was in no way disappointed, it is a delight to see such firmly moulded features, speech, and manner after our accidental and slipshod personalities. I am much impressed by the expensiveness of everything, as soon as I am able to I must move or I shall be ruined. The only cheap things I have seen are a pair of gloves and a package of envelopes. House rent is quite as high as in Boston unless

---

[7]   Louisa Loring, Katharine's sister, was also an invalid and suffered from weak lungs. Katharine, engaged in nursing them both, found herself in demand, rushing between them. Leon Edel in *Henry James: A Life* suggests that 'Louisa Loring and Alice James were engaged in a fierce subterranean competition for the nursing and attention of stalwart Katharine'. (p. 308)

you go to some distant quarter where you would die of loneliness, people not having the time to go and see you, and where your rent would soon be doubled by cab-fares. Italy I imagine is the only cheap place unless you are willing to bury yourself in some provincial town. I give Campbell $1.50 less a month than I gave Mary, but she does just half the work, and has brought the science of dawdle to perfection. Besides being the servant she is an excellent creature however, and gives me a dose of robust comfort every morning, such as 'your illness is a very pleasant one, Miss, with some ladies it isn't pleasant at all', so you see I have my consolations. You would think so if you could see my head for when it is not upon the pillow it is elaborately coiffée in Camp's last 'idea', so that although I am thinner and more mildewed of tint than ever I never have had such varied and dressy locks before. As I did not seem to mend and had another bad attack of gout in the stomach which kept me in bed for nine days I consented against my conscience and my purse to send for Dr Garrod, whose whereabouts Kath. of course knew by instinct.[8] We read his book two years ago and Beach said that he was the only man in the world who knew anything about suppressed gout.[9] I have since heard that he is the supreme authority. On Saturday afternoon therefore a round, genial ball of seventy rolled into the room with whom I passed the most affable hour of my life, an old fellow all rounded and smoothed by tradition, with all the graces of the mendacious Slave and the honesty of the angular Oliver. He listened with apparent interest and attention to my oft-repeated tale, which by the way to save breath and general exhaustion I am going to have printed in a small pamphlet, he understood without question or explanation all my symptoms, especially the emotional ones. He said of course he could say nothing until he had seen me again and given me a thorough examination. I do not expect anything very satis-

---

[8]   Alfred Baring Garrod (1819–1907), English physician who specialized in the treatment of gout and was the first to relate gout to increased uric acid in the blood. His book was *Treatise on Gout and Rheumatic Gout*, 1859.

[9]   Beach was probably Henry Harris Aubrey Beach, a Boston physician.

factory, but he may give me some hints as to diet. These details, medical, are for William's delectation. Give him my love and tell him that I shall hope to surpass even my 'Boston level' giddy as it was. My present collapse is no mystery to me, so many long months have led up to it.

10 December: I have seen today a Nation a month old and feel as if I was once more in the current of human life having learnt more from it of European events than I have in the whole month that I have been here, though I see two daily papers. I have decided to move on Saturday – and shall go to 7 Bolton Row upon which Bolton St. abuts. You had better send this to Aunt Kate as I shall not be able to write again in sometime as I have a large number of claims upon me. With love to all.

Ever yours affectly
Alice J.

Tell the artist philosopher with my love that he is kept green in my memory by the waiter whose tragic solemnity of demeanour only equals his own.[10]

To William James   [Harvard, MS 1473]

40 Clarges St.

23 December 1884

Dear William

I was delighted to hear such good news of your eyes and of the prowess of the 'human turtle', that your letter brought.[11]

[10] The artist philosopher was, of course, her brother William.

[11] William had described his baby son Herman, who was born 31 January 1884, as a 'wonderful human turtle'. Herman was to die of whooping cough on 9 July 1885. Commenting on Alice's illness William had written 'I hope you will often think of me as I was winter before last immersed in the same aureate darkness. Those were strange days indeed when I was suddenly plunged there alone, to await more and more news of poor Father's death.'

I was much amused and entertained by your description of the 'aureate darkness'. It is a perpetual pleasure and I dread the time when I shall have to come to the surface. We have as yet had no fog and much less rain than I had expected. It pours all the time at Bournemouth, Kath. writes. My life passes with clock-like regularity. I have seen one or two people, no one new except Mrs Humphrey Ward, a niece of Matthew Arnold's, a scribbling lady belonging to the middle-class, woollen type.[12] She, as well as Mrs J. R. Greene, are afflicted in the most melancholy manner with writer's cramp in both hands and arms.[13] She told me that her sister-in-law wrote for her for three hours a day 'and though I am very fond of her she irritates me dreadfully, at moments'. The emotions of the sister-in-law not given! But I had a truly delicious call from Mary Wilkinson,[14] no pen can describe it and although it only lasted for twenty minutes, or so, I was more done up than I should have been by Mrs Morse, Grace Norton and Anna Palfrey rolled into one. 'Are you fond of history, Alice?' – 'Do your brothers live anywhere near you in America, Alice?' But the funniest thing she said was, *a propos* of Emma's misfortunes,[15] about people being able to bear anything that came, or something of that sort – 'Oh! yes I have found that out by experience. I have always feared that if my husband should be very ill I should not be able to keep awake, but last winter he was very ill and I did not sleep at all!' She looked very smart and invited me to drive in her carriage, a very neat brougham I saw her getting into, the proceeds probably of Jamie's rail-road that her husband, according to Mrs Wilkinson, has stolen.[16] Mrs W. told Harry a little while ago that Jamie had gone off on a holiday

---

[12] Mrs Humphrey Ward was Mary Augusta Ward (1851–1920). She was to publish her best-selling novel, *Robert Elsemere*, in 1888.

[13] Alice Stopford was the wife of historian John Richard Green (1837–1883). She revised her husband's *Short History of the English People* and it was probably this she was engaged in at this time.

[14] Mary Wilkinson was the daughter of Dr J. J. Garth Wilkinson (1812–1899), the British Swedenborgian and close friend of Alice's father.

[15] Emma was Emma Wilkinson Pertz, Mary's sister.

[16] Jamie was James J. Wilkinson Garth.

for three weeks and left this precious rail-road in care of Mr Matthews and when he returned Mr M. would not give it up and they did not 'know what to do about it!' – I look back and long for my salon in Boston, as doubtless from her perch in purgatory Mme Dudeffand is longing for hers. It seems like the centre of all wit and wisdom, with those excellent beings all permeated and perfumed with goodness!

My doctor came last week and examined me for an hour with a conscientiousness that my diaphragm has not hitherto been used to. When he came to the end he was as inscrutable as they always are and the little he told me I was too tired to understand. He is coming next week when, as there won't be as much percussing and stethescoping to be done, I can get more out of him. I shall not tell you 'till then what he told me. I think he takes the gout as a foregone conclusion simply and is deciding what other complications there are. Meanwhile he has left me a pill of which he thinks all the world and I am to have my spine sponged with salt-water, I was much disappointed by his lack of remedial suggestions, all great doctors are chiefly interested in the diagnosis and don't care for anything else apparently. They ought to have a lot of lesser men, like tenders, to do their dirty-work for them, curing their patients etc. I shall let you know if he tells me anything interesting. I am much afraid that it won't be immediate dissolution, but on the contrary a long drawn out process. I sent some cards to the children. I hope they will go safe, give them lots of kisses, also much love to Alice and Bob. Don't write except just when you feel like it.

Always affectly
Alice

P.S. It occurs to me that I have never mentioned Harry. His kindness and devotion are not to be described by mortal pen, he shows no outward sign of impatience at having an old Man of the Sea indefinitely launched upon him, I am afraid that he will find me attached to his coat-tails for the rest of my mortal career.

I sent out to a chemist to have some powders put up in *cachets*, they came back in papers, when remonstrated with the man said he supposed *cachet* was an American form of a latin word. This is in the heart of Mayfair!!

H. seems *very well* and is *much* less stout.

To Catharine Walsh   [Harvard, MS 1532]

Bournemouth

31 January 1885

My dear Aunt Kate

I don't know when I last wrote to you but it must be a good while ago as so many weeks have gone by since I wrote to any one. I was glad to hear from your last letter that you felt yourself again and that you were going to Newport. I was getting so incrusted with grime in my London quarters that I felt a change to be absolutely essential, of course I had no alternative but Bournemouth, Harry and Kath. being my only anchorages. I am sorry to come to the sea but I shall never have to see it as my windows don't give on it at all. Kath. comes in of course every day and does all my marketing for me. They seem to be quiescent for the present but I tremble every time I see her lest their plans change. Louisa seems to be doing well and of course from my point of view seems like an Amazon, but she may take a fancy to move at any moment. I have not seen her but I hope to be strong enough to see Mattie Whitney next week, who is a nice little body. I have very pleasant rooms and infinitely better food and cheaper than in London where I was greatly over-spending my income. I am on the high ground-floor which gives upon a busy but noiseless road so that as I lie in bed I can see the passing, and I feel as if I were more in the world than I have felt since my progress in the arms of two stewards thro' the emigrants on the deck of the Pavonia. My doctor turned out as usual a fiasco, an unprincipled one too. I could get nothing out of him and he slipped thro' my cramped and clinging grasp as skillfully as if his physical conformation had been that of an eel, instead of a Dutch cheese. The gout he looks upon as a small part of my trouble, 'it being complicated with an excessive nervous sensibility', but I could get no suggestions of any sort as to climate, baths or diet from him. The truth was he was entirely puzzled about me and had not the manliness to say so. I got from him however a very thorough examination. He said I had no organic trouble, that my organs were simply disturbed in their functions. My legs are produced by a functional disturbance of the lower half of the spine. 'Is this produced by gout?' 'Oh! dear me yes I have seen people with their legs powerless for years from this cause!' He assured me that it did not lead to paralysis, a grim spectre which has been staring me in the face for a long time. My legs have been entirely useless for anything more than hobbling about the room for three months and a half, and most of the time excessively painful. I asked the doctor whether it was not unusual for a person to be so ill and have no organic trouble and he said, 'yes, very unusual indeed'. – I should have thought he would therefore have liked to do something for me – but it was only my folly in going to a great man their only interest being diagnosis, and having absolutely no conscience in their way of dealing with one. I have very cheerful accounts of my health from Boston, a letter from Mrs Lodge who hears that I have 'completely recovered'. A delightful letter from Mrs Kellogg wondering why I don't write. If you should be writing to her, please tell her of my condition as I don't know when I shall be able to answer her, and will therefore not write again unless she knows why. I have been very sorry not to write to William but I have been too nervous and feeble. I saw Sara for a few minutes in London – quite a transformed being, in her appearance, at any rate she has been extremely affectionate and kind since I arrived proposing all sorts of friendly offices. She proposes coming here to see me, but I hope not for some time as I dread any excitement, my nerves having been so shattered by that horrible night five weeks ago. I am sorry to send so dull a letter but I have no annals but those of a sick room. Give my best love to Cousin Helen. Tell Elly V. Buren[17] how sorry I am not to be able to write to her. Let me know the Ripleys' Paris address as soon as you know it.[18]

Yours as always
A.

To Catharine Walsh   [Harvard, MS 1535]

7 Bolton Row W.

21–24 November [1885]

My dearest Aunt

You may have observed a considerable hiatus in our correspondence on my side, I shall not however waste my energies upon trying to whitewash the past but expend them, as you will doubtless prefer, upon a pencil sketch of the present. You know of course that I have pitched my tent at no. 7 Bolton Row, where, as it faces Bolton St. and overlooks a vast sea of mews behind, I have all the light vouchsafed by Heaven at this season of the London year. The rooms are very good and as our landlady is a Swiss she is possessed of a larger repertory for the manipulation of the potato than were her origin British. Miss Ward, my fourth keeper, promises, and until now has performed very well, but the standard of morals is so low and human nature so debased on this side of the water that I am prepared for the darkest revelations at any moment. She is a 'reduced lady' and consequently cheap, she is as intelligent as any creature can be stultified by the Church and Toryism. She goes to Celebration on an empty stomach between eight and nine a.m. and a gloom is cast over the Sabbath by an exclusive devotion to 'Lenten Lessons' and the 'Christian Year', but as

[17] Ellen James van Burren Morris was Alice James' cousin, daughter of Henry James Sr's sister Ellen King James.

[18] Relations on her mother's side.

she rarely moves or turns a page I am in hopes that the labours of the day are lightened by a good deal of soporific refreshment. I am going to provide myself with a weekly Zola to cheer up the Lord's Day. Katharine's sudden flight was a great shock as you may imagine. We had counted upon six or eight weeks more. Poor Louisa is still very ill, I have great doubts (between ourselves) myself about her ultimate recovery. Her lungs are said to be perfectly sound now and that it is only nervous prostration. I am afraid that being the case that she won't gain much this winter as they have got to go to the Riviera for her chest and that is found to be very bad for nervous troubles. The present break-down all came from six inches of snow at the end of September! I should think that my experience and hers would make, if it were known, the European climate maniacs pause and consider. Don't for the world repeat what I say about Louisa's condition, it is only my own impression, Kath. is as optimistic about her as ever. I am gradually working the Bournemouth poison out of my veins – was it not extraordinary my planting myself in a spot to which the doctors say you have only to go to find out whether you have rheumatism, or not? Whether I am much better or not, I don't know, I am gradually getting stronger and am able to do a great deal more, but as always happens as my physical strength increases my nervous distress and susceptibility grows with it, so that from an inside view it is somewhat of an exchange of evils. To have a tornado going on within one, whilst one is chained to a sofa, is no joke, I can assure you. I get into the sitting room about twelve o'clock and stay until between five and six and I manage to get about the room half a dozen times a day which is a great gain. I have much less severe and constant pain and my legs feel almost as comfortable as they did before I left Bournemouth and got them so dreadfully bad by the journey. I suppose you have heard of my 'invalid chair' – a variety of the Bath family – presented to me last summer by the munificent Kath. It has rubber tyres and bicycle wheels so that there is absolutely no jar and one can lie out in it like a bed if necessary. I got out in it about a dozen times in Hampstead and you may

imagine, after six months of the British bedroom, how I
enjoyed the glimpses of that enchanting spot. I have only got
out once since we came to London, it is very difficult to
regulate the weather and my various attacks at the same
moment, after the New Year things will be better doubtless.
I see Henry every day, he is as good as good can be, of
course. He looks and seems very well, barring an occasional
headache, the frequency and severity of which he says are
much reduced by guarana. I only wish I could take it but it
always makes me faint.

I was very glad to see Helen R.[19] – and much amused by
her unqualified surprise at 'finding me the same', whether she
expected to find me developed into a higher or lapsed to a
lower organism I could not make out. What a sad break up
for poor Mrs Gibbens to lose Mary and her health too at her
age.[20] I have written this bit by bit as you see, please forgive
all shortcomings and send it to William, I shall write to him
soon, but I have lots of debts to pay off as I can. Much love
to C. Helen, and any receptive cousins.

Address here.
Always very affectly yours
A.

To William James   [Harvard, MS 1474]

7 Bolton Row W.

3–7 January [1886]

Dear William

I hope you won't be 'offended', like Frankie,[21] when I tell you

---

[19] Helen Ripley was related to Alice's mother and to Aunt Kate.

[20] Mrs Gibbens was the mother of William's wife, Alice, who was suffering
from lung trouble. Mary Gibbens, younger sister of Alice, married
William Salter of Chicago in 1885.

[21] Frankie was Francis Boott whose hyper-sensitivity was often referred to by
Alice.

that I played you a base trick about the hair. It was a lock, not of my hair, but that of a friend of Miss Ward's who died four years ago. I thought it a much better test of whether the medium were simply a mind-reader or not, if she is something more I should greatly dislike to have the secrets of my organization laid bare to a wondering public.[22] I hope you will forgive my frivolous treatment of so serious a science. I have a great many very kind and sympathetic letters to thank you for, with many amusing and Venner-like predictions[23] as to the date of my recovery, I am glad to observe that you have grown wily by experience and deal of late altogether in years instead of months, as at first – it is safer.* [Alice's asterisk.] While I am on the subject I may as well add that, as you know, the tendency of the age is rather to overdo the sympathetic and that there is a fortunate provision of nature which keeps one from seeming as flimsy and dismal to one's self as one does to one's affectionate friends. My ill-health has been inconvenient and not aesthetically beautiful, but early in youth I discovered that there were certain ends to be attained in life, which were as independent of illness or of health, as they were of poverty or riches, so that by turning my attention exclusively to them, even my torpid career has not been without its triumphs to my own consciousness and therefore not to be pitied. This is meant not as biographical but simply to cheer you up, in return for all your like efforts on my behalf. It may seem supine to you that I don't descend into the medical arena, but I must confess my spirit quails before any more gladiatorial encounters. It requires the strength of a horse to survive the fatigue of waiting hour after hour for the great man and then the fierce struggle to recover one's self-respect after having been reduced to the mental level of Charlie Moring.[24] I think

[22] The medium was Mrs William J. Piper whom William was interested in for years and about whom he wrote a paper, entitled 'Certain Phenomena of Trance'. Henry James was to write in connection with her in 1890 that he had 'a general aversion to her species'. *Henry James Letters*, vol. 2, p. 302 (7 October 1890).

[23] Oliver Wendell Holmes had written a novel entitled *Venner: A Romance of Destiny* (1861) about predestination.

[24] Charles Moring was an acquaintance from Cambridge.

the difficulty is my inability to assume the receptive attitude, that cardinal virtue in women, the absence of which has always made me so uncharming to and uncharmed by the male sex. The days of the week roll by as like each other as peas in a pod. It is a very curious and disciplining process, in view of my privileges of the past, to live shut up to little Wardy's centimetre of mind, to whom every thing from Warwick Castle to a gas-fire is 'pretty and sweet'. But it has its consolations and I simmer with a Goethian-like sense of my own superiority. A few virtuous matrons have come to nibble at me but no one worth recording, they all seem like the tamest of tame Boston, Boston minus a capacity for understanding one's jokes or one's misguided flights of rhetoric. Annie Richards is as good as possible and Sara came in the other day on her way to Cambridge for the holidays. She looks dreadfully and seems more lifeless than ever so that one feels like a flea beside her. A. Richards thinks she is very much hipped, but that is all nonsense, any one looking as she does must be really ill. She was very kind and affectionate. Poor Clover Hooper's death is sad indeed, a dreadful shock – it has enabled Ellen, however, to write to me, as Kath. says it evidently takes an immense emotion to make it possible for her to express a lesser one.[25]

7 *January*: This scrawl has been written at various moments and meanwhile yours of 24 December has come in. I shall be curious to hear what the woman will say about the hair. Its owner was in a state of horrible disease for a year before she died – tumours I believe. I am glad to hear that you are all well, Harry writing and drawing! Give my love to Alice, but don't let her know you address me as 'dearest Alice' it may complicate our relations. I am sorry about the Childs, but still more sorry that you have the support of them on your hands![26] Where is the Valario-Washburn child? and has Mrs Washburn Mêre died?[27] I have vainly striven to

[25] Clover Hooper, Mrs Henry Adams, a pioneer woman photographer, had been depressed since her father's death. She committed suicide by swallowing some of the chemicals she used to develop photographs. Ellen is Ellen Gurney, her sister.

[26] The Childs, see note 44, *The American Letters*.

[27] Mrs Washburn was presumably Lucy's mother.

learn for a year. Fanny Morse writes to me about the sky and the leaves and the dear knows what invalid pap. It seems to be taken for granted by many that as soon as one is ill one has necessarily become an imbecile to be fed on skimmed-milk. Your discovery that the climate has largely to do with my condition amused me extremely and throws a curious light upon Harry's and Kath's. letters if they have given no impression of the poisonous effect of the deadly, damp, raw nerve exacerbating chill of the air. Until lately every joint in my body was constantly pierced with rheumatic pains flying from my head to my feet, from my stomach to my hands, how I should have lived without salicene I don't know. The same *betterment* has taken place since I came to London that was so wonderfully marked when I was here four years ago.[28] I think it is the lessening of the damp through the pavements and houses, and being so much more protected from the East wind which blows perpetually. London is anything but depressing to me, I adore the darkness and the roar of the city is a constant satisfaction. The only thing I dislike is the layers of grime with which one is incrusted. You know that statistically it is the healthiest city in the world. I never felt cold until this year. All through the summer at Hampstead as well as now I have my couch within three feet of the fire, I have two suits of winter underclothing a flannel lined wrapper, two very warm shawls over my shoulders a very heavy rug over my legs and these constantly supplemented by a duvet and fur cloak, it is simply the chill of the tomb which penetrates to the marrow of one's bones. But enough you see you get enough of me when I once start. Give lots of love to Alice and the chicks. Let me know about the hair.

Always
Your loving sister
A.

Tell A to send me one of her good letters when she can.
*There is however the same finality of tone, as if you had

---

[28] Alice had spent six months in England with Katharine in 1881; part of the time they had spent in London, living in Clarges Street, round the corner from Henry's Bolton Street rooms.

been exclusively surrounded by the receptive, which is delicious!!

To Catharine Walsh   [Harvard, MS 1534]

7 Bolton Row W.

11–15 February 1886

My dear aunt Kate

You have doubtless lived long eno' in the world to know that people within sight and sound of the battle field don't generally know anything about the scrimmage until everything is over, and have consequently not been alarmed about Henry and me. Henry happened to be in Bournemouth or he would have *heard* at least what was going on as the house on the corner of Picadilly next to no. 3 had its windows broken. I should very likely have heard the shouting too if it had not been one of my bed days so that I was at the back of the house, with the sitting room door shut and occupied just at the moment with violently ringing my bell for the housemaid having discovered that smoke was rising up from under the fender owing to the carpet and rug being on fire from having been judiciously laid close up to the grate! Wardy was calmly enjoying herself at the Pantomime at Drury Lane; and said when she got in 'I think there must have been some trouble as I see that the windows in the house on the corner are broken and the shops are all closed along Picadilly'. And trouble enough there had been! The next two days, especially Wednesday, London looked like a city that was besieged, they say all the shops were shuttered and barricaded.[29] It has been dreadful for the poor tradesmen many of whom have lost their little all, and who are as badly off comparatively as the working men. It seems pretty sure that none of the working men had to do with it, nothing but roughs and

---

[29] She is referring to the demonstration of London's unemployed in Trafalgar Square on 8 February 1886, which turned into a riot.

thieves who were evidently upon a lark, from their reckless and random conduct. The most astonishing thing was that no lives were lost with such a shower of missiles of every description flying in all directions. There were numberless poor ladies dragged from their carriages and robbed of their jewels and frightened to death, the footman in many cases running away!! The conduct of the police was absolutely disgraceful, tho' Wardy thinks it was very natural that they did not want to get themselves hurt! Things are all in order again except the broken windows which are all boarded up, but great anxiety remains I think in the minds of every one, which is proved from the fact that 100,000 gentlemen have enrolled themselves to act at any moment they may be called upon as special constables in the City. A lively little lady who comes to see me, Mrs Montague Cookson, whose husband is a lawyer and a defeated Radical candidate, was here yesterday and I asked her whether there was wide-spread anxiety that the British workman would turn at last and she said that there was the greatest chance simply from the fact that there was not work to give him and that whatever relief there was could only be temporary. She goes every week to the East end and works under some clergyman who told her that he never had known such destitution in his life, that thousands of families were living in one room who had tasted no food all winter but 'sop' which consists of crusts of bread which they get from the parish and which they soak in water and these the families of cabinet makers, etc. honest hard-working men who are only crying out for work, and 'how can you wonder!' as she exclaimed. Wardy and I jog on together comfortably enough, the former as serenely sapient and infinitesimal as ever, and I stronger from month to month and with less constant physical distress, tho' at best it is a weary ache. Since Henry gave me a screen I have had less rheumatism. Wardy used valiantly to take command of expeditions in search of the sources of the drafts, and one morning she made three but was unable to discover that the window on the landing had been surreptitiously opened an inch and the consequence was that I was laid up the next day with rheumatism in my head, unable to move or breathe for twelve hours. The thermometer at my right elbow next to the fire will be 72° while at my left two foot off it is 59°, if you put a candle near the crack of the hall door it blows right out even when the landing window is tight shut, so you see the desirability of a screen. Henry's friend Lady Clark told him she was afraid I did not get air eno' in Bolton Row![30] Sir John came to see me and was struck with my youth and beauty, I wish it had been my mind for the former must fade. I am afraid he is not an accurate observer, for nine or ten years ago when Henry first knew them and he was about thirty-four years, Sir J. told him he thought he was about fifty-two and this before he was bald. Wardy has just come in and I asked her if the shops were getting repaired 'Oh, I have never been to see them!' On Tuesday she found herself in a great crowd in Trafalgar Square and in the middle there were men haranguing and shouting, I asked what they looked like – workmen or roughs, 'Oh, I would not for the world have looked at them!' Her ideal is to reduce the field of one's speculation, observation, and reflection to a minimum, she has an indulgent contempt for my erratic mental orbit, but I cannot flatter myself that I have developed her in the least, I think I have only stupefied her.

15 February: I have not been able to write for a couple of days. The blackness continues and I feel exactly as if I were a perpetual Rembrandt, but the afternoons are lengthening suggestive of the dread approach of summer and the rural districts. Sara D. came in yesterday, it is pleasant to see her but after five minutes talk that deathly 'gone' look comes over her face and you feel as if you had sapped her life blood. She retains all the rigidity of Kirkland St. and her old pretensions to elevate the tone of the conversation, which produces a ludicrous effect in this atmosphere fetid with scandal and the voice of the evil-tongued. Every now and then some new being comes to see me, but they are mostly still struggling, some of them began in October and when they do arrive most of the call is passed in an elaborate account of the diffi-

---

[30] Sir John Clark was a diplomat, a son of one of Queen Victoria's doctors. He lived with his wife Lady Clark in Tillypronie, Aberdeen, where Henry James visited them in the seventies and eighties.

culties which they have overcome to get here. It is amusing
to find Boston's favorite graces so perfectly reproduced. Mrs
Cookson is quite the most amusing person from her being of
a nervous organization and having a strain of hyperbole like
a refreshing trans-Atlantic blast. Their *au pied de la lettre*[31]
nature is inconceivable, the other day I said something to
one of them about things being more or less chaotic at home,
'Why, I thought there was very little that was wild about
Boston now'. I also ventured to another into the subtlety of
saying that So and So had no moral nature, 'Why, what a
very odd person, how very peculiar'. It rather arrests the
flow of analytical and rhetorical gymnastics. Farewell,
forgive the length of this. Love of the warmest to C. H. I
have not invested my Xmas presents yet as they pay me
interest at the bank, there is no hurry. Send this to
Cambridge.

Your loving niece
Alice

To Alice H. James   [Harvard, MS 1453]

7 Bolton Row, Mayfair

7 March 1886

My dear Alice

My friends and relations are being by degrees imposed upon,
in order of quantitive not qualitative, merit, so you must
needs take your turn with the rest and bear up under the
affliction of a '*long*' letter; which seems to be the quality
universally discernible in my effusions, tho' William kindly
added lately 'strong minded', or some such gratifying epithet.
My orbit round my pale and minor luminary, Wardy, offers
me so little variety and stimulus that I feel as if all my letters
were precisely alike, so I advise you not to form a club á la H.

[31] Literal. This is a favourite expression of Alice James.

H. for reading my epistles aloud, your sisterly ardour might receive a mortifying check. All goes very well here, and you will have heard thro' A. K. of how unheroic our share in the riot was. It was all owing to the police misconduct of the [affair] who were ordered to Pall Mall and went to the *Mall* near Buckingham Palace by mistake and then with British idiocy stuck there.* [Alice's asterisk.] It has been a most unfortunate circumstance, having led to the arrest of the Socialist leaders and the probable restriction of public meetings – all of which would have been prevented by a line of police men drawn across the head of Pall Mall, before whom the mob would have melted into thin air and the poor tradesmen not have lost their all, as happened in some cases. H. moves tomorrow to his new quarters with which he seems more and more contented. One of his friends, Sir John Clark, is terribly distressed lest he should suffer unendurably from the Western sun! They are too comic! The weather is very bad they say, at least K. L. writes to me a great deal about it from *The Times*.

But one day is the same to me as another, only varied by a little more or less goose-flesh, but there are happily few gradations in the cosy-low studded blackness. I look with horror to the moment when I shall have to step out into staring day. My social existence is expanding slightly, some weeks I have a rush of four – usually all on the same day – and then I go for a week or ten days without seeing any one but the ever-faithful Annie Richards who has developed into quite a personnage. Within the last ten days Mrs Gurney has called upon me three times![32] and I must give you a word of warning. The first time she burst forth immediately about your spouse, 'I do so wish I could go to America!' I murmured something to the effect that there was not much to be seen there 'Oh, but I am so afraid that it will be so long before *He* comes again, but I think Mr Gurney would not like it!' I thought, but did not say, that I was quite sure that

---

[32] Mrs Gurney was the former Kate Sibley. Her husband Edmund Gurney (1847–1888) was a writer on philosophy and founder in 1882 of the Society for Psychical Research; he was interested in both hypnotism and hallucinations.

Mrs J. would not like it, for sad as your present lot may be I should not advise you to fall back upon Edmund, you would not improve matters. One of my intimates, Mrs Cookson, who is an enthusiast about Mrs G. takes a very dark view of Edmund as a husband. There must be a very unmanly element of irritability and discontent about him. How would you like to tell a story to a room full of people and have your husband exclaim at the end, 'You began your story with a very good point, you talked a long time and ended it at last with a very broad base'. Mrs G. is a very redoubtable soul to enter the lists with, so be well prepared. Her calls are all on account of William. Mrs Pollock came a few days ago and also burst forth into a *Te William*, but her state is not so dangerous as Mrs G.'s, as Boston and Carry Dixwell were celebrated with equal fervour. The hysterical curiosity and midnight darkness in which they are all in about Americans and things American is ludicrous beyond description, Henry says it is growing hourly. A Mrs Buxton, descended upon me (Heaven only knows why) last week, she was the most juiceless of Cambridge mére de famille with a daughter compared to whom Ellen Tappan is a Mme Becancier, imagine my emotions on hearing afterwards that she was a granddaughter of Sydney Smith![33] Such shocks meet one on all sides. Mrs Litchfield, *nee* Darwin,[34] asked me what was the matter with me, I told her that the doctors called it suppressed gout – 'Does it come from drink?' 'Not in my own person!' 'But did your parents drink?' I answered that they were not to my knowledge victims of what William euphemistically calls 'progressive nervous degeneration'. She says her father's trouble was a gouty diathesis and they are all victims to it. Three of the sons have invalid wives besides! Henry was at a musical party the other night and the Princess Louise of Lorne after gaping at his beauty asked to have him presented, which he was, whereupon she blushed extremely and in a most embarrassed manner blurted out 'How *much*

---

[33] Sydney Smith (1771–1845) canon of St Paul's was known for his sense of fun and his aversion to evangelicalism.

[34] Henrietta E. Darwin, daughter of the naturalist Charles Darwin, had married R. B. Litchfield.

you do write, do you ever write two things at a time?' The rest of the conversation consisted of deciding upon whether Mrs Henschel had a brother or an uncle who sang in Boston. She thinks that the society in Boston must be delightful. I am afraid I sound extremely frivolous, I would tell you something about the Irish question, the unemployed and the Dilke scandal the three absorbing topics if I knew anything about them.[35] The Irish question is still in the clouds; one person tells you that such poverty has never been known, another that it is no worse than usual, that the meeting the other day was all got up by the Fair-trader. Mr Mundella said in Parliament the other day that there are 13,000,000 working people in Great Britain.[36] The chief trouble is, of course, over population, and yet I have never seen but one reference to the subject. You read all the time of most 'deserving cases' of a man of forty with twelve children under fourteen years, another man of thirty with six under eight years and so on ad infinitum and no human being seems ever to say to them that instead of posing and whining about their twelve starving 'Gifts of God' and asking charity, they should be sent to the penitentiary and kept there for as many years as they have children! It is thought that public opinion is veering a little in favour of the Dilkes, because the *Monstrosity* and his lady are found weeping by their fireside! I wonder what the fictions of his infamy are about! Farewell dear Alice and when you have a spare moment send one of your delightful letters and tell me all the stories you can about the babes. They are a delight, love to William and the children.

Your loving
A.

*When they might have run across Green Park and headed them off in Picadilly.

---

[35] Sir Charles Dilke (1843–1910), liberal politician, had been named as correspondent in a divorce case by the lawyer Donald Crawford.

[36] A. J. Mundella was President of the Board of Trade in Gladstone's government.

To Frances Morse   [Harvard, MS 1510]

7 Bolton Row
London

11 April 1886

My dearest Fanny

I have at last 'got round' to you on my list of the unanswered.
That I should have been so long in reaching this happy
moment for me, is owing in a small degree to certain disabil-
ities on my part, but chiefly to your own naughty self – the
fewness, the shortness and the simply literary quality of the
notes which you have *imposed* upon me! I shall have to allow
that the [l. g.] was of the best; but why will you assume that
because my caloes have softened that my heart has too and
that I shall not want to know all about your dear self and
belongings infinitely more than ever before? What you said in
your last about feeling as if you 'knocked very loudly at my
door' deserves five years in the penitentiary. Now I shall
have done and proceed to tell you all about my interesting
self by which I shall expect you to be deeply thrilled. You
probably have heard that I have been all winter in Bolton
Row.[37] I passed through some rather dark hours last spring
which I fondly hoped might lead me into celestial light, but I
evidently did not deserve the best, so only got the second
best, London fog in all its glory! The silly sun has a way of
coming out every now and then of late and turning me from
a delicious Rembrandt into a glaring chrome, it is most
unprincipled of it! I live side by side with a human fragment
by name, Ward, 'the Epitome of the hierarchy' as Mr Cross[38]
aptly calls her, for whatever inner consciousness she may
have is simply a chess board upon which the bishops and
pawns of the Establishment play puss in the corner all day
and all night. The death of every bishop and the resurrection
of every curate is known to her by instinct, and you may

[37] The house Katharine and Alice shared in Mayfair.

[38] John W. Cross, George Eliot's widower, who was married to her in the
year of her death, 1880.

imagine, given my past, what a state of internal ebullition I must be in. It has bred great spiritual pride within me, I fear, as I have never boiled over upon her once under the intensive provocation; her power of effacing herself before her betters and the absolute nullity of her being I suppose is practically useful, though sadly wanting ideally. Then there is something so excessively ludicrous too in the conjunction of our two personalities that I am reconciled. I am seeing just now a good many amiable ladies, who inflict the burden of coming to see me upon themselves, with great good-nature. Among others, your friend Mrs Helen Nicholson called, I thought her very pleasant but eminently a person whom one has to know well to know at all. She enquired very interestedly after you. I have seen no one of any especial interest, simply modified or exaggerated Boston, but with an *au pied de la lettre* nature absolutely appalling to a creature so given to irresponsible speech as your foolish friend; to be perpetually confronted with the nonsense one said last week to Mrs So and So, does *not* make life worth living. I have often laughed over the memory of my having tried to extort from you that Mrs J. R. Greene was *charming*! How thankful I am that my efforts were vain, for if they had not been I should not have been writing to you! She has been to see me twice and Heaven forbid that I shall have to go thro' the terror again. Henry says she is much worse since her husband's death before which she was comparatively innocuous. Henry and she are supposed to be mutually desirous of leading each other to the altar! I suppose this will sound base in the pure ether of Malboro' St. – but it is a very refined remark for London, I assure you.

A propos of altars, or rather not altars, but matrimony, I received a letter this a.m. from Mrs Duvenick at Montrose.[39] William says that the alliance has been received very kindly in Boston, but I must confess that it shocked me terribly. As far as Lizzie is concerned of course, she is old enough to know what she wants and then there was always about her an unperceptiveness with regard to personal shades of difference

---

[39] Lizzie Boott had married her painting teacher Frank Duvenick.

which keeps me from being greatly surprised at her choice, but there is something tragic to me in the last years of Mr Boott's innocent life being invaded by the perpetual presence of an unlettered, idle, smoke-impregnated boy. It seems a nemesis overtaking him for all his linguistic fussings and all the little worriments he has inflicted so liberally upon his hearers and best friends. His loyalty to Lizzie is absolute and he has swallowed this large human pill without allowing the world to see the twitching of a muscle. He writes that 'the blind God has come without his bondage this time, at any rate' – touching isn't it? But I have no doubt I am going thro' the most superfluous vicarious anguish, after the manner of my generation. This tendency is so often brought home to me in my own case! Pray dearest Fanny don't think of me as a forlorn failure but as a happy individual who has infinitely more in her life than she deserves. You know that ill or well one is never deprived of the power of standing for what one was meant to stand for and what more can life give us? – I hope this won't affect you as a somewhat similar remonstrance to William, who replied as if I were a hyena? 'I see you are still quite untamed and I shall condole no more but stand tremulously watching your course from this distant shore.' The middle of May I shall go to Leamington for the summer, where I shall settle myself in the busiest street where there will be as much humanity and as little nature as possible – so low have I sunk! Give a great deal of love to your Mother and Mary and remember me most kindly to your father and personally forgive this empty scribble, and do, oh do! if you answer this, tell me whether Mrs Washburn is dead. I have just heard of Martha's engagement. Give my love to Lucy when you see her and tell her I think she might write to a fellow. How strange it must seem to leave Jim married.

Always dearest Fanny
Your loving A. J.
My address is Bolton St.

To Catharine Walsh   [Harvard, MS 1533]

London

23 April [1886]

My dear aunt Kate

I have been hoping for some time past to get one of your graphic letters telling all about your visit to William and Alice. Two days ago I received a delightful letter from the latter saying how much they had enjoyed your visit and what good friends you had become with the boys. I am sadly afraid that the Great-aunt will entirely cut out the lesser one! I was very sorry to hear about your bad cold, what a victim you seem to be to them. All goes well here. I grow gradually stronger from month to month and have fewer 'attacks' and less constant pain. My nights are not the periods of terror that they were for fifteen months, owing to the improvement in my digestion, having got rid of a well known form of trouble produced by the contraction of the pleuro-gastric nerve which takes place with the act of falling asleep, and which produces all manner of horrible sensations. I find too that I can see people with less ghastly fatigue than I did at first, tho' they are very fatiguing still owing to the curious law of nature which obliges them always to come at one and the same moment. I have two or three intimates who show a more than Boston absorption in me, they come two or three times a week, stay for a couple of hours in a, to them, very hot room, becoming from moment to moment more apoplectic, without any tea and bread-butter which they would naturally at that hour be consuming by the quart and the loaf, and then write me a note the next day to explain away all that they said. There are two views taken of me that rather neutralize each other, unfortunately, one 'so subtle, just like your brother', the other 'and above all so original', this by a lady who every now and then finds a little refreshment in Plato and Emerson, don't you think I must have put on a good many frills since we parted? – It may sound fatuous but I divine from a certain greenish tinge which is coming over Harry's features, that after the manner of canines, a little modest day is dawning for me, rather late, to be sure! Nothing more absolutely elementary than the British feminine mind as far as I have observed it could not be conceived of. But enough of myself, of which I am afraid you have had more than enough. I have had flowers twice from Mentone from Mrs Duveneck, whose emotional centres cannot have been greatly disturbed by recent events as she is 'calmly happy and sketching'. I should think a little delirious joy, at any rate, for a week or two, to blind her to the terrors of her situation, would have been grateful, but then Lizzie has a happy way of not seeing the terrors that she does not want to see, so there is no use making oneself wretched about her of all people. Harry seems to be very well and happy, he enjoys his new establishment extremely, and all seems to go smoothly. He pays Mr and Mrs Smith for wage and board, no more than I paid Mary and Margaret, of course, the washing is all extra. He told me of dining somewhere the other night where Lord Derby introduced himself in order to compliment him upon *The Bostonians* which he had been reading with great delight and exhibited the most intimate knowledge of Boston and things Bostonian.[40] Although he never has been there, he said, that every European diplomatist should marry an American woman to which Harry replied 'they almost all have', which he allowed to be the case. Harry tried modestly to divert his attention from *The Bostonians* by discoursing on other matters to which he listened very politely but made no other reply than to say with the utmost gravity 'Miss Birdseye is Shakespearian'.[41] Harry was invited awhile back to Lambeth Palace where he was received with great enthusiasm by the Archbishop of Canterbury who told him that he was an immense admirer of his works and had copied page after page of *Roderick H.* into his notebook.[42] They ask him to dinner very often but he

---

[40] Lord Derby was Edward Henry Stanley (1826–1893), statesman who moved from Conservative to Liberal allegiances, also a President of the Royal Literary Club.

[41] Henry James is widely reputed to have modelled Miss Birdseye on Elizabeth Palmer Peabody, the Boston reformer. See note 99, *American Letters*.

[42] *Roderick Hudson* (1875), Henry James's first published novel.

does not go, for dinner is at eight and 'Chapel at half past seven'. He had another amusing experience a short time since he went to the Roseberrys[43] and found the people all standing in a circle shoulder to shoulder in terror lest they should turn their backs to the Prince and Princess Beatrice[44] and the Countess Erbach who were standing in the middle. After awhile Mr Phelps, who had been presented to the Countess who is the sister of Prince Henry, came to him and said she wished him to be presented, so Harry was led up and found the Countess possessed of an intimate knowledge of his works, and she went on to say that the English novel had entirely died out, that when they wanted an English novel they always turned to the old ones and when they wanted a new book they always got an *American* one. This in a little German court! Harry departed from her as soon as possible, but was sent for again as she wished to present him to Beaty, who curtseyed very low and made some infantile remarks to him, during which Harry observed the German ambassador backing himself up to the supper-table, for fear his back should be seen by Harry and his young woman. Can you imagine anything so inconceivably dreary as the existence led by 'Royalty', how they must long to see a back! Americans have got it all in their own hands socially, at any rate.

This long story has been somewhat long in the telling and I am afraid it will be longer in the reading. I am trying to use a 'reservoir' penholder instead of a smutty pencil, but it has great variations and is at moments very anaemic and trying. I shall probably go to Leamington at the end of May but the time is not settled. I decided upon Leamington last autumn having heard of some excellent lodgings in the busiest street with a band in front of them every day, where Nature is *not* and where Man is! Kath. has a wild plan of coming to transport me but I very much doubt her being able to accom-

[43] Archibald Philip Primrose, fifth Earl of Roseberry (1847–1929), Liberal politician, Foreign Secretary in 1886, became Prime Minister briefly 1894–5. He was married to a Rothschild heiress, Hannah de Rothschild.

[44] Beatrice was the youngest daughter of Queen Victoria; she had married Prince Henry of Battenberg in 1885.

plish it. If she has not a crown of Glory somewhere I don't know who will have! Her whole life and occupations broken up having to give up all she most wants to do and all taken as a matter of course. I wonder how much of courseness there would be about it if she happened to wear trousers! Oh, the goodness of women!! But you certainly don't need any instruction so I shall stop my chatter. Give my best love to dear C. Helen and to any Cousins who may desire it. Address until you hear from Leamington – Care of Brown Shipley and Co.

Always
Your loving niece
A. J.
When writing give my love to the Tweedies.[45]

To William James   [Harvard, MS 1475]

London

19 May 1886

My dear William

I am going to inflict a few lines upon you now as it will be some time I am afraid before I shall be able to write again. I am going off on the 26th and am much exhausted with the prospective terror of the journey, sending picture postcards and galvanizing Wardy into the performance of the last rites. Katharine proposes to arrive on the 22nd and take me in charge but I shall not believe it until I see her. A hard shell has formed itself round my mind so that expectation or disappointment will never more be felt by me. I am awfully sorry to leave London and should stay except for the expense. Leamington fortunately *is* cheap so that I shall gain that if nothing more. Our days run only varied by more or

[45] The Tweedies, Edmund and Mary Tweedy, were the foster parents of the orphaned Temple cousins.

less headaches, more or less slamming by the Count in the drawing room,* more or less Wardiance and more or less epidemic of me among my intimates. In view of my postcards I counted up my cards and found that to my surprise I had had sixty-five individuals, most of them have come more than once and many very often, so I think we may call it a *succes d'estime*. Mrs Buxton the grand-daughter of Sydney Smith came again yesterday and she was more than ever removed by twenty, rather than two generations from a joke. She is very intimate with the Mat Arnolds and said that M. A. was going to lecture this *summer* in America, and that he had not prepared, she was sure, any lectures. She seemed to think his ways reprehensible in this respect. An intimate friend of his, Matt, told Henry 'Oh! you know he is very clever about getting houses lent to him'. This is a remark as characteristic of 'intimate friends' as it is of Matthew, I imagine. Last Sunday p.m. was made memorable by the advent of Mr Pollock led in by his wife's rippling laughter.[46] She is a sweet creature, and eminently by a man to be fallen in love with being, so what could have induced her to rivet Fred to her side! Mrs Clifford says that he and Mr Leslie Stephen have the name among their own kith and kin of being *desperate flirts*![47] He was quiet for the most part, but every now and then he suddenly jerked his profile round and shot forth a volley of deafening sound at the side-board. Henry saw his Mother introduce him to a lady who was standing near, one evening at her house, when he immediately turned himself completely round and stood with his back to the lady and his nose to the wall. What will he do when he goes to Court! I was very sorry to miss one day when I was laid up, Miss Cross who brought her brother John, the widow of George, to see me. He seems to have become quite an historic character – and a complete wreck

---

[46] Sir William Frederick Pollock (1815–1888) the queen's remembrancer, he was also a writer and had numerous literary friends. He was married to Juliet Creed.

[47] Leslie Stephen (1832–1904), man of letters, was the first editor of the *Dictionary of National Biography*, father of Virginia Woolf.

physically owing to the Georgian episode. Henry says he would have departed this life if she had not, owing to the rarefied atmosphere in which she kept him. His sisters are the most excellent beings and Florence the youngest is to be married and I have had to buy her, grievous to relate, a wedding-present. Dr Holmes and Amelia have arrived and being in a more desperate plight could hardly be imagined.[48] The latter told Henry six delegations came out to the ship, that they have had to get a secretary who is constantly employed answering notes. Did you know that Mrs Holmes at the age of sixty-five had absolutely lost her mind? It must be rather a terror to Wendell. Charles Atherson came a few days ago to see me and exhaled a perfume of resinous purity and prosing virtue which filled my heart with joy. He gave me many details of your household which I was glad to get, the undimmed beauty of Alice's orbs and the position of the study table etc. To keep William from being jealous I will add that a fair lady wrote a little while ago, that she had met him and that he was 'looking *so* handsome!' Henry and I smiled! I have got a tale to unfold, with regard to the Gurney household, to *Alice* some day which will astonish and grieve her, and a beautiful story to tell of John Morley's interior which will make her eyes dim with tears of another flavour.[49]

21 May: I was interrupted here by the advent of Mr Lowell from whom I had the most inspired call – such a work of supererogation on both sides! He apparently receives and can give no general impression of anything and his judgements of people are absolutely infantile, he is just like a boy. But he is very kind, genial and friendly and has the simplicity and unknowingness of the world which can only emanate from the Western world. *Smith* has just brought me from Harry, William's letter over which I have wept as I did over John Morley's virtue, and for which I am as 'inexpressibly grateful' as Ed. Gurney for *The Bostonians*. Poor Harry has

---

[48] Dr Oliver Wendell Holmes (1809–1894), essayist and poet, was the father of the Jameses' friend. See note 25, *The American Letters*. Dr Holmes was married to Amelia Jackson.

[49] John Morley (1838–1923), editor of the *Fortnightly Review* and liberal politician.

been pining for something of the sort, and coming from you I know it will give him infinite delight. After toiling with endless conscientiousness over a book for months it is hard lines to have no recognition of it but a few lines of superficial criticism which you know to be written by a child, but which sets the tune for the general public. The English papers are in one way *worse* than ours owing to the absolutely authentic fact that there is no independent literary criticism known. It is all *unblushing* cliques and sets worse even than Trollope made out. I am indeed sorry to hear of Mr Richardson's death, what a loss! he was undoubtedly the first of his time. There is no problem to settle about my summer, it was all decided upon early in the winter. I have not thanked Alice yet for her *delightful* letter. I was delighted to hear all she told. Tell as much as you can about the boys.

Always your loving sister
A.

*More or less nausea from his matutinal soap and pomadé.

To *William James*   [Harvard, MS 1476]

Leamington

10 September 1886

My dear William

I have two fraternal, sympathetic and amusing letters to thank you for. The fraternity and amusingness are very grateful to my heart and soul, but the sympathy makes me feel like a horrible humbug. Amidst the horrors of which I hear and read my woes seem of a very pale tint. Kath. and I roared over the 'stifling in a quagmire of disgust, pain and impotence',[50] for I consider myself one of the most potent

---

[50] In July 1886 William had writtten to Alice: 'You poor child! You are visited in a way that few are ever called to bear, and I have no words of consolation that would not seem barren. Stifling slowly in a quagmire of disgust and pain and impotence!', quoted in Strouse, p. 295.

creations of my time, and though I may not have a group of
Harvard students sitting at my feet drinking in psychic truth,
I shall not tremble, I assure you, at the last trump. I seem to
present a very varied surface to the beholder, Henry thinks
that my hardships are such that I shall have a crown of glory
even in this inglorious world without waiting for the next
where it will be a sure thing; Mrs Cookson, who saw me in
all my greenery, yellowy shades of last winter never can
imagine that I am invalid at all and the landlady says, 'You
seem very comfortable, you are always 'appy with yourself,
Miss', – this may seem to you a small area within which to
rejoice but it has the advantage of always being at hand. I
heard a while ago that contrary to my strenuous injunctions
Harry had written to you that I had consulted Dr Townsend.
I did not want any report of the engagement to be spread
abroad except from myself, but I had not the energy to write
at the time. The excellent Henry's pathological apprehension
is as vague as his financial and both apparently a direct inheritance from Father, so that any account of his of my insides,
or rather what may have been said about them, by the time it
had reached your distant shores, could hardly have much
scientific accuracy, it will be a consolation therefore to
myself, though I fear boresome to you, to say just what is the
matter with me. I thought it wrong, being so ill as I was last
autumn, not to see a physician and find out whether my legs
were getting to be a habit or not, so I called in Townsend
who gave just the same diagnosis as Drs Torrey and Garrod,
a gouty diathesis complicated by an abnormally sensitive
nervous organization, the legs' neurosis brought about by
anxiety and strain.[51] He assured me that they could not, the
legs, be hurried, that time would do it assisted by his
medicines, but I found that they were very strong tonics and
that it was going to be only the old Neftel system, drugs
instead of battery so I gave him up. I was very glad that I
went to him however, as he gave me much good advice and
relieved my mind about the genuineness of my legs. He said

[51] Dr John Cooper Torrey, Alice James was later to write 'was the only
    man who ever treated me like a rational being'. (*Diary*, p. 207, 31 May
    1891.)

what I have been told often before that I should be much better at any rate, when I reached middle life, this seems highly probable as I have had sixteen periods the last year. Dr Townsend is personally the flower of that type which makes the Briton valuable. I never came in contact with a more beautiful soul, manly, impersonal, intelligent, kind as a nursing mother, but with too pale-eyed a purity and unhumourousness of being to thread the mazes of trans-Atlantic neurasthenia. But it is a gain to know such creatures exist in the world – there is an awful possibility they say, that just that type may be horribly penurious! in the old world there seems a canker in every flower, but perhaps it is only on the tongue.

I have no excitements, occasionally a new old-maid adds herself to my circle, but my main stand-by is a Miss Palmer, who has a tumour and an income of 10*l* a week! She has the conversational methods of old George Bradford,[52] is perpetually trying to escape from the terrors of the sentence in hand, or rather on tongue, to fly to those she knows not of, in the next, but George is a perfect woman of the world as compared to her, tho' she does read her Testament in Greek. Though I have no human excitements, I have been having the last month some very serious entomological ones, owing to the appearance in my bedroom of black-beetles – euphemism for cock-roaches, they are one and a half inches long, three quarters inch wide and half an inch thick with endless number and length of leg – a truly British edition of our diaphanous water-bug. They are odious and some houses are so over run with them that they have them in the beds. Wardy returns from her matutinal repast having 'partaken of the Spirit of our Lord' and has no more drastic measures to propose than to stand in the middle of the room with her petticoats gathered up and say 'Oh, I'll keep my eye upon him!' The reckless invertebrate unimpressed by the potent orb, goes gaily upon his career, whereupon I rise from my bed, go down upon my ricketty knees and extinguish the

---

[52] George Patridge Bradford was a classmate and friend of Emerson and ran a school in Newport which Alice attended. She was to refer to him in her *Diary* as 'the flower of New England maidenly bachelorhood'. (p. 84)

creature with a towel and the landlady exclaims 'Whatever
shall we do, how I wish Miss Loring were here to tell us!' A
moribund Yankee is worth twenty of the deadly, stupid, lazy,
doughy lumps, when there is anything to be done. They
make me feel, just the look of them sometimes, as if I must
shriek and scream or be stifled, it is perpetually like running
your head into a feather-bed. The minds of the most intelligent even are simply cul-de-sacs, more or less long of course,
but the dead wall you will always come to in time. They are
absolutely without the Irish brain cell and they have consequently a structural inability to conceive of an Irishman as
having the ordinary human attributes.

11 September: Since I began this the well ventilated Kath.
has arrived to spend a couple of weeks and I am happy. I had
a call yesterday from Helen Paine an ancient friend sister-in-
law to Mrs Julia Bryant P. who said she would go out to
Cambridge and tell you about me; so do not be surprised if
she turn up. All the information you will gather from her
will be that 'she is just the same!' I have been considering and
deciding upon my probable future for the next three or four
years, and I see no chance of my being well enough for the
journey for a long time to come, the *jar* of the voyage coming
out having had such a disastrous effect upon my back I shall
have to be very *well* before I run the risk again, in view of all
this I want you and Alice to go to the store-room in Boston
and take all or any of the furniture which you may need or
like. I suppose you have some of Mrs Gibbens's things which
she will want. The carpets especially, I think there are only
two, the red rug and the parlour rug, are only in danger of
being destroyed. The red-rug will do I should think in some
way for your study and the other perhaps Alice might use.
The beds you may have use for, take everything and call it if
you like a loan, it will be a help to me as what is left you will
doubtless be able to have put in a smaller room and I shall be
at a less expense – I have to pay now almost $100 storage
which I greatly grudge. The only thing you will have to do in
return will be to see to it all yourself as I do not want Mr
Warner to have anything to do with it.[53] He will give you the

---

[53] Mr Joseph Banges Warner, Alice's lawyer. See note 72, *The American
Letters*.

keys. The keys of the trunks are in the safe at Higs. Mr
Warner will give them to you. Tell Alice that the contents of
the trunks are marked upon them, and she can take all the
blankets and linen of which there is a very small supply. The
blankets may be all gone by this time.* The only thing I
should like to leave untouched are the barrels of crockery, as
you have a set you will hardly want it and I feel rather sentimental about it, I will slough it off in time. The pictures will
be better on your walls if possible. The old clock needs to be
so much over hauled that it would be quite an expense so you
had better leave it dormant. You must not regard this as a
favour to you it will be one to me. The enclosed letter from
Mrs Gurney will interest as telling about Mr G.'s mishap.
Love to Alice and the babies.

Your loving sister
Alice – I shall go to London about the 15th of October.
*And anything else she wants.

To William James   [Harvard, MS 1477]

8 Gloucester Road
Palace Gate
London S.W.

9 October 1886

DICTATED

Dear William

'Your splendid noblest letter' of the 27th was handed to me
just before leaving Leamington yesterday morning, and I send
a line to entreat you not to take any of the furniture that you
don't want, simply to relieve me of the expense of storing. I
only mentioned that part of the matter by way of making it
easy, if you should have any scruples about taking it. Pray
don't take any of it simply to spare me because that was not

my object in offering it; for I shall always feel that the dear old things belong quite as much to you as to me. As to returning them, that is not part of the programme.

What I said about Dr Townsend was meant for Aunt Kate's ears, as I had recently received a letter from Ellie Morris saying that she had just heard from Aunt Kate 'that Alice was slowly recovering from the various treatments to which she had been subjected'. She also still talks about my being afflicted with atrophy of the muscles.

Your admiration of my scrawls is doubtless deserved but it is rather embarrassing when read aloud. I feel a power within me for even higher things. Thank Alice very much for her delightful letter, which I shall soon answer, and give her my love.

Yours Alice

P.S. Alice is so much better than we had any reason to hope, after her coming from Leamington, that we fear a crash in the near future. When I can get an hour's time I am most anxious to chronicle for your benefit her triumphs over the clergy and the lodging house grabber and her attitude towards dishonest slovens.

Yours ever sincerely
K[atharine] P. L[oring]

To Alice H. James   [Harvard, MS 1455]

8 Gloucester Road
Palace Gate
London, S.W.

8 December 1886

My dearest Alice

1000 thanks for your beautiful letter which reached me the day before yesterday. I was much thrilled of course by the

news with regard to posterity. I shall approve and congratulate only upon one condition and that is that you show
yourself able to produce one of the nobler sex.[54] She *must*
have your eyes moreover and a Gibbensian softness of
outline, unalloyed by that James asperity which has led to
sour spinsterhood in the one feminine blossom which the
race rose to bringing forth. I have another delightful letter to
thank you for, which came I think since I last wrote, but it is
hard to remember. Your letters are always an immense
pleasure both to Henry and me. What you say of Ellen
Gurney gladdened me greatly, I thought what I heard could
not possibly be true.[55] I felt as if some sacred thing had been
desecrated, I had just had such a beautiful letter from her! I
am glad to have dropped a consolatory quotation into
Edwin's consciousness, I remember the quotation but not
the fact. You had not told me about Florence James I am
very pleased that you found something to like in her. I
should think, however, that the High Church tendencies of
her family was their least evil. I am delighted that the
furniture came so *a propos*, do anything you want with it.
The old kitchen traps will be useful in the country. I am
sorry about Bob but what else could have been expected?
Harry had a most characteristic letter from him in which he
announces in the end with the greatest pride and unction
that he 'knows nothing of the rest of the family'. Poor Mary
perhaps has to follow suit, such is the case often in the Holy
bonds of matrimony, sweet and seductive bondage![56] I have
just been consoling myself this morning with some pages of
Father's book. It makes him so actually present! William can
have no haunting thought of having inadequately fulfilled
his filial function![57] Mrs Ed. and Mrs Russell Gurney (Aunt)

---

[54] Alice H. James was pregnant with her fourth child who did turn out to be
a daughter, Margaret Mary born 24 March 1887.

[55] Ellen Gurney was to suffer a breakdown after the death of her sister and
husband.

[56] Mary Holton James, her brother Robertson's wife.

[57] William had edited his father's papers and published them as *The Literary
Remains of the Late Henry James*, 1884.

Mrs Cookson, and Mrs Stanley Clarke are all devote readers
of the volume. The last alternates her perusals with converse
with the Prince of Wales! I am so happy that William is so
well and working so much. There is a great interest here in
the Harvard occasion. I see plenty of people, eno' for my
amusement and strength, but no one very interesting. A Mrs
William Sidgwick, sister-in-law of Henry, is by far the most
intelligent person whom I see.[58] She has a fine mind and
threatens to bring Mr Henry Sidgwick but Heaven forbid, my
nerves are not robust eno' for a stammer yet. This is only a
line of love and greeting to acknowledge your letter. Hoping
that your stout heart will stand you in the good stead it has
hitherto, believe me with love to all.

Your loving sister
A. J.

Harry went five days ago to Florence, but I have not heard
from him yet. I am afraid I did not thank William eno' about
the photo.

To Frances Morse   [Harvard, MS 1511]

8 Gloucester Road
Palace Gate
London, S.W.

9 December 1886

My dearest Fanny

I was going to write to you when your last letter came by
return of post, but I refrained thinking it cruel not to allow
you a little breathing time before the incubus again descended
(I have not divided that up right) upon your shoulders. I was
delighted to hear but you are so naughty about your letter

---

[58] Henry Sidgwick (1838–1900), was an English philosopher who worked
on Ethics. He was also, like William, interested in psychical research.

that I am going to say to you what Mrs Kemble[59] said to me
yesterday – she was tempted to say to people who wriggled
when she asked them to *read* to her, 'I did not ask you to
please me but to *read* to me!' paraphrasing what Jaques says
to Amiens in *As You like it*, when he asks him to sing to him.
Just write to me and I will decide whether your letters are
worthy to be read or not. I must hasten to send 1000
congratulations upon the new generation you have entered
upon. I am glad that all things went smoothly with Mother
and child. I am sorry your dear Mother is languid and weak.
What a long life of ill-health she has had! I had heard of your
Uncle's death, did he have an illness or did he die suddenly?
– I was delighted to have your account of the Celebration,
everyone speaks of it as a success. Cleveland's speech I
thought truly touching, he must be a *good* creature, as well as
a strong one.[60] I was made so happy in Leamington and then
again in London, by seeing dear Lucy, with her illusive
vocabulary and her extraordinary mildness of nature, which
amounts to a *positive* quality in her. She made us laugh as if
she had been Mark Twain in petticoats. There is no doubt
about it there is a refreshing 'freshness' in the Yankee genius
which is not found in the excellent but soggy Britain. I am
very comfortably settled in pleasant little rooms close to
Henry, who, however, is at the present moment in Florence.
There are some kind and charitable mortals who come and
see me in a most praiseworthy manner, but no one distinguished or very exciting, only pleasant and good. Your
friend Miss Nicholson came once, but I felt that she loathed
me, or rather loved me not would be more accurate. Mrs
Marau, terrible being, has just been trying to get into
scrimmage with me, but she succeeded not, and I am very
much in hopes it will lessen our interviews. She is a savage
pure and simple, with all her savagery revealed in her countenance. I am constantly thinking of and anxious about Lizzie
Duvenick but I suppose there is no need of the last so many

---

[59] Mrs Kemble is Fanny Kemble, the actress.

[60] Stephen Grover Cleveland (1837–1908), Democratic President of the
United States 1885–1889 and again in 1893.

women of forty have had babies successfully. She seems to be doing very well through the preliminaries. I am in the throes of seeking a new 'useful companion', Wendy having been sloughed off successfully before leaving Leamington. It is dreary and weary business! The new one will be the fifth unknown quantity which I have let loose upon myself in two years. In the midst of the starving and unemployed to find one good person one would think would not be hard, but the starving and unemployed do not want to work and they *do* want to *drink*. This last point is my chief terror in changing as it is a favourite accomplishment with companions. If you want to see the London problem handled without gloves, read 'The problems of a Great City' and be thankful you are not working amongst the London poor. The world is in a curious and hopeless tangle, but with us it seems a simple matter as compared to this seething cauldron. By my preaching attitude in the beginning I have cut myself off from saying that I am ashamed to send so stupid a scribble, but it will carry plenty of love to all of you, so here goes dearest Fanny.

Always your loving
A. J.

To Alice H. James   [Harvard, MS 1456]

34 De Vere Gardens
London W.

3 April 1887

My dearest Alice

This morning comes the thrilling postcard from William giving the happy news of 'la belle fillette!' and your consequent deliverance.[61] I have been eagerly and anxiously waiting to hear and I am correspondingly rejoiced. You have

---

[61] The birth of William and Alice's daughter, Margaret Mary.

my warmest sympathy and congratulations. That 'he is a girl' delights me, it will be so good for the boys, elevate the tone of the house and be some one for me to associate with in the future! You and she will be two against three, Mother and I, however, maintained the fight more unequally still, two against five and I think I may add not altogether unsuccessfully. Your beautiful letter came three or four days ago and I was waiting for this news to answer it. Your stories of the boys were exquisite and you never can give too many. Your account of little Billy shocked me, his health I mean, I had no idea that the trouble had been serious. Children out grow these difficulties in the most wonderful way. You will have an anxious mind about him, I am afraid, for some time. You will be sorry to hear that Henry has had a light attack of jaundice in Venice. I hear from him and from an outside source that the attack is a light one, but jaundice is a depressing and tedious infliction and he has had a bad time with his head, but a note this a.m. says he is sitting up and eating a mutton chop. He has an excellent doctor and an impassioned Gondolier taking care of him, Mrs Bronson in the foreground[62] and Miss Woolson in the background[63] at Bellosguardo upon whom he is going to fall back when he is able to travel to Florence which will be in a few days from now, so I think we may have no anxiety about him. I am enjoying his beautiful rooms of course immensely, at first it was like an Arabian nights transformation after the squalor of my two years. Alas! the magic has gone, but the comfort remains. The Smith's are a rare but not a rich study, such perfection as servants and such poverty-stricken human beings! I well understand Harry's groans over them and if I

---

[62] Katherine De Kay Bronson, wife of Arthur Bronson, who lived in Venice in the Casa Alvisi. She had been Henry James's fellow passenger to Liverpool on a stormy journey in 1875; she also entertained Robert Browning in Venice.

[63] Constance Fenimore Woolson (1840–1894), grandniece of James Fenimore Cooper, who wrote popular fiction and who had come to Europe half in love with Henry. He left Venice to recover from his illness in Bellosguardo, where Woolson and Henry James shared the same roof, if not the same appartment.

were shut up to them for a year I should without the slightest doubt kill either myself or them. Hug your Irish to your bosom!

All you tell me of Ellen Gurney interests me deeply, my heart aches incessantly for her. What a battle she must be fighting! William says 'the heart is a tough organ', which is true enough but the following form of the same idea appeals more to the feminine mind – 'A force de s'élargir pour la souffrance l'âme en arrive à des capacités prodigieuses, ce qui la comblait naguère ai la faire crever, en couvre à peine le fond maintenant.'[64] Be sure and give her, Ellen, my love whenever you see her also to the Childs and any one who seems appropriate. I was glad to hear good news of Bob tho' the purchase of a house sounds rather dangerous as it usually brings about a necessity, in the case of rolling stones, for an instant move. Harry had a characteristic and literally excellent letter from him a short time since. I have knit a little plain shirt and Nurse has knitted three which will be sent you au fur et à mésure.[65] I have settled down with little Nurse for a long tête à tête, much the best thing I can do. She is a good creature but any hermetic attachment is a discipline. She is as peculiar in her way as Kitty Prince but the British element in her keeps her simply unworldly not compact of otherworldliness.[66] I was delighted to see on the postcard that the little maid was the 'portrait de sa mère', may she be so within as well! Although it is not always the fairest that have the fairest lot here below. The Miss Lawrences[67] were

---

[64] 'By enlarging its capacity for suffering, the soul achieves an amazing strength; what formerly overwhelmed it to bursting point, now scarcely covers the base.'

[65] 'In due course.'

[66] Kitty Prince was a cousin, the daughter of Henry James Sr's elder brother William. She married her physician William Henry Prince whom she met, having spent a year at the Northampton Hospital for the Insane. She was, according to Strouse 'quite spectacularly unstable, in and out of mental hospitals all her life.' (p. 73)

[67] The Misses Lawrence were, according to Henry James 'two virtuous maiden gentlewomen of fortune, who live in a very pleasant old house in Whitehall and are fond of entertaining'. (*Letters*, vol. 2, p. 161)

telling me a pretty story of Sir James Paget the great surgeon and his wife, who were engaged nine years and have been married forty, and he told them the other day that he could not conceive of existence without her, and she is phenomenally ugly and he is very good-looking. Mr George Meredith the novelist said a picturesque thing about her, she has an enormous running-back forehead and a long pendulous nose and some one was descanting upon her goodness when he said, 'But that brow like the skull of a camel which has been bleaching for long ages on the sands of the desert!' The Misses Lawrence are twin ladies aged fifty years who dress in bright green suits with scarlet flowers in their bonnets and are excessively lively and absolutely inseparable, they say 'Oh! that always disagrees with us!' 'We have got such a headache' etc, etc, one day a friend hearing of the death of Mrs George Meredith and knowing they were very intimate with Mr George said 'Why one of you must marry him' 'Oh! we never could do that!' These simple anecdotes will not be too exciting food for you, I trust, but eno' is as good as a feast so I won't bore you further. I shall anxiously look for a letter and trust to hear that the report on the postcard was more than fulfilled. I am as always

Your loving sister
Alice J.

3 April – I am going to answer William shortly.

To William James   [Harvard, MS 1479]

24 April 1887

My dear William

Your letter, date unremembered, but number three since I wrote to you came yesterday, I sent it and its enclosure to Henry, off directly to Florence. I am very glad that the furniture comes in at an appropriate moment but I insist that you take nothing that you are not likely to use and want, merely for the sake of storing. The barrels of china and two boxes of books which I want to keep had much better be left, also the trunks in the store house. The china consists only of the dinner-service for which I have an especial affection and which would be too handsome for you to use in the country. There are no toilet-sets. I want Alice to look into the trunks and extract from there any blankets and linen etc. which she could use. There is not much but it may be useful to you and will otherwise probably become, if not already, the prey of moths. But remember not to take anything to store simply. I am quite able to pay the cost and should feel much easier to have it so. The trunks have their contents marked upon them, I think.

I am more and more delighted with the sex of the babe, your 'affectional-side' as Aunt Kate would say will have a chance to develop in your relations with her, I feel as if I must hurry home and protect the innocent darling before she is analysed, labelled and pigeon-holed out of existence. I am surprised to hear that her name is doubtful. I supposed that her sex made that a spontaneous and undiscussed homage to Mrs Gibbens's maternal and grand-maternal devotions.

I am indeed distressed to hear about Bob. Poor, poor Mary! She has need of all her courage, how bad it must be for the children now they are getting so old. As Bob has been drinking ever since he was in the army, off and on, my unpsychic intelligence leads me to decide that his 'progressive nervous degeneracy' is effect and not cause, the result however is equally distressing and disastrous. The poor creature seems to have no inner existence of any kind, he has always made upon my mind the impression of a human bladder. My heart is wrung for poor dear, dear Ellen Gurney, how can you be so cruel as to wish her to live, nothing would rejoice me more than to hear that she was gone. I am sorry that Alice still keeps weak but I hope that by this time she is herself again. I do not see how I came to forget the photo in my letter, I meant to speak of it. I think it is lovely and I prize it greatly. One of these enclosures will please you, the other amuse I hope. I sent Father's book to Mrs Gurney, having heard from Mrs Edmund that she hankered after it greatly and I was glad to find that it had not gone amiss. The paper which you sent for Mrs Edward Gurney went astray in the move. I have only seen her once this winter, she has been in Brighton. If it was a joke she lost nothing, her gift lies not in that direction. The absence of the humourous quality in the people I see is something extraordinary. Altho' American humour is the fashion I have only dared once to read those comic cards you sent from the hotel at Nantucket and then I tried them on Mrs Andrew Lang whose passion and profession is American humour and they fell flat and I felt flatter.[68] It is a horrible moment politically, but you know quite as much about it as I do. Nearly all my friends are imbecile Unionist abortions.[69] Their hideous, patronizing, doctrinaire, all-for-Ireland's-good, little measured-out globules of remedies make my blood boil so I never speak on the subject. Their stoopidity, the impossibility of their ever suspecting that the situation is one to be treated imaginatively makes them on this subject as hopeless intellectually as the beasts of the field. The out and out Tories one can respect. Lady Playfair told me she had seen great strong men at dinner fairly shake and tremble with rage in talking of Gladstone![70] Upon certain organizations his name is like a red-rag. I do not know whether to feel flattered or not by your saying that you had had so 'many pages' from me. I had hoped you were wondering at and pining under my long silence, I having only written when you wrote, once to Alice, and once to Aunt Kate since before the 15 January. I have written again to Alice since the young one came. I shall take it as a veiled compliment showing how the richness of the quality had to be accounted for in your memory by quantity. I have not thanked you for three

[68] Leonora Blanche (Alleyne) Lang, wife of the Scottish folklorist, poet, and journalist Andrew Lang (1844–1912).

[69] On 18 April 1887, *The Times* published a series of letters purporting to show that Parnell had secretly encouraged the Phoenix Park Murders, the stabbing to death of Lord Cavendish the Irish secretary, and Burke the under-secretary. The letters were a forgery but it took Parnell more than a year to prove his innocence.

[70] Lady Playfair, the American born Edith Russell, was the wife of the baron Lyon Playfair (1818–98), British scientist and reformer.

charming letters of yours which arrived in due time. The wealth of sympathy they revealed in your nature was very beautiful to me and was received most gratefully, reverently, not to say moistfully. I only took exception to your saying that no matter how ill one was, 'This is life', and consequently of value and to be clung to. As, vivre c'est sentir la vie I never expect to be deader than I am now, nay, not even after the worms have gorged themselves, I breathed a gentle remonstrance or feeble protest. I have however to thank you for a moment of vivid life called forth by your unaccountable want of having in any way felt or perceived the 'Princesse'. I was vehemently indignant for twenty-four hours but now I shrug my shoulders, the Princesse being one of those things apart that one rejoices in keeping and having to one's self.[71] It is sad however to have to class one's eldest brother, the first fruits of one's Mother's womb among those whom Flaubert calls the bourgeois, but I have been there before! Having had a holiday I was unnecessarily shocked at finding myself there again. There is some East wind for you! A striking contrast to the mild Southern zephyr in which your own Alice bathes you.

Give her lots of love and kisses to Harry and the babe. Always your loving sister A. J.
Henry is quite well again!

To William James and Alice H. James   [Harvard, MS 1480]

34 De Vere Gardens
Kensington W.

16 June 1887

DICTATED TO EMILY ANN BRADFORD

Dear William and Alice

Hearing through Aunt Kate, that Mrs Gibbens's name is not

---

[71] Alice is referring to Henry James's novel, *The Princess Casamasima*, published in 1886.

liked, I send a line, from a bed of illness, to ask why you do not choose the name of 'Margaret'? There could not be prettier name, or a worthier aunt. The name is entirely new in our family, and in infancy she could have that most delightful of nicknames 'Peggy'. Please do not send my letters to New York, unless expressly told to do so, also please remember to charge me with four of Father's photographs, Mr Warner will pay you. Kindly remember to tell him about the furniture insurance being lessened for another year. I have been running down very much the last six weeks, and had a bad little illness last week; but Katharine is come to the rescue, and I shall get off to Leamington as soon as I can pull myself together for the journey. Before K. arrived I fell so low as to send for an MD who had been variously and highly recommended. After examining my heart, which he seemed to consider an unnecessarily vivacious organ, he looked at me and asked, 'Does the protuberance of your eyeballs increase rapidly?' I am only sorry, not to be able to gratify William, by saying that my reply was 'Yes'; but truth forbids. He also remarked, 'You won't die, but you will live suffering to the end'. The last gentleman of the trade I saw, was going to make me perfectly well in four months! Farewell with lots of love to all.

Yours as ever
Alice
(E. A. B.)

To Sara Sedgwick Darwin   [Harvard, MS 1438]

11 Hamilton Terrace,
Leaminton

4 October [1887]

My dear Sara

I have been long in answering your pleasant letter but since it came my little world has had many convulsions – digestive, mental and sentimental. I was very glad to hear from you that you had enjoyed your visit so much and that all had gone well whilst you were there. I hear that you have been to Spa since you got back, your venturing so far afield again makes me hope that you are more robust than is your wont. I am getting on famously for me. I saw a new physician last spring whose advice I have followed with great benefit, so far. He holds out the hope that in eighteen months or two years time I shall be strong enough to have some special treatment for my poor spindles, but we shall see, it does not do to hope for extravagant results. He is a very interesting and peculiar being and I have not decided whether he is a genius or a maniac, he seems to have the qualities of both. For many small reasons I have decided to spend the winter in Leamington. Entire quiet and a reducing of myself, if possible, to a lower level of imbecility even than that already fixed by nature, has been decreed for me – intercourse with the bovine native I find most conducive to that result. In London the friends are rather many and altogether too stimulating for jangled nerves. I shall be densely dull and lonely of course, but the sands of my little hour-glass will run out as swiftly here as anywhere.

I am very comfortable in my quarters altho' the clerical animalcule of last year is still below, but he has not begun his midnight revelries yet. I am haunted however by the fear that I may be suddenly taken ill unto death and that before Henry can arrive to protect my little ecclesiastical, nurse will introduce the curate to my bedside. Imagine opening your eyes and seeing the bat-like object standing there! I am sure it would curdle my soul in its transit and at any rate entirely spoil my post mortem expression of countenance. It is terrible to be such an unprotected being as I am.

My soul was rejoiced to get a box from the U.S. today, containing sweet potatoes and Indian meal – and some diaphanous hot-water bags. My diaphragm has been lying crushed for the last six months under one of British manufacture, as dense and solid as the Empire. Did not you palpitate over the yacht race? But you are a degenerate daughter I am afraid. With kind remembrances to Mr Darwin.

Always affectly yours
A. J.

To Catharine Walsh   [Harvard, MS 1539]

11 Hamilton Terrace
Leamington

15 November [1887]

Dear Aunt Kate

Thank you for your two letters, the last received yesterday. I have been having a bad siege with my head or I should have written before to say how grieved I have been to hear of poor Cousin Helen's 'stroke'. It is an immense relief to hear that the dear, good soul does not suffer. I was of course immensely touched and grateful for her kind thought of me. I hope that Helen Ripley got her share. Tell me when you write, she is the one who needs it most. I wish I were where I could be of some service, but the most I can ever hope to do in this world is to keep out of the way. I have constant 'attacks' of all descriptions, more frequent than ever, but not so bad at the time and I get up from them quicker and feel stronger in the intervals. They are extremely inconvenient and I much prefer the rarer kind. My new doctor turns out to be a very remarkable and original being quite after my ideal, as he never wishes to see me and is quite satisfied to treat me through a third person. He gave a very remarkable diagnosis of my case and nature after seeing me once for twenty minutes during which time I lay with my eyes shut in explosions of laughter owing to the comicality of his manner. I shall give him a good trial. I have been delighted to hear of you from Katharine who gives charming accounts of your blooming condition. I am glad the umbrella is to your taste. Silver tops are all the rage and have the advantage of durability. Don't you think K. looks older? – Her existence must be a mild purgatory. Some days the rights of women will be respected, I suppose.

I am glad also that the photo pleased you. My room is very pleasant and the most comfortable in the way of temperature of any that I have had. It has no sun however being North. The bedroom is South and I get all the sun there is in the morning before I rise as I do not get up until 12.30. 'Little Nurse' is not little, her figure is exactly like a bookmarker and her face like a sheet of note paper, as Fanny Morse said. She is a good healthy creature and I look back upon my year with the diseased jelly-fish as something heroic.[72] 'Father thinks you have improved me very much, Miss, that I am much more intellectual than I was.' 'Oh! I am glad to hear it, Nurse.' 'Yes, Miss, I made several remarks about books the last time I was at home.' She is on a microscope scale a perfect illustration of her race, abrupt and arbitrary streaks of supreme intelligence traversing a bog of absolutely, passive imbecility. My solitude is almost complete, an anaemic Yankee appealing not at all either to the taste or the compassion of the Leamingtonites. After my London experiences my disgust and fatuous amazement are great at being so suddenly let down to my natural level. About once in three weeks an old maid comes to tea and such an old maid! dressed in my cast off things which I send her to give to the poor and which she intercepts to adorn her own decrepitude. It is weary work having to suppress all but the one syllabled reflection, but owing to my extraordinary capacity for maintaining the same perpendicular I am not likely, 'likeunto' to Bowles's butler to assume the horizontal in the river Leam. 'Whatsomever, Miss, 'is Lordship died, and it was likeunto this, Miss, thank you, Miss, thank you, the butler became un'appy in 'is mind and put 'imself in the Leam, Miss, thank you, it was likeunto that, Miss, thank you.' The only news on the 'ouse is that the curate lately

[72] Alice's previous companion, Miss Ward or Wardy.

took unto himself a dog who chose of all places in the house
for his midnight misdemeanours the rug outside my bedroom
door. After a second performance he was h'ordered out of
the 'ouse and the craven Clerk had as usual to succumb
before the militant old-maid in the 'droring-room.

Please send this scribble to Cambridge, with my love to all
and thanks for an excellent letter from William which I shall
shortly answer. Let him meanwhile rest assured that no race
to which I belong is an inferior one. If there is any means of
saying anything to Cousin H. which she can apprehend you
will surely give her my heartfelt thanks and love for all her
goodness to me, of a life-time. Also give my love to Henry
W. You never speak of Ellen V. Buren Morris! Is she well?

Always your loving niece
A.

To Alice H. James and William James   [Harvard, MS 1481]

11 Hamilton Terrace
Leamington

20 November [1887]

My dearest Alice and William

At the risk of oppressing you by a too prompt reply to your
charming letters I must unburthen my soul of its load of
gratitude. They equal each other in quality but Alice
manages to enclose more of the domestic atmosphere within
an envelope than any one else. The 'echoes of the little men'
are my delight. I am glad that my photo was acceptable, but
I am sorry to see by William's that Time has laid its mark
upon his 'thoughtful and noble countenance', but the genial
Lodge who saw it, says it gives no idea of his beauty, which
beauty by-the-way, seems to be one of the facts in the
progress of the race a solid gain about which there is no
dispute. Your Cambridge news is very interesting, but what

a horror about Ellen Gurney, was ever a man so heavily weighted as Edward Hooper?[73] And when one looks back at their youth, when we first knew them, who could have conceived of such an end! And poor Elly Emmet what a purgatory life must be to her![74] Being with Alice this winter must do her good, her strong and gentle spirit must soften her. To think of having no other armour than 'grimness' with which to meet 'the strings and arrows etc.' with all its cracks and crevasses for letting in despair. Surely there is nothing so true as that we are simply at the mercy of what we bring to life and not at what life brings to us. May God help her. I am disgusted with what you say of Margaret Warner. She seldom writes but when she does she is always very friendly and she used to be very admiring of Harry. How extraordinary it is that that brazen instrument of a Lydia Perry should have brought forth those charming verses, so full of such tenderness and grace. *A propos* of Grace, I am amused to hear that the ancient houri of Kirkland St. is still sowing her belated crop of wild oats. I suppose her mouthing ineptitude, her three-century old anecdotes and her snobbish pretentiousness are as great as ever. Instead of Froude why does not Charles expurgate her? – was there ever anything so exquisitely delicious as Charles pruning Carlyle![75] Aunt Kate sent me a most pleasant letter from Fanny Meeker* likening Bob to Father, what a desecration! One must remember, however, that all she knows of Bob is sound and if one is not too long within its vibration it is surely very superior sound. How lucky that his property is in trust, but it makes his position rather ignoble. I have sent you some

---

[73] Edward William Hooper (1839–1901) was the brother of Ellen Gurney and Clover Adams.

[74] Ellen James Temple (1850–1920), younger sister of Minny, had married her cousin Christopher Temple Emmet in 1869. She had been widowed in 1884 by which time they had six children.

[75] Charles Eliot Norton had edited *The Early Letters of Thomas Carlyle* (1886) which attempted to redress Froude's depiction of Carlyle, partly by missing out the material published by Froude which Carlyle had explicitly wished destroyed. Henry James wrote to Norton 'You seem a most perfect and ideal editor...but your demolitions of the unspeakable Froude don't persuade me that Carlyle was amiable'. (*Letters*, vol. 3, pp. 145–6.)

P.M.G.'s[76] to give you an impression of the state here, it is a plunge back into the middle-ages. I am in a terrible ferment at moments over it all, desolate at not being in London, but glad too, because if I had to see my Unionist friends I should explode from blood-boiling. It is a wonderful time to be living in, when things are going at such a pace and deeply interesting to sit by and watch mankind going up and down in the earth each with his own little panacea. Tolstoi with his shoe-making and his non-resistance, Cunninghame Graham[77] ramming his bare head into a phalanx of life-guards, and in between the Herberts and Howards tying their shoes with whip-cord and waiting upon their servants and 'Wilfred' having Lady Anne bludgeoned by the Irish constables because 'the Arabs when they go into a row always take their wives'.[78] Gladstone will come in with a rush before long.** How fine and noble is the conduct of the Irish during this waiting time, and that masterly mystery of a Parnell never breathing an audible breath through it all.[79] I have been reading lately with great enjoyment George Sand's letters.[80] You, Alice, must read them if you come across them. The picture of her latter days among her grand-children is lovely. She is such a great, healthy, rich, generous, human creature with such bursts of eloquence. She says

---

[76] *Pall Mall Gazettes.*

[77] Robert Bontine Cunninghame Graham (1852–1936), writer and radical politician. On 13 November 1887, 'Bloody Sunday', Cunninghame Graham had attended an illegal gathering in Trafalgar Square and had, allegedly, hurled himself at the police phalanx.

[78] Auberon Edward William Molyneux Herbert (1836–1906) was a radical MP, an agnostic, a vegetarian, and a disciple of Herbert Spencer; George James Howard (1843–1911) was a liberal politician and amateur artist; his wife Rosalind Frances Howard (1845–1921) was an advocate of home rule and women's rights; Sir William Lawson (1829–1921) was a Liberal MP who supported Gladstone's home rule policy and opposed Balfour's coercion measures.

[79] Parnell was not vindicated in relation to *The Times* letters until March 1889; in the meantime he maintained a distance from the controversy.

[80] An edition of Georges Sand's letters, translated by Raphel Ledos de Beaufort, had been published in England in 1886.

somewhere that she has always been happy because she never did anything wrong, never had any mauvaises passions! This might be called carrying the anti-morbid to its extreme limit and perhaps stretching it a little. Think of poor, dear Fanny Morse whose excellent mind has been stunted from the cradle by the burden of uncommitted sin which she clings to as her dearest possession, perhaps if she fell once it would fascinate her less. At the risk of stirring William's evil passions I will state that Harry's virtues transcend as ever the natural. Has he told you of his seeing Coquelin who is so enchanted with Harry's article in *Century*, and says it is the first time he has been understood.[81] He is a very brilliant talker. A lady asked Harry if there really was any difference between the English and French conversation. Oh! the conceit of these British! Your remarks about our inferiority as a race were very crude. I will put you right some day when I have energy, it is a subject which I have mastered. It strikes me sometimes that I may seem rather inflated, it comes from perpetually measuring myself with the lesser, the nurse, the landlady, and the decayed gentlewoman, when I come across the greater, perhaps not to be found upon this continent, unless you and Alice immigrate, my proportions will seem less magnificent. But I shall make you dizzy with too much reading as I am with too much writing. Love to every one Mrs Gibbens and Margaret and Elly Temple. How I wish I could see Margaret Mary!

Always you loving sister
Alice
This need not go to New York.

P.S. I forgot yesterday my main object in writing which is to say that I am delighted that the furniture is available. Use everything you can out of the trunks and the pictures too and the mirror, you will want things for the walls of the new

[81] Constant-Benoit Coquelin (1841–1909) was a French actor, associated with the Comedie-Francaise. He created the title role in Rostrand's *Cyrano de Bergerac*. He had been a schoolmate of Henry James's from the 1850's in Boulogne-sur-Mer. Henry James had published an article in January 1887 in *The Century*.

house which I am delighted is so successful. Do not have any view to my wanting them, if I ever do it will not be for years. The little gain I have made is simply negative feeling less tired and having less acute pain, but as usual it is simply an exchange of sensations as I am much more nervous than I was. My doctor says that in eighteen months to two years I can try the two remedies that exist for legs like mine, galvanism and certain douches of Charcot's given on the Lake of Geneva by some physician.[82] Galvanism now would be fatal to me, this he said without my having told him how nearly it had done for me in Bournemouth. Since Kath. has again been wrenched away from me and has now definitively passed from within my horizon for years I am stranded here until my bones fall asunder, unless some magic transformation takes place in my state. So do not consider me in using the things but use them up. There are some shawls in the trunks which Alice would find useful and might save from the moths. Why don't you use the Wilton rug? It will wear for years.

It seems so sad to think of you with your love of kin left alone in Cambridge with the family melted like snow from about you, but our dead are among les morts qui sont toujours vivants. Your wife allies you to the present and your children to the future, but I live altogether in the past, I have a momentary and spasmodic consciousness of the present, but the future beyond the next half hour is a black abyss on the borders of which I stand trembling but into which I never allow myself to glance.

Be sure to tell me, some one, what the baby's eyes are like. If she dares not to have Alice's eyes I shall cut her off without

---

[82] Jean Martin Charcot (1825–1893), French neurologist, founder of the Salpetriere clinic; his work on the difference between hysterical and organic paralyses were ground-breaking; he also undertook a study of hypnotism. Galvanism was the then fashionable treatment of nervous disorders by applying mild electrical currents to the body. Henry James records in a letter to William in January 1885 that Alice applied this treatment 'with her maid's help' and had induced 'an approach to paralytic stroke'. 'Of course she will never touch Galvanism, at least in that way, again', he added. (*Letters*, vol. 2, p. 63.)

a shilling. What was the use of bringing them into the family if they are not to descend to future generations and make them illustrious and lustrous. Forgive me my first pun!

*How sad the lucubrations of the follower are with the touch of the Master hand left out.

**A Conservative Lady asked Lord Hartington if he did not wish Gladstone were dead.[83] 'God forbid!' was the answer, 'What would become of us, he has got to get us out of this mess.'

To Alice H. James   [Harvard, MS 1459]

11 Hamilton Terrace
Leamington

3 December 1887

Dearest Alice

1000 thanks for your dear letter with the details of Ellen Gurney's death. I am indeed as you say 'triumphant' that her bruised wings are folded, no more desperate flapping to prolong that weary flight. In view of what might have been one cannot murmur at the manner of her end, but with our imbecile, physical clinging to what we know to be dust and ashes the thought of that poor wandering body violated by that hideous iron monster has given a ghastly wrench to my feeble frame.[84] And that walk for poor Edward Hooper, was ever man so tried! How noble she seems and what a desolate void her going makes for you. Beside our silent and

[83] Spencer Compton Cavendish, Marquess of Hartington (1883–1908) consistently opposed Gladstone's home rule policy and favoured coercive measures in Ireland.

[84] Ellen Gurney, who had suffered a nervous breakdown after the suicide of her sister Clover Adams in 1885 and the death of her husband in 1887, had thrown herself in front of a train. Her brother Edward at this time suffered a breakdown.

dignified dead, how trivial we living folk seem, do we not? We are being lopped on every side, may the tender shoots that have sprung up about you and William over grow all your scars and make your days fragrant with their innocence.

God bless you all!
Your loving A.

I wrote a few days since a letter which as usual consisted of things unsaid. Please send us a picture of Margaret Mary taken with you. This last is essential.

To William James [Harvard, MS 1489]

11 Hamilton Terrace
Leamington

11 December 1887

Dear William

I have grieved in the past over my inability to send an Xmas present to the boys, it has lately occurred to me that my grief can be assuaged by the unsentimental process of giving them a couple of dollars to spend for themselves upon some object they want. Will you please take the enclosed to the PO and give $3.00 to Harry and $2.00 to Billy if you think that a proper division. I remember being much pleased by a present of the kind myself. Put them in the enclosed envelopes with their other presents. I am not sure of the rate of exchange so perhaps have not sent enough.

I have been much knocked up, crushed and broken in fact, by the manner of Ellen Gurney's death which haunts one like a nightmare. That such an end should have come to *her* of all people in the world with her exquisite personal refinement is too hideous. It brings home to me cruelly what paralytics we all are, so remote from our nearest and dearest that we are helpless to save them from such a desecration of their personal sanctity even as that. It is ghastly! Harry

wonders if 'Mr Gurney could look *down* from some super-
natural sphere', if he could look down surely he looked
beyond as well, and his vision did not end where ours does,
at the blackest point of the dark valley! One's memory of her
goes so far back, even to the old Newport days, when she
came to stay with Mrs Tappan and filled me with awe, owing
to her Boston *parfum*. I think she was truly attached to
Father, she wrote me a beautiful letter after Clover's death
saying she had had the night before what seemed to her a
vision of him. It would be curious to know whether they are
within sight and sound of one another now.

What sort of children are the Hooper girls? It is like losing
a second mother for them.

I want you to tell me when you next write whether there is
a shadow of ground for saying that the Anarchists were
illegally sentenced. The shrieking and hysterical Pall Mall is
in a great way about it. On the subject of *Labour* and
Anarchy one is shy of putting perfect confidence in Edwin,
but what I should do without the Nation on the Irish business
I know not! When Godkin is right he is so right and goes so
to the root. I sent a letter of Mr John Cross's to K. to send to
you as I thought it might interest you. 'Johnnie' is better in
this way than as a devotee of Dante, an attitude which I
suppose he assumes in order to remind himself that he is the
Widower of George. Two of his sisters came for a few days
last week. Though strangely dislocated in mind and manner
they are most excellent creatures and for tonic quality have
the same relation to the Leamingtonians that the Yankee
does to the Londoner. I am nigh suffocated with exclama-
tions, chaff, reflections, not to say a 'la Annie Roche'. Is Mrs
Mackay of the gleaming tooth and glassy eye still alive? Also
Juliet the fair? 'ideas', 'rentres'. I asked nurse one day
whether Katharine and I were in any way different from
English ladies, 'Oh! yes, Miss, *entirely* different! 'Why, how?'
'Not so *aughty*, Miss'. Alas for our Vere de Vere aspirations!
Tell me when you next write whether the Miss Rebecca
Hunter who threw herself off the 40 steps was my Becky?[85]

[85] In 1858–9 Alice had attended a girls' school in Newport run by Rebecca
Hunter and her widowed mother.

I have always forgotten to ask, and if so how shocking. I had quite a human letter from Sara about Ellen, more red corpuscles in it than her pallid effusions usually have. From the reviews of the 'Life', what a delicious and exquisite being on the line of simplicity Darwin must have been.[86] The extracts from Father brighten up Mr Cabot's paper a bit. I have just got a letter from Mrs Russell Gurney saying, 'I have been following your Father's footsteps again in his relations to W. E. Channing', have you seen anything about it?[87] I am reading the Old Testament straight through with great interest owing to its rhetorical fatness, taken en masse it has a shocking effect upon the mind, a work more calculated to destroy all religious belief never was writ, I fancy. The picture of that sanguinary, rapacious and vainglorious deity is most repulsive. It will take many generations I suppose, before the mental muscles throw off their automatic reverence for it. I continue to grow stronger but I pay a great price for it as I grow *au pure et à mesure*[88] more nervous. Heaven forbid that any of you should know what it is to have half of your body helpless while the other half is the battle-ground of an army of fiends. There is some comfort in good solid pain. Remember the babes' and *Alice*'s photo.

With loads of love

Yours A.

---

[86] *Life and Letters of Charles Darwin* edited by Frances Darwin had been published in 1887.

[87] William Ellery Channing (1780–1842), Unitarian minister who was profoundly influential on New England writers such as Emerson and Lowell. He was said to have brought humanity to theology and equally a religious spirit to literature.

[88] In proportion.

To Frances Morse   [Harvard, MS 1512]

11 Hamilton Terrace
Leamington

28 December 1887

My dearest Fanny

Thank you so very much for your two letters which have recently rejoiced my heart. The first was the most beautiful you ever writ. I sent a note to you, to say farewell, to Queenstown but it was returned marked 'too late', owing to the gale which raged at the moment. How I shuddered for you! As you do not dwell upon the horror I shall not at this late period. I am sorry that your poor, dear Mother is so poorly, what a price she has to pay for her fun! I shall hope however that by this time she is acclimatized. All you say of dear Boston and its critters is a joy to me. I hope Lucy will come out all right. Of course she knows what she is about. I was greatly interested in what you say of Cleveland which is most true and encouraging. We feel very proud of him from here. I suppose his re-election is pretty secure.

I am just as you left me fulfilling as usual my career of ups and downs, getting the black future behind me five minutes at a time. My good landlady tried to bring some colour into my Xmas day with some feeble bits of holly and some succulent crumbs of pudding but only succeeded in throwing a very high light upon the pallor of the situation and forcibly illustrating your recent quotation of the 'busy ineffectiveness' of our kind. I had yesterday an excellent letter from Mr Boott, telling Lizzie's having a Xmas tree for the boy with eighty presents upon it! She seems to have a perennial spring of youth within her – or is it simply from having pitched her key so low from the start! – My nerves are still all quivering from the shock of Ellen Gurney's end. That *her* hyper-aesthetic personality should have had such violence done to it is a hideous incongruity and the longer one contemplates it the harder it is to be reconciled to. Her going makes a great void, although of late years I saw so little of her, but she goes far back in our lives and was greatly loved by Father and

Mother. I wonder very much sometimes whether Father and she have come together. She wrote me a beautiful letter just after Clover's death in which she described a sort of vision she had had of him that night. It is a struggle this fitting oneself to the middle volume of life from the pages of which all the ripe and mellow are vanishing so fast leaving our own crude generation to fill their places. Can Time *ever* round our angles and deepen our tone so that some day we shall impose upon the innocents behind us and seem to them low-toned and harmonious? I suppose so, as human experience seems to renew itself and revolve perpetually in the same narrow circle of emotions.

6 January 1888: Happy New Year to you all! I have kept this foolish scrap hoping to be able to add something that would make it worth sending, but I have been afflicted by 'greetings' which have had to be immediately answered, being a slave to what Mr Trowbridge used to call 'etiquette' I shall be rewarded in Heaven doubtless and at any rate you have escaped a deluge for I send this off to catch tomorrow's steamer.

Love to all. I shall write ——

To Sara Sedgwick   [Harvard, MS 1439]

11 Hamilton Terrace
Leamington

30 January 1888

Dear Sara

It seemed at Xmas-tide very cold-blooded and [——] not to be sending you a word of greeting, but I was much oppressed by the attentions of the superfluously fond trinitarian so the moment passed. My Blarney inheritance[89] would lead me to

---

[89] On her mother's side her great-grandfather had emigrated from County Down to Philadelphia in 1764.

gloss over your iniquities but that conscience which has been super-imposed upon me by my long residence in the puritan capital obliges me to *proclaim* that I *have* 'reviled' you and that very audibly too! You sign yourself 'your devoted', I should prefer less devotion and more sound, Madam! As you say naught to the contrary I take for granted that you are fairly well. It will be a great pleasure to you to have the Arthurian family with you, but the babes I am afraid will be productive of a certain number of headaches. There is nothing new with me, I peg away as usual at the black future working it off five minutes at a time and so keep my head above water. I have gained in strength by the quiet here but I long for the social flesh pots of London. I am much oppressed by the clerical atmosphere in which I am smothered, the black-coated creatures swarm all over the place after the manner of certain lower organisms. The wives of two vicars and one vicar in person, over six feet in length, have broken loose upon me. This worm beneath, whom we have always with us, gave nurse a tract lately descriptive of a profligate patient converted by a nurse. It is a bad moment for him to have chosen as I have been absorbing a good bit of the Old Testament lately and am almost an Atheist in consequence, it is succulent though as literature. The only person of consequence that I have seen is Miss Rose Kingsley whom I like as far as I have gone, unfortunately her responsibility to 'my West Indian blood' makes her rather too florid and tropical in her demonstrations, as someone said.[90] I get into a great ferment about 'the human race' and cannot allow myself to read anything more on the Irish question. How are our friends the Liberals going to dove-tail Mitchelation and Trafalgar Square into one another?[91] They seem all tarred with the same brush though the Unionists seem to have a thicker coating than all the others put together for cynical

[90] Rose Kingsley (b. 1845) was the daughter of the writer Charles Kingsley (1819–75) and Fanny Pascoe Grenfell Kingsley.

[91] Possibly a reference to John Mitchel (1815–75) the Irish nationalist and publisher in New York of the *Irish Citizen*. He was elected MP for Tipperary but since he had been convicted of sedition was not allowed to take his seat. A biography by W. Dillon had been published in 1888.

complacency in pursuing 'ways that are dark' 'commend to us the purely good'. I have always been so grateful that I was born bad and never by any chance could become good. But I shall tire you to death. Give my regards to Mr Darwin and believe me your moderately affectionate friend.

A. J.

To Francis Morse   [Harvard, MS 1513]

11 Hamilton Terrace
Leamington

19 March 1888

My dearest Fanny

As it is against the law of the land to incriminate oneself I will not recount the number or the dates of the agreeable letters which I have had from you since I last wrote. I have been most grateful although no echo has reached you, I am afraid. But are you still alive? – the papers are full of the horrors of the storm and from here it seems as if no one could have survived to tell the tale. What a new attraction added to life where existence is already overburdened with meteoric eccentricities. I was glad to learn by your last letter that your Mother had readjusted her nerves to her native air, how sad that so many of us should be born out of our atmosphere and have to exhaust all our energies in keeping our jangled notes in tune, or an approach thereto. I had a great pleasure in getting a letter from Lucy awhile back which stirred my stagnation with a blast Californian of the accidental, the never-before-happened, most vivifying in the midst of the rigidly foreseen. One has not to lament that Lucy was born upon an alien soil she could only have flowered in Yankee-land. I am going on very well here as to the body though the soul continues to be rather starved, but according to our topsy-turvy methods I shall doubtless feel it my duty for sometime to come to feed the mortal at the expense of the imperishable and shall therefore remain *in statu quo* for the summer at any rate.

I think since I last wrote that Miss Rose Kingsley has added herself to my circle. Have you ever seen her? She lives near by with her invalid mother. She is amiable, instructed, and intelligent a l'Anglaise filled with fervour over the discovery just made by the little Island, that you can have a pleasant talk with a *Carpenter*!! She does very well occasionally but makes one altogether too moist as a consistency with her gush. But, oh! what a curdling of the lactic flow when the Irish cock is turned on! Let the carpenter beware upon what side of St George and Channel he was himself born for should he be one of the unconquerable race of patriots the lowest human attributes will be denied him and he will be likened, without a twinge of shame or the faintest breath of compassion, to Hottentots, Kilkenny cats or whatever euphemism recommends itself at the moment to the gushing humanitarians. Had you heard that Mr and Mrs Barnett[92] are going to take forty Whitechappellers to Florence to develop their taste for art, at £10 per head! Isn't it iniquitous when you think of the actually starving? 'Living', as Miss Mary Cross says with Zolaesque precision, 'right in among the insects', does not seem to enlarge the intelligence of the bitten I wonder if it lessens the number of the biters! I should not like to risk it!

How dramatic the situation in Berlin! What a theme for the moralist, for all time, that man with a foot and a half in the grave becoming the arbiter of the fate of millions! – no one since Napoleon I suppose, has had such power. His hoary old Father, with his hymns and his Fitzwilliams, going out too in such a blaze of glory![93] The cast-iron anachronism which he helped to build up carries within it, I suppose, the

[92] Revd Samuel Augustus Barnett, social reformer, one of the founders and Warden of Toynbee Hall, Whitechapel. He and his wife had been the joint authors of *Practical Socialism*.

[93] The German Emperor Frederick III had acceded to the throne, a dangerously sick man, suffering from cancer of the throat, after the death of his father Emperor William I on 9 March.

seeds of its own destruction which will blossom sooner or later, according to the length of days allowed the pacific Frederic, let us pray they may be many for the crumbling tho' necessary will not be agreeable to contemplate. Give my warmest love to all your circle in which of course Mary is included and believe me dear Fanny.

Lovingly yours
Alice James

Did you hear of the child who asked what God had for dinner and when he was reprovingly told that God had no dinner exclaimed 'oh! then I suppose he has an egg with his tea!'

To Sara (Sedgwick) Darwin   [Harvard, MS 1440]

11 Hamilton Terrace
Leamington

21 March 1888

My dear Sara

Had I obeyed the impulse of my sweetly responsive nature I should have answered your letter, from Wetherby Place, by return, but Providence staid my hand and thereby averted a calamity – give thanks to the Most High! Surprise and ecstasy fought for supremacy within my bosom at the unexpected birth which was not looked for for six months at least, tempered by a shade of anxiety lest it should be a sign that you were passing from our midst. I plucked up hope, however, when I read the bad names you shower upon me. Surely one need not be classed as infernal simply because one refuses to swell the bloated ranks of the self-righteous. Spelling the word in Irish doesn't recommend it even to an Irish-maniac.

I hope you enjoyed your London. Isn't Mrs Leonard very attractive. I shall not have the pleasure of seeing you later for I have not the faintest idea of pulling up my stakes for a long time to come. I am very comfortable here and am growing stronger. My soul rebels but I trample upon it.

What have you been reading lately? Have you read that prettiest of stories 'la Mendaine de Colette'. It quite captivated me perhaps because it came after one or two of the pagan, miasmatic, exquisite Loti.[94] What an *artist* the creature is! Do you remember 'Un Dining' in 'Propos d'Exil', you seem fairly to see, not to use another word, the old creature crumbling, a decay tho' in which there is no germ of a new birth. Miss Kingsley is *surprised* to hear that Loti is 'the dullest of mortals', I do not know why because he is evidently simply a creature able to receive and reproduce with utmost perfection sensuous impressions, he apparently never made an intellectual reflection in his life. I do not like to blow the fraternal trumpet, but Henry's article in the *Fortnightly* on Guy de Maupassant is most brilliant, methinks.[95] I wish he did more of that kind of thing, but he thinks it unworthy, I believe.

Isn't this German situation most dramatic? To think of the death of that hoary old sinner with his hymns and his bastards reducing us all to such 'Grief'. I suppose the cast-iron anachronism which he helped to build up will begin to totter in the hands of his grandson.

But the Tories and Mr Bradlaugh please me more than anything that has happened lately![96] But I hear you crying for mercy so farewell.

Your *devoted*
A. J.

---

[94] Piere Loti (1850–1923), adventure writer, whose novels are set in the tropics. *Propos d'Exil* (contes) had been published in translation in 1888 as *From Lands of Exile*.

[95] Henry James's article on Guy de Maupassant had first appeared in the *Fortnightly Review*, March 1888; it was later included in *Partial Portraits* (1888).

[96] Charles Bradlaugh (1833–1891), politician and advocate of freethought; he was repeatedly expelled from the House of Commons for failing to swear on the Bible; disliked by many liberals, he found support from some Conservatives who expediently exploited Liberal divisions.

To Sara (Sedgwick) Darwin   [Harvard, MS 1441]

11 Hamilton Terrace
Leamington

5 April 1888

Dear Sara

Harry sent me yesterday a letter from Mr Boott the second which has come. He seems to be taking it all with great philosophy and of course owing to his age his sensibilities are somewhat lessened. The fact of her having suffered intensely at first and then having died entirely unconscious of what was approaching greatly lessened the shock of the event.[97] He is the simplest of mortals after you get beneath the skin which to be sure is a very irritable surface with him, and he seems chiefly struck with the discrepancy between Lizzy's plans and those of the Almighty. He seems as he says 'like the victim of a huge practical joke' to be left at the end as well as at the beginning of life with a helpless baby on his hands and now chained thro' it to this perfectly incongruous man! That Lizzy's perfectly normal organization should have produced such a complicated and abnormal situation is not to be explained by us. He is going to carry her body to Florence in May and bury her under the 'cypresses she loved so well'.

Her husband had just made a fine portrait of her which is to be exhibited in the [Salain]. Rather tragic that seems, when you think how she would have delighted in any glory which may have come to him thro' it.

I am amused at your being mentally exhausted by Miss Sellar in view of her similar attitude, or perhaps rather I should say physical condition, in presence of your great brain power, before which you know I also tremble. Would it not be hygienically more economical to reveal to each other your relative cerebral equality? I was at first rather échauffée by your remarks about G. de M. but now I am only calmly

---

[97] Lizzie (Boott) Duvenick had died of pneumonia on 22 March 1888. Frank Duvenick sculpted a bronze effigy of his wife.

amused and have decided that à la London you have not read the article as you seem too conscious that I recommended it to you as a student of de Maupassant. Doesn't the low level of contemporary criticism make you blush to the tips of your fingers for belonging to the Anglo-Saxon race. Said at this moment this may seem personal it refers strictly to this journal.

A propos of French novels I think you rather 'strain at a gnat etc' if you read the Bible, I never either have heard that the former course imposed upon innocent youth as sacred and inspired volumes. I too recently took a long draught of it until I trembled for all my ardent natural religion which the picture of that sanguinary and vainglorious deity almost extinguished. A pull after at the 'Service of Man' soon fanned the flames again into its usual fervour. I feel as if I had said all this before, forgive me if I have! I have just been reading 'Robert Elsemere' one of the most beautiful books for purity and moral elevation I have ever read, methinks.[98]

Mrs Kingsley never writes me a note but what she is 'reading night and day' one of Harry's books 'for the sixth or seventh time!' She also sends me butter because I am 'my brother's sister', for a freeborn American woman this is pretty humiliating.

Yours with love
Affectionately
Always your A. J.

P.S. Forcibly recall me, with my regards, to Miss Sellar when she comes.

I saw somewhere that General Gordon had told rather a robust fib to the Mahdi, it was an occasion I suppose upon which God *was* willing! Seeing it was the Mahdi.[99]

---

[98] Mrs Humphrey Ward's best-selling novel, *Robert Elsemere*, was published in 1888.

[99] General Charles Gordon (1833–85) was killed at Khartoum by the Mahdi's followers. Gordon had disregarded his instructions and instead of withdrawing from the Sudan and leaving it to the Mahdi had sought to overthrow him.

To Frances Morse   [Harvard, MS 1514]

11 Hamilton Terrace
Leamington

24 June 1888

My dearest Fanny

Since I last wrote two events, one all of sadness, the other all of gladness have shaken our little universe, have they not! – Let us take the glad one first. Was there ever anything so good as Lucy's engagement? – Since the news came I have seen everything thro' rose-coloured spectacles. How happy it makes one to think of that dear waif anchored in that race whose goodness makes one feel as if, all unaided, they had invented *Virtue*, at any rate they have eliminated from their practice of it all its usually unseductive attributes. I am very eager for details. William says that *he* was 'took sudden', and some one else reports that he has been pining for long. To your hyper-refined being this will seem vulgar curiosity but it is a natural craving in a less highly developed form, so when you next write tell me all the gossip, *scandal* if possible connected with the affair. I suppose they will be married without delay and live in Marlboro' St! I know that 'Jim' was your friend especially, but I found when I came to know him that for my flaccid brain Chas was the easiest to get on with.[100]

I had an excellent and like himself letter from Mr Boott a few days ago which makes me hope that our long and by me greatly enjoyed correspondence will have no interruption. He seems to have taken it all in the simplest and most unrebellious way, very touching to contemplate. But he was always under his easily exacerbated surface, the simplest of mortals. Then kindly age comes to his help and softens the blow no doubt. The fact that Lizzy has gone still eludes one and will ever remain one of the most inscrutable freaks of providence. It has surely been the only violent action of her life and how curious that her harmonious personality should

[100] Lucy Washburn married Charles Putnam.

have brought about so incongruous a combination as those four. Let us hope that the raging Anne will be permanently dismissed. What a new sense to the word *superfluous* a motherless babe gives, does it not? Lizzy had written a few days before her illness that they were coming to England for the summer and that meant for me a sight of them. A great bit of the past has gone with her and out of the present how much of faithful friendship!

A propos of faithful friend. I had such a loss a fortnight ago in missing the more than excellent Russells who came here for three days. I was more than sorry for they are all compact of *American* faithfulness and goodness.[101] H. was so much touched by Mr Russell and his constant allusions to our dear old Wilky, he exclaimed – 'Think of hearing any one speak of Wilky in London where you never hear a creature's name mentioned twenty-four hours after they are dead!' The rapidity with which English grief assuages itself is most remarkable, all the torn fibres heal by first intention. I have been crying my eyes out over the beautiful Emperor, of all the stories of kings there surely never has been one more pathetic or romantic. But what a relief that he has gone, the spectacle of that benignant heart being eaten away by that moral cancer Bismark would have been too ghastly! For form and *kingliness* of sound are not the proclamations of the young one magnificent – but what a note of carnage! It is said that after Bismark an American Countess is his inspiration – it seems to be no longer 'cherchez la femme' but cherchez l'Americaine.[102]

The weather is very cold and rainy so I am much impeded in my chairing but I have been out several times and find of course an exquisite world prepared for me. Yesterday I got as far as the 'Centre of England' an ancient oak about 20kms off. I tried to *realize* but I do not know whether I succeeded perfectly, not having what Mrs McKay of the gleaming tooth,

---

[101] Probably William Eustis Russell (1857–1896), Mayor of Cambridge, who became Democratic Governor, married to Margaret Manning Swan.

[102] She is referring here to the death of Emperor Frederick III who ruled for just ninety days. His son, William II was not yet thirty when he ascended the throne.

calls 'historic sense' i.e., pumping up emotion at a given spot.
Why under the sun do you call Helen Paine amiable? – She is
I should say distinctly lacking in that desirable quality. She
is possessed of all the solid virtues but of the graceful who
could have fewer? Do you think I am very base? – nothing
new if you do! I must tell you the most delicious Captain
Costigan episode that H. told me about the last time he was
here. He was invited to dine by an Irish editor one day last
winter – to come at seven and and meet two men. It was an
ex-fashionable quarter so that the house was one of the old,
shabby, big ones, and the drawing-room consequently
fiercely cold as it was intense weather and hardly any fire in
the grate. In the middle of the room was the table set for four
with a large hole in the cloth. He sat en tête-à-tête with his
host until 8.15 when one of the other guests came in, the host
meanwhile as serene as the Captain himself. They then sat
down to dinner, which consisted of kidneys, a pair of birds
and some raisins and nuts and of course some very bad wine.
Henry in despair asked if he might sit near the fire and
insisted upon getting hold of the scuttle himself so that he
could empty it into the grate. Meanwhile the door was
always ajar and the other man finally suggested its being
shut – 'oh! yes I will do it myself' – and the good soul – the
host – strolled out into the hall and after a great fumbling
came back and said – 'I am very sorry but the truth is the lock
is out of order and I have been meaning for a long time to
have it put in order but I have always forgotten it, very
careless of me! and he remained unruffled and serene to the
end! Imagine this in London, it sounds funnier when heard
than written, but what a refreshing human oasis in the arid
desert of buttered respectability in which H. is penned.
Forgive my length and thinness. Give my love to your
Mother, Father, and Mary and believe me as always your
loving,

A. J.

————————————

To Alice H. James   [Harvard, MS 1482]
and William James

11 Hamilton Terrace
Leamington

21 August 1888

My dearest Alice and William

I have two delightful letters to thank you respectively for. I
never rejoiced so much as in hearing that the house of
Dollard has escaped from bondage,[103] but the death of the
one brother I trust will haunt you to your grave! I am glad
you are enjoying your place so much and that the young
ones are so hearty. I had meant if I had rented the cottage
properly to give the boys a pony, but tho' the cottage rented
the C. B. and Q. has become anaemic so that I am impotent,
may the great-aunt long survive to make up for my
deficiencies![104] I am doing very well, there is no excitement
within doors save the arrival of a black beetle and his mate
upon the premises so that my consciousness is filled with his
lusty personality alone. I wish you could see the British
cachet of the creature, he having in perfection that look,
which all the products of their genius have, of as much stuff
as possible having gone into the making of him. I am getting
out more or less and seeing endless robust and juiceful bits,
flowing with milk and honey from every pore. My outing
however has been suspended for the last ten days by the
thunder-bolt, which I have long expected, having fallen at
last, i.e., Bowles being drunk. He did not lie down in a ditch
or pitch me out of the chair which is their usual way of diver-
sifying the monotony of their profession, but he curveted
quite eno' to reduce my stomach, always on the look out for
sensational opportunities, to despair.* His successor, as an
object intended to personify Temperance and to soothe the
nerves of a fluttering spinster, would convulse you for all

---

[103] Alice is referring to William's shoemakers, the Dollard brothers.

[104] Alice owned a seaside cottage in Manchester, Massachusetts; she owned
stock in The Chicago, Burlington and Quincy railroad.

time, he is that rubicund! His fore-fathers have evidently thro' all the generations of Adam down suckled beer with the maternal milk, but I shall cling to hope to the last and meanwhile rejoice that his ten digits are less en deuil pour le roi de Chine than Bowles's, the human touch which mingles with all my scenic impressions and which the four dilutions to the contrary notwithstanding, I could so easily do without. Imagine my surprise and amusement on having a slip of paper sent up to me, as I was going to bed the other night, to the effect that Mrs Morrell Wyman[105] had been asked to call upon me by Mr Denman Ross[106] and to inquire very particularly about my health! D. R. is the 'fourth dilution' isn't he? I never laid eyes on him. Where and how and why has he fallen in love with me?** Annie Richards writes this morning that she has heard that Charles quelled a mob at Ashfield – was it of hens and chickens? – H. hears from some Englishman that he has met his 'charming friend Miss Lodge', can you imagine a less Virginesque figure? – I was enchanted of course to hear of Lucy and Charles P.'s marriage. I never saw him except at the shanty for a few days, but then I felt that beneath his carpet-slipper and maiden-aunt-like virtue there lurked a subtle charm that might lead the heart of woman far. There is some explanation of Mr Boott's behaviour about H. and the picture, in the fact that we have since heard that he was 'very much offended' that Harry did not admire it eno' when he was in Florence. As H. says 'one can never imagine that smallness of the reason for any of his actions'.

I have been much impressed by getting your letters and one from Aunt K. in having none of you mention the elections, showing how different your insides must be from mine, which cramp themselves so convulsively over every little public event here.[107] I seem perfectly grotesque to

---

[105] Mrs Morrell Wyman was Elizabeth Aspinall Puslifer who was married to Morrell Wyman (1812–1903), Professor of Medicine at Harvard Medical School, famous for his work on the drainage of the pleural cavity.

[106] Denman Waldo Ross (1853–1935), an acquaintance from Cambridge, became a famous art collector.

[107] The forthcoming American Presidential elections which Cleveland was to lose to the Republicans.

myself, a wretched, shriveled alien enclosed between four walls, with such an extraordinary disproportion between what is felt and what is heard and seen by her – an emotional volcano within, with the outward reverberation of a mouse and the physical significance of a chip of lead-pencil. Henry's genius not tending to 'race-consciousness' or 'pivotal beliefs' as A. K. would say prevents his being as much of an outlet as might otherwise be. But just you see if I don't have a career somewhere! When perhaps Bismarck and some people who think a good deal of themselves now may have to take a back seat – a certain wife and mother scientifico-philosopher whom I could mention, e.g., isn't Bismarck a hideous spectacle? – like some huge moral cancer eating into the life of forty-two millions of the human race!

I was afraid that you (William) would feel Mr Gurney's death as a great loss.[108] But what an interest death lends to the most commonplace, making them so complete and clear-cut, all the vague and wobbly lines lost in the revelation of what they were meant to stand for. Mr Gurney's death apart from his psychical value, was not to be greatly lamented on his own account as he seemed to have little hold upon life. I only saw him twice but he made an impression of weakness upon me which I find is shared by other outsiders. He showed with me an almost feminine irritability, and talked of his low-tonedness and of the great effort all work was to him and seemed to be little in love with existence generally. His marriage was from all accounts a most singular blunder, but it must be admitted that however great his faults to her may have been she is singularly calculated to drive a compli-cated and easily exacerbated organization wild, by her tactlessness and her inconceivable literalness. She is the sweetest of tempered mortals with a perfectly healthy and absolutely British simplicity of construction, exactly like her healthy, blooming, story-less face, labouring under the

[108] Edmund Gurney, fellow psychologist and friend of William's had killed himself by inhaling chloroform. In her *Diary* Alice wrote in August the next year: 'They say there is little doubt that Mr Edmund Gurney committed suicide. What a pity to hide it, every educated person who kills himself does something towards lessening the superstition.' (p. 52)

impression that she has gone thro' the profoundest subtlest and most tragic experience and telling! you about it by the hour. The second time I saw her she revealed indirectly her domestic woes and told me her life had been spent on the verge of suicide from the cradle, I believe. Notwithstanding her boring power, one cannot but be fond of her, owing to her singularly generous temper and her clearly healthy uninteresting beauty. Clearly, I am afraid, can no longer be applied as I am sorry to hear she took to painting herself last winter. The story of the marriage which I heard from a man and several women is this. Some half dozen young men were on the search for beings, one of them found a being in a lodging-house in Pimlico, a daughter of a solicitor who had died leaving a large family in poverty. They flocked to see her and Mr Fred Myers who seems to be more of an idiot even than usual persuaded Mr G. to marry her.[109] He wrote to his friends saying he was going to marry a young woman much beneath him but who as his wife would have a rise in life and larger opportunities; he wasn't in the least happy but happiness wasn't in the least in his line, so that didn't matter. To another friend he wrote making him exclaim 'why Gurney writes as if he were marrying a house maid!' This I know at first hand from the friends. Mr Fred M. joined them in Switzerland after a week or two and began 'training' Mrs G. in French manners and the musical glasses, when Mr G. wanted some pruning done he got Mr M. to do it. Apart from the cruelty can you imagine anything so ludicrous? – She poor soul, as she said had given her all and got a stone in return! His snubbing of her in public was proverbial; for him it must be said that she was very provocative of it for she talks on all subjects human and divine with supreme infelicity. To have taken the poor, sweet, inept, and blundering creature for 'a being' shows an unexacting standard in the British youth. Mr G. was distinguished for his fidelity and devotion to his friends and was high-minded in all ways, but not meant by nature for a

---

[109] Frederic William Henry Myers (1843–1901), poet and essayist, interested in spiritualism and helped to found the Society for Psychical Research in 1882; co-author (with Gurney) of *Phantasms of the Living* (1886).

husband. They say he wanted to break off the engagement.

A. K. I suppose will be with you when this comes, give her my love. I wrote to her at Sharon not long ago. Be sure and give my love to Mrs Gibbens and Margaret. With kisses to the infants.

Always your loving sister
Alice J.

* Bowles told the people at the Repository when he got back that the lady was very different from usual.

** and why does he in this shabby fashion let his passion percolate thro' the bulky Mrs Wyman?

To Sara (Sedgwick) Darwin   [Harvard, MS 1442]

11 Hamilton Terrace
Leamington

9 September 1888

My dear Sara

Your elegant expression to the effect that 'we have not exchanged letters for some time' cannot certainly be controverted, but I confess to being curious to know whose shortcomings it is intended to cast in shadows. I feel much flattered that Mr Darwin should have 'regretted' *my* silence (he is, to be sure hardly in a situation to have mourned over *yours*!) I am also thereby indebted and grateful to him for your agreeable letter. Under the satisfaction there lurks however a hideous fear that you may be living in that worst form of matrimonial bondage, a community of letters, dread thought! I shall have to reform my spelling and my grammar to say nothing of my general flippancy of tone and raise all – impossible task! – to a standard meet for British inspection. Patriotism, if not friendship ought to have kept you from such a betrayal. I had heard through the excellent Annie, who always keeps me *au courant*, of your going and returning from Spa. I am glad it did you good – why did you not stay to compete in the beauty show, from your own account you would doubtless have drawn the prize. I am sorry to hear that Mrs Arthur is not in good health, it must have given you an anxious summer, with the children too.

I had a very bad illness in the spring of which I suppose you did not hear. It was the same in kind but very much more dreadful than any I have had before. I was much in hopes for a time that it was to be my last, but there was no such luck for me. I shall have to go over it all again and live meanwhile with a new terror added to my already terror-bestrewn path. I was for some two or three months struggling to recover lost ground but now I have got back to where I was before, I think. I have got out between the showers whenever I have been able and have had rich feasts upon endless robust and juiceful bits – this refers to the landscape and not my semi-weekly joint. My only adventure has been that one day my chair-man was drunk! I vividly realized the sensations of our cook when she was told that William was engaged to be married. 'Mrs James, I am that shocked that I feel cold within me!'

19 September: I had to stop here and since have been a prey to neuralgia in the lower parts of my interesting physiognomy while the rest of me was actively engaged in carrying on a very successful sick headache. I have at last emerged into the light of day. Such occasions if you only think so are very amusing, they give entire repose and time for one's sins to file past one's unrepentant soul. Can you conceive of creatures prostrating themselves before God and saying fifty times in a day that they are miserable sinners. Where is their self-respect or sense of truth, if they *are* sinners why don't they stop, if they are not why lie about it, above all to God! Excuse my heat, but Miss Kingsley talks to me about 'the *dear* Archbishop' and I don't shriek at her, so you must do me *that* justice. Do you remember Mrs Kellog a pretty little lady who had your Uncle Sam's house in Cambridge – she was here the other day and told me that in the house she is in in London there is a woman from Oregon, who *is* Oregon with a vengeance and brings down the house at the table d'hôte every night where she is considered *fascinating*. I asked for a sample – one night they were talking of wholesalers and retail when she said at the top of her voice 'I don't care whether he is in retail, in wholesale, or in cocktail!' Thunderous applause and anguish of Mrs K. H. has written what I think an admirable story called *Two Countries*. I believe it is to come out in a book and be called *A Modern Warning*.[110] I think though that only a feminine soul will understand it. There seems to be a difference of opinion about Cleveland at home, is the Nation right? I hope so as I have been feeling much distressed on the subject. Aren't you amused to *now* find that proving the non-authenticity of the Parnell letters is of trifling importance? The *Standard* furnishes me with much amusement from time to time. I have not read the new Charles Lamb letters, edition, I mean.[111] I have been meaning to send for it. You remember the virtuous Mrs MacKay of the flowing drapery and flowing talk? Mrs Kellogg recalled William saying one evening in the Quincy St. piazza, 'Here comes Mrs Mackay, with her hair falling down, her teeth falling out and her clothes falling off – a perfect Bacchante!' My tipsy chairman told them at the repository when he got back that, 'the lady was very different from usual', it is all in the point of view! To Bowles there must have been shocking irregularities in my conduct!

Forgive this endless futile scribble, but I have just been reading a novel in which the hero has 'left his eyes in her mind', fortunately he 'had a closely-fitting nose', so that he did not leave that behind him too or the poor thing could not have lived to the end of the the third volume. Pray give my kindest regards to Mr Darwin but tell him that he is *not* to read my letters.

Always affectly yours
A. J.

[110] 'A Modern Warning' first appeared under the title 'Two Countries' in *Harper's New Monthly Magazine*, June 1888. It was included in *The Aspern Papers*, published in 1888.

[111] Charles Lamb's complete works and correspondence was published in six volumes, 1883–8.

To Catherine Walsh   [Harvard, MS 1537]

11 Hamilton Terrace
Leamington

8 October 1888

My dear Aunt Kate

Many thanks for your interesting letter with all the details of your Chocurua visit which as H. says gives an impression of hospitality on a great scale, 'la grande vie'.[112] I am sorry you lost a week of it but I have no doubt that your peace of mind about H. made up for it. Have you ever heard any of the details of the 'elopement'? The blushing bride would bury all mishaps, of course, in her bosom. I am glad that you enjoyed the rest of your summer, the photos of Sharon came safely and I thought they were lovely, the trees fairy-like and inspired as compared to the dense stodgy giants by which I am surrounded. Thank you greatly for them. Are you 'offended' with the Tweedies that you never go there now? What about the famous 'quit-claim' – I don't want to be grasping but it would give me unholy joy to be even with Katy. A wave of amused indignation rolled thro' my being at your cool proposal for disposing of Grandmother's portrait. My highest ambition is that,

> By foreign hands *my* dying eyes were clos'd,
> By foreign hands *my* decent limbs compos'd.

but as the highest is not always attainable one must needs put up with the next best, therefore so long as Death eludes my grasp I remain as much alive as possible and have not the slightest desire or intention to dispossess myself of the *few* ancestral posessions owned by our race. I am very glad that you should have it and I am also very glad to have been told where it is. I greatly regretted to hear that my things had been moved to Cambridge, as I particularly desired that they should all be kept together in Boston as being so much more

---

[112] Chocorua was an old farmhouse on the shore of Lake Chocorua in New Hampshire that William James had bought as a summer residence in 1886.

accessible to send Kath. to or for me, should I ever return. But it is of no consequence now. If poor Mr Loring had not met with his accident I was going to ask K. to send the pictures, clock etc across to Henry who is very eager to have them and to whom they are to go at my death and then to William's children. I fail to see that Lilla can have the associ-ations with the picture that we have, dating back to 14th St. I think it would be very good to have the picture photo'ed and to give one to the Stamford Walshes, one to Jay and to Lilla and Dick. If you send the *bill* to me I can easily send you a P.O. order and then they will come from me. There has been a sudden plunge into winter and I have got my double windows up and am getting myself hermetically sealed for my eight months hibernation. I have been out I suppose, on an average once a week but now that the time has past it hardly seems as often, there are however compen-sations in all things, the days I go out are *twice* as long as the enclosed ones! My experience with Bowles is a striking illus-tration of how we are the sport of chance, for three years I have only felt *safe* under his guardianship no other man in Leamington would I go out with, I now find that he is a 'fearful drunkard', and that it has only been thro' some fortunate accident that the weather, my wellness and his inebriety have never been before in conjunction! Why should I be going to Oxford? – to lead a deaf and purblind don captive to the altar or what? – deaf to my twang and purblind to my faded charms! It is very strange to live alogether with people who 'can't imagine that I ever walked' and who take me as having always been an ancient, grey-haired spinster. This sounds as if I wished to give an impression of a Hebe-like dawn! I greatly enjoyed seeing Mrs Kellogg who looked so handsome, elegant and American and was so entertaining, affectionate and sympathetic, also American! *A propos* of William she recalled his exclamation about Mrs McKay, 'Here comes Mrs McKay, with her hair falling down, her teeth falling out and her clothes falling off – a perfect Bacchante!' – which as you may imagine carrried me back to Quincy St. with a vengeance! As William like the dissipated Jap. student is fond of 'flattery and sponge-cake' tell him

that in writing to a friend the other day I quoted something
he said and added 'this is from *him* at whose feet I always
sit!' I am looking forward very cheerfully to the winter as I
have several friends whom I really like and who come often.
I have been fallen in love with, I am afraid, by two sisters,
Miss Maudes, daughters of a vicar![113] but who do not believe
in the Trinity, which may account for their inclination me-
wards.   Forgive all this egotism but I have to be my own
Boswell and it would be a pity for you to lose a little local
colour by artificial bashfulness in me, put on simply for
looks, or rather sound.   *A propos* of the Trinity, some one
read a letter of Mrs Max Muller's[114] – who is a niece of Mrs
Kingsley giving an account of a visit they had had from
Prince and Princess Christian, all the pronouns required in
relating the tale and referring to them were written with
capitals, exactly as if they were the two *Persons* of the
Trinity.   He, She, Him, and Hers, now if they could only fit
the Holy Ghost to one of the minor Royalties, or better still
the Queen as being more pervasive, what a comfortable and
tangible solution for the Ms. M's of the elusive problem.
What a crowing cock the young Emperor seems to be and
what bitter lessons he has before him to learn before he is
brought in touch with humanity and his age.   But he is a
substantial and dignified figure compared to *our* papier-
mache Royalties.   Harry has just this minute enclosed to me
a note from M. Jusserand[115] of the French Embassy written
in English and very funny about the Whitechapel murders[116]
and the Police, he finishes with the following: 'when I meet
you I shall tell you how yesterday having to go out to post a

---

[113] Constance Elizabeth Maude, as well as being the daughter of a vicar, was
a musician and a writer.

[114] Georgina Adelaide Muller was married to Max Muller (1823–1900),
who was an orientalist and a philologist and the first professor of
comparative philology at Oxford.

[115] Jules Jusserand (1855–1932), diplomat and literary historian was a friend
of Henry James.

[116] The Whitechapel murders, committed by 'Jack the Ripper' in 1888
remained unsolved.

letter after midnight, when I opened the door and issued out
of the house, an inert body, a woman's body, fell along [sic]
me to the ground remaining partly inside, partly outside the
door. I found after a careful examination first that the body
was still warm, second that the cause of its inertness was its
being dead drunk. I behaved I dare say in the most approved
Good Samaritan fashion. To the Whitechapel fiend might be
appropriately applied an expression which I have heard you
use, 'He is simply a form of *evil*!' a very gross one too, he
causes a species of Terror throughout the country and he
has set all the other cranks flourishing knives. That canny
Scot Sir J. Rose has had the good fortune 'to be dead without
dying' as some one says.[117] He has left twice as much money
as was supposed, fortunately *in trust* as several of his children
are spendthrifts. The eldest son I believe is given to
bohemians, and the youngest dreadfully in debt. He married
an Earl's daughter for whom his father had to pay £10,000,
a large sum considering that the Earl is the poorest in the
peerage and has to live in Belgium and that she was one of
twelve olive branches. I am very glad that poor handsome
Mrs Clarke's struggle with existence poverty and fashion,
should be over![118] But the extraordinary morality that exists,
Sir John dying at the Duke of Portland's whose relations
with Mrs Sloane Stanley have been so notorious! Mrs Clarke
lets her daughter whom she has lately brought out be seen all
over London with her Aunt and told a friend that she
regretted the fact that she should have to let her go about
under her auspices but they could do nothing to offend Amy
because she had got Stanley's place for him from the Prince!
Then can you wonder at the French holding up their hands at
'English Virtue!' On looking over this I am afraid that the
tone may strike you as low, but remember my *milieu* and that
one can't be always on stilts unless one is Sara. Give my love

[117] Sir John Rose (1820–88), Canadian Statesman and financier. He was
distantly connected to the Temples.

[118] Mrs Clarke was the daughter of Sir John Rose from whom she had
inherited £70,000.

to all the folks and believe me.

Always your loving niece
A.

Send this to William.

P.S. Here is some Parsonic colours laid on thick, which I
have just read in the *Morning Standard*. Lady Shrewsbury
ran away from her husband and four infants with the Earl,
her husband divorced her and she married the Earl, he being
twenty and she thirty. The Rector would say, I suppose,
that it only showed the robust fibre of his 'Christian Spirit',
'I wonder what hue it took on to Polly Chubb, Anne Boosey
and all the rest of 'em, when they went astray in the village!

To William James   [Harvard, MS 1483]

11 Hamilton Terrace
Leamington

4 November 1888

My dear William

It was an awkward moment for you to choose to ask me
whether I was homesick, for I must confess that a certain
portion of your very charming letter of October 14th just 'to
hand' has rather forcibly impressed me with the drawbacks
of a random and good-natured civilization, where rights are
not passionately clung to and where affectionate relatives
permit themselves to rattle round the country with the
crockery of their kin. You will not need to know further
what portion of your letter I refer to. When I heard last
spring that you had moved the things, left over, to
Cambridge I was much amazed and annoyed and wrote to
remonstrate, but reflecting that the milk was already spilled
I tore up the letter fearing to seem unamiable. I made I find
a sad mistake! When I asked you to take all or whatever of

the things you might find useful I expressly requested that you should take nothing whatever to store, simply, I cannot therefore conceive how you felt free to transport the remainder to wherever it was most convenient for you, without a word of consultation with me. I unfortunately, but very transparently, spoke of the storage to make the gift seem less to you. I do not remember to have spoken of it a second time or to have intimated that I felt incompetent to pay for what I considered the proper care of my things. My having chosen so expensive a lodgment for the things showed on the face of it that the objects were precious to me and that I had provided for their safety in a fire- and thief-proof building, as nearly as possible, in a place also where they would be accessible and above all concentrated. I made therefore another sad mistake in supposing that what was so plain to my order of mind could not be entirely unperceived by yours. I have no words to express my extreme annoyance at your having paid the storage. You doubtless meant to be kind, but you know that kindness imposed upon an unwilling recipient – and that I was an unwilling recipient you can't have had a shadow of doubt – is likely to go astray and receive small gratitude in return. I am sorry I have been forced into this ungraceful attitude which a postcard from you asking my wishes would have entirely obviated. If you had not said in your letter that the things were en route I should have telegraphed to Chocorua and Cambridge to try and avert the catastrophe.

I am delighted to hear that the place is so satisfactory. Eat oatmeal and wear homespun if necessary in order to cling to it on the children's account. What enrichment of mind and memory can children have without continuity and if they are torn up by the roots every little while as we were! Of all things don't make the mistake which brought about our rootless and accidental childhood. Leave Europe for them until they are old eno' to have the Grand Emotion, undiluted by vague memories. A. K. described an Earthly Paradise, where Nature, Humanity, and Architecture were in friendly rivalry and all the generations from Grand Mother to infancy displaying new and unsuspected perfections – especially Grandmother! I rather imagine that ladies who come into the

world featured, eyed and completed like Alice have little difficulty in managing shirking man, she would hardly need to be
explained even to a Warwickshire peasant.   Does Simon
Hassett with his operatic stride still ornament the streets of
Cambridge? It is gratifying, however late, to have come into
'beauty' as you and I have done.   How has it come about? –
as the classic mould of our features can't have changed it
must be that the popular eye has been educated up to our
expression.   I have been told always that expression, when
once secured, increased with time so no doubt we shall be
more and more talked about, when our hitherto more
fortunate contemporaries, Gibbenian and other, who have
depended on the bloom of youth for their stock in looks are
quite forgotten.   Henry is somewhere on the continent flirting
with Constance.[119]   He seems like the 'buttony-boy' to have
broken out all over stories.   The best for its data is 'The
Modern Warning', which will be considered unnatural by
the bourgeois.   I feel as if I were the heroine.[120]   The Sackville
affair seems to be very lamentable all round.[121]   Politics,
politics, what horrors are done in thy name! The German
race must have some shreds of humanity in its composition,
it can't therefore be denied that the Empress Fred[122] must be
sadly wanting in tact; as some one said she must be too intelligent, no Royalty can succeed who has any shadow of mind.
Did you hear that Bismarck said when she was married 'That
little washerwoman will spoil the handsomest and healthiest
race in Europe!' if it was wafted on a breeze to her ears it
may account for the subsequent tension.   The curious thing is
that Sir M. Mac. has no respect in London from the

[119] Constance Fenimore Woolson.

[120] Henry James did perhaps partly model his heroine, Agatha Grice, on
Alice both in her atttachment to her brother and her susceptibility to
hysterical attack.

[121] Lionel Sackville-West (1827–1892) diplomat, American ambassador,
was recalled from Washington owing to alleged intervention in the
American presidential election.

[122] The Empress Fred was Victoria, the eldest daughter of Queen Victoria
and wife of Frederick III of Prussia.

'profession'. He was not admitted to the College of Physicians and would not be allowed to perform an operation they say in a London hospital. He is called Sir Immorell Mackenzie.[123] H. had the French ambassador to Spain dining with him one day, who told some stories, rather amusing. Spain is the most democratic country imaginable. The ladies of the court happen to be all very old and ugly and when the poor creatures go to Court for functions they have to run the gauntlet of the crowd, who exclaim, 'Look at that one, she is worse than the last' and so on. One day a mother and daughter were side by side waiting for the crowd to let the carriage move on and were both of them incredibly ugly, when a fish wife called out 'Look at those two they are uglier than all the others put together!' when the great lady put her head out of the window and said 'Yes, my dear, and they are both very much more sorry for it than you can be!' Some one said imagine an English great lady chaffing with the crowd on her way to the Drawing-room! 'Our Clara' gave himself away the other day in a delicious manner.[124] He was speaking somewhere and said that the Tory party was making great gains as proved by the Municipal Elections which were worked on party-lines (they are supposed not to be, is the proud boast!) and there had been seven Tory gains, the next day when the whole story was known there were found to be fifteen Liberal gains! Clara had to laugh on the other side of her mouth! The Parnell Commission drones on and is nothing but 'Parnellism and Crime' read aloud.[125] I had a cheerful but touching letter from Mr Boott, touching

---

[123] Sir Morrell Mackenzie (1837–1892) physician, specialist in throat diseases. He was summoned to Germany to attend to the crown prince, afterwards Frederick III. He failed to diagnose the cancer and later justified his treatment of the case in 'Frederick the Noble', 1888, for which he was censured by the Royal College of Physicians.

[124] 'Our Clara' was the nickname of Arthur James Balfour (1848–1930), later Prime Minister but from 1887–92 Chief Secretary for Ireland, responsible for Coercion Acts.

[125] The Parnell Commission had been set up to investigate the letters which turned out to be forgeries implicating Parnell in the Phoenix Park murders.

from its breath of old-agedness. It is wonderful how much one misses Lizzie from one's consciousness, she didn't furrow the surface deeply when here but her continuity told more than one suspected. Her having so violently discontinued herself was a great shock. I hope the beginning of this will not be entirely indigestible but it is necessary to have an understanding every now and then. With love to Alice and Mrs G. and Marg.

Always your loving sister
A. J.

To Frances Morse   [Harvard, MS 1515]

11 Hamilton Terrace
Leamington

18 November 1888

My dearest Fanny

What is left of me after the dismay and heart-sickness of the last ten days at the result of the election is going to try to write you a letter, charge the Republican party with the poverty of the infliction. The bolt fell so out of the blue as I kept hearing that it would be such a close fight. Tell me if there can be any explanation of why it was such a *bad* defeat?[126] Was it Lord Sackville sending over the Irish vote[127] or the ignoble conduct of the Government in turning him out that sent over shakey Mugwumps?[128] I suppose until Home Rule is granted or every Irishman now breathing is extermi-

---

[126] President Cleveland had been defeated in the Presidential election by the Republican Benjamin Harrison.

[127] Lional Sackville-West, the British Ambassador, had written a letter, used by the Republicans during the campaign, in which he seemed to support Cleveland. This seeming collusion between the British and American governments alienated Irish supporters. Sackville had been dismissed, October 1888. See footnote 121, *The English Letters*.

[128] The Mugwumps were the derisively named liberal or independent

nated our politics will remain vile. You may be thankful that you did not have to read the English papers during the episode. I felt that, as Julia de Kay used to say, 'a pelican in the wilderness is a festive bird to me', at the moment, and now will the odious Blaine get us into further trouble?[129] – Harry has written a story called *The Modern Warning* in which he has managed to get into the skin of a transplanted American woman in an extraordinary manner, it is so easy to fall in love with the incrustations and flowers of mould. I should like you to read it and see if you think it fits. The English being pachyderms having no superficial nerves, don't care in the least what anyone thinks of them so that the French, the Irish, and the Yankee with their quivering nerves of patriotism awaken nothing but contempt in the fat complacency of their bosoms. I hope you are impressed with the didactic tone of this, I feel as if I were *Charles* in person speaking from the highest peak of Shady Hill! Forgive me, I forgot that you could not bear to have that sacred name taken in vain. *A propos* of Charles I heard a good deal of 'Charley' in a delightful and Lucyish note which came a short time since. The highest tribute yet paid to the robust fibres of the Putnam virtue is the following – 'This family, I am happy to say, is just the same as when I came into it!' Think of their having withstood Lucy's corrupting influence! I have three delightful letters to thank you for filled with good and sad news too. How hardly the poor Russells are being treated by fate just now! Mrs Henry looked *so* ill when she was here that I should think that her *years* at any rate would not be many. Poor little Sally too what possible need can *she* have for trouble with that face of hers. Mrs Tappan's death, judging from a Dixey-like note in which illness, death, and the buying of clothes were confusingly intermingled, must have been a relief to her and poor Mary. In two of your letters you ask me about Mrs J. H. Ward, so I will proceed to

Republicans who had abandoned the party ticket in 1885 to actively support Cleveland.

[129] James Gillespie Blaine (1830–1909), Secretary of State in Harrison's administration; his anti-British sentiments were popular with the Irish-Americans.

tell you what I know. She came to see me twice, I found her very kindly and pleasant reminding one somewhat in her appearance and the sound of her voice of Mrs Fields, but she has never been as pretty as Mrs F. and is quite without the 'opaline' taint. I have been told from a variety of sources that her complacency is something sublime, it is so beyond all limit that it is grotesque and unheard of and comes to in a great measure from her being *altogether* without humour. *Robert Elsemere* which you ask my opinion of I thought at the moment of reading one [of] the most absorbing books I ever read. It is of course very defective as a novel being so inartistic in form and unequal in execution. Theologically I am so ignorant and uninterested that I had no judgment about that part, but with these very large omissions, I never was so touched and moved by a book before, a book which breathed a deeper feeling, a greater moral elevation or purity of tone, as H. said 'it makes one think better of London that such a book can have been written in it'. He told me to write to Mrs Ward so for the first time in my life I addressed an authoress. You dearest goosey where have you lived? Are your friends in the NORTH END (I don't know why I dignify the quarter with capitals) of so sublimated a nature that you can't even suspect the weaknesses of your educated brethren, and are surpised at their longing for applause? Miss Jewett is more than right and is honest like Dr Holmes.[130] To make a sudden transition have you any pamphlets or printed account of the working of the system of Associated Charities? – I have been so sorry to learn that Mrs Lodge is so far from well. Miss Mary Cross has come to spend Sunday in Leam., she says to see the historic monuments but her kind heart I think includes me as one of them. She used to devote herself to that criminal class of starving curates and clerks whose chief occupation is to bring children into the world to starve. She used to attend the accouchements as Nurse until she had to give it up because after she had been up all night with the Mother she was expected to take the previous twelve out in the perambulator thro' the day! You constantly see adver-

---

[130] Sarah Orne Jewett (1849–1909), writer, who became Annie Fields's companion after James Field's death in 1881.

tisements in the papers from clergymen and curates saying
that they have £150 or £200 a year and from eight to fifteen
children and they request to have some half of them adopted!
The poor are more honest and say when you go in 'we have
had no luck with the burying'. Altho' such a hidden violet
my influence is telling. Nurse came in on Sunday much
excited saying 'the Vicar preached such a beautiful sermon
just *your ideas*, Miss'. Perhaps its a lapsing spinster rather
than a developing vicar. Forgive my frivolity and give my
love to *every*one and write me all you can about the elections.

Your loving A.

To Sara (Sedgwick) Darwin   [Harvard, MS 1443]

11 Hamilton Terrace
Leamington

9 December 1888

My dear Sara

I was indeeed sore and humiliated over the news from home,
the more so as the bolt descended from out of the blue, I
foolishly not having had any fear. I saw in one of the papers
an analysis of the votes cast and it was an encouragement,
altho' also an exasperation, to find that the Mugwumps had
increased rather than diminished – what an incomprehensible muddle our presidential method of elections always is.
It seems pretty low to say so, but it is not human not to hope
that Blaine's ill-health will prevent his being Secretary of
State, for if he is *where* shall we all be? Lord Salisbury will
need to chuckle on the other side of his mouth. How more,
even than here, is the Irish question a lurking one at home.
The Phelpses[131] always meant to go back at any rate, how

---

[131] Edward John Phelps (1822–1900) had served from 1885 as Ambassador
to Britain in Cleveland's administration; he was married to Mary L.
Haight. Henry James said of them that 'he is a wrinkled old Democrat
politician, but very capable, very well-dressed and well mannered...she

distressing if that vulgar Whitelaw Reid[132] should take their place. I see John Hay is mentioned.[133] Did you read a very comic article by Mr G. in a recent Nation on the subject? – and also a most deeply humiliating account in the last Nation of the bribery in the last election. Had you the faintest idea that it existed to any extent? – let us bury our heads in shame! I received yesterday a very pleasant letter from Theodora. Give her my love and thanks when you write and say that I will answer it when I feel 'high-toned eno'' and have risen sufficiently out of the base personalities in which my nature keeps me sunk to when *she* sounds so superior.

I have no news. Henry has been galavanting on the Continent with a *she*-novelist, when I remonstrated he told me he thought it a 'mild excess'.[134] I hear he has been refused perhaps simultaneously (I have put 'perhaps simultaneously' in the wrong place, dazzled doubtless by my wit, please move it along) in company with Mr Bryce[135] by the widow historian Green![136]

He has sought consolation with the novelist, Mr Bryce, in India! I suppose it will shortly become our duty to read Mr B.'s three volumes upon our native land – rather an appalling prospect to beings endowed with patriotic hyperanaesthaesia. I am still to stay here for the winter as I find the quiet very advantageous. I don't do much more, but I don't have to pay

---

a remarkably nice and graceful little woman of the Pure American tradition.' (*Letters*, vol. 3, p. 215.)

[132] Whitelaw Reid (1837–1912), editor of the *New York Tribune*.

[133] John Milton Hay (1838–1905), poet, historan, and diplomat; friend of Henry Adams, jointly authored *Abraham Lincoln: A History* (10 vols, 1890).

[134] Constance Fenimore Woolson was at Bellosguardo, Florence.

[135] James Bryce (1838–1922), historian and statesman. Had published *The American Commonwealth* in 1888, aiming to portray 'the whole political system of the country in its practice as well as its theory'. The book acquired a high reputation in the USA.

[136] Alice Sophia Melia Green (1847–1929), better known as Mrs Stopford Green, Irish historian and widow of the historian John Richard Green. Advocate of Home Rule.

so heavy a price as I did a year ago for doing nothing. I see very few people – I don't seem to draw at all in Leamington. Last winter the Kingsleys were in raptures over me, calls, notes, books, fruits, and gush such as was never known before but in midsummer they suddenly collapsed and I have heard no more. I am told by 'one who knows' that such is their habit, somewhat surprising when one is not prepared. My attractions being based entirely upon my 'Great Brother' as they call Harry in their least excessive moments, makes it more puzzling still. There is a most delicious Philistine who calls upon me and makes literary remarks owing to my unfortunate family connections. The other day talking about George Eliot something was said about her excursions from the conventional whereupon she said – 'That terrible rationalism leads so to Mormonism and that kind of thing'. It was physically impossible not to laugh. 'Why, isn't Mormonism a plurality of wives?' Imagine the immortal George and the complacent rationalist likened to the vile and degraded Mormon! Nurse told me that Calvinists were 'a kind of Jew and they are never baptized'. Don't you think John *must* have heard and shuddered! 'A *kind* of Jew' too is delightful, suggestive of possible modifications of the crystalized Hebrew.

It is comfortable to think of Annie back in London, more attainable for funereal rites in which function I am always in imagination employing her. I am not going to die however, the doctor here said I might, but the doctor at home in whom I believe says I *can't*! I shall be a non-wandering Jew! When you are all comfortably tucked away I shall still be here lamenting. My smug, comfortable friend of whom I spoke above is praying for my soul having by chance discovered its darkness!

Farewell and write only when you feel like it, as I don't relish being sent, you know where. My principles don't allow me to use certain words to which you seem very familiar.

Yours as ever, affectly
A. J.

P.S. Isn't the boom in American girls too comic!

To Alice H. James   [Harvard, MS 1457]

11 Hamilton Terrace
Leamington

10–11 December 1888

My dear Alice

Thank you a thousand times for your letter and William's P.S. so full of forgiveness and mansuetude. I can easily imagine from past experience William's bewilderment and I must have seemed to him, as of old, like some Fury descending into the blue of the serene and simple atmosphere which surrounds all his personal relations. I never for an instant imagined that any other brain had assisted in, or sanctioned the move, it had in too much perfection our William's cachet! I read somewhere 'that the constructive, without the imaginative, sometimes leads to the destructive', with W.'s vast powers of construction it would be too much to ask him to throw in imagination, as well and so far he hasn't been very destructive so I grant full forgiveness, especially as there was such an excessively comic side in the way he put the business, which seems to have escaped him and which I have refrained with the utmost generosity from pointing out, knowing how much less sharp the arrows of indignation (!) were than the poisoned ones of ridicule! I wasn't made ill by the affair as you suggest, but I was ill after I sent the letter with all the 'mines' proclaimed and implied in it and would have gladly called it back and let all the old plates be ground to powder without remonstrance rather than assert my proprietorship from the house-top. About the pictures; I heard, or I dreamed that I had heard that you had no room for them, I consequently supposed that they were all boxed and stored in the warehouse. H. having a great blank wall in his library I thought it a pity he shouldn't have the

Venice, the clock, and Grandmother Walsh's picture, as he cherishes so much all associations with the past. Do not do anything about it until I write, he doesn't use the room as it is entirely uninhabitable in winter – the whole flat is a draft-trap. The crossing is now so bad too. Its alright for A. K. to have the portrait, I was however annoyed at having it assumed, or rather having her assume, that I had no liking for it.

Harry and I were both deeply stricken by the Election and I devoted a whole night to tears, but as they seemed not to improve the situation gave them up. I was amused to receive three letters, yours, one from A. K. and Theodora Sedgwick ones (written in such Nortonese!!) in which none of you even mention the word. I have long thought that patriotism is a centrifugal emotion intensifying at the outskirts. It all seems so dreadful from here, hearing both too much and too little. Is there any justification for the article in the *Nation* of November 22nd on the bribery practised? Let us bury our heads in shame!! My heart is warmed every now and then by the sight of Gam. Bradford pegging away at his hobby.[137] Mr Bryce's book is spoken of with the greatest praise in all the papers, it'll become one's duty to read it soon. Have you heard that he and Henry have both been refused, perhaps simultaneously, by the widow historian Green, H. drowning despair in Italy, Mr B. in India! *A propos* of H. he has got to Paris and will be back in a fortnight, I suppose. He is, as always, as good as bread and the staff of my life, of course. I received a letter from Marg. Warner which entirely confirms my impression that his disapprobation is an affair of features and consequently but skin deep – (a play of words which will not bear close examination) she speaks of the boys with admiration – 'Billy is a dear soul and Harry very bright and interesting – Mrs Alice's face very sweet and handsome and I like to talk to her when we can really have time to say a great deal, I carry home always something to

---

[137] Gamaliel Bradford (1831–1911), a banker who, having made sufficient money, retired from banking in 1868. He devoted himself to politics, joined the Mugwumps and opposed Republican policies of high tarriffs and imperialism.

Joe when I have called there'. – so, Madam, what more compliments can you want? – I shall give you none!

Mrs Lodge has always given me to suppose that her affection for the family was based upon William's Beauty! How sad to think of her fate, how curious she so satisfied and unprepared, and here I am all packed up! Perhaps it will seem to you that I am not as packed up as I imagine, but if so, I am like other great ones, George Sand e.g., who writes a long letter to a friend telling him why she is going to commit suicide and in the end says to be sure and have her two mattresses corded! Last year I read her in her grandmother period when she is admirable, lately I've been reading her earlier letters when she seems to have been morally simply a boy – up to middle life. At the core of all her fine phrases on love, friendship, and humanity there is simply the boyish ideal of escaping all control, but it is very fine and most interesting to see her sloughing it gradually off. What a loathesome pervading of French domesticity there is, of soiled peignoirs, cheveux parfumés, maux d'estomacs and dirty hands – an all-using-of-the-same-towel atmosphere! I was much amused with Mr Godkin on French love of privacy! *A propos* of the *Reverberator*. They haven't their George Flack's, but give me George![138] He hits in the light of day and doesn't the moment his nearest and dearest are in the grave turn a lens of the first magnitude upon their physical and moral warts and wens for the disgust of coming generations. Geo. Sand confides to a friend that she is going to separate from her husband, she having found in rummaging in his secretary the day before, when he was out, a letter addressed to her upon which was written that it was not to be opened until after his death, whereupon she calmly opens it and finds therein a list of his griefs and her shortcomings. She entreats the man to burn her letter as soon as read, which he not only doesn't do, but her son publishes it! But you will be sick of Geo. and all this may be ancient history to you. If it is forgive me! but my existence is somewhat restricted, intellectually confined to Nurse and Miss Clarke. Nurse told

[138] George Flack is the gossip-writer in Henry James's novel *The Reverberator* (1888).

me that Calvinists were a kind of Jew who were never baptized. Don't you think John must have heard her and shuddered! 'A kind of Jew', too, as if there were possible modifications of the crystallized Hebrew. I heard an American and an English account of the Moshers in Paris, the former very distasteful and the latter rapturous, the goodness of the group being dwelt upon. It seems odd that Mrs Mosher who with Mr Breed seem to constitute the demimonde of Cambridge should now stand for pure virtue, it shows the difference in the standard in the two centres of civilization.

14 December: The only thing that saves you from another ream is that I have been down with a head. Another *Nation* with more appalling accounts of our infamy, one would fain pray that the two oceans might rise and sweep us and our shame from the face of the globe! Farewell

Love to all. Especially W.
Your loving sister
A. J.

To Catharine Walsh　　　　　　　　　[Harvard, MS 1538]

11 Hamilton Terrace
Leamington

29 December 1888

DICTATED TO EMILY ANN BRADFIELD

My dearest Aunt

Thank you a thousand times for your letter and its roseate enclosure. I rarely have seen a lovelier shade of pink! I shall invest it in some luxury, otherwise unattainable. I feel very rich, of course, at not having to pay the tax, and have abandoned trying to devise means of reducing Nurse's food, so as to make two ends meet. I am sorry not to be able to write myself, but we have been through a 'circus' the last week. What do you suppose a young couple, who took the dining room for a fortnight, sprung upon us as a 'Christmas Box?' An Accouchement!!! We feared it all Monday and Tuesday the battle began and raged until 11.30 p.m.

My first feeling on Monday was to be immediately carried over to the Regent Hotel; but after Nurse had towed my heart back to its moorings by Digitalis and poured a sufficient amount of Bromide upon my gunpowdery nerves, I returned to my ordinary passivity, although not serenity. It seems to have been more silliness than villainy in the people. It was very curious to lie here, and to hear the Xmas rejoicings through the gossamer walls on one side, and the groans of the woman in labour in the room above, where the mystery of Life and Death was acting itself out. How my heart burned within at the cruelty of men! I have been haunted by the thought of Alice and all the child-bearing women ever since. The little waxen image held a feeble spark of life which flickered out at the end of an hour, beneficent Death, rescuing it from a mother who was 'glad' when she heard it would not live, and who had not prepared a rag to wrap it in.

Miss Clarke gave the doctor a rag out of which he cut a shirt, and fortunately had a yard or two of flannel to wrap it in. But I must do justice and say that the father has impersonated woe with great perseverance, but as he has, when not tramping up and down stairs, devoted his attention to keeping up his strength with brandy and soda, I think he makes a neat illustration of William's mechanical theory; centres of emotion so thoroughly lubricated must exude somewhere.

Please thank Ellen Ripley for her charming calendar, and tell her she will hear from me before long.

You might send this to Cambridge, as I shan't be able to write them for some time.

With best wishes for the New Year
Your grateful and loving niece
Alice J.

Alice sends this because of her recent troubles; she has

improved the 'Liege's letter before she sends it off – At first I
could hardly understand it. I don't want this back. But send
me back the one which Alice sent me.[139]

To William James   [Harvard, MS 1484]

11 Hamilton Terrace
Leamington

29–31 January 1889

My dear William

Your letter enclosing Lilla's – what an excellent letter by the
way – was of course a great satisfaction to get. Henry and I
had been anxious so long and Helen Ripley and Lilla had
only given us partial accounts. Aunt Kate's letters have for
several years showed signs of a loss of memory, but she
seemed as vigorous as ever, until the second letter she wrote
after having got home from Chocorua, which showed the
most curious change and enfeeblement, each successive one
more so. I suppose she did not write to you or you would
have perceived the change, it was so very marked. From
what they wrote us we had no idea of how serious and
distressing her condition is, but yours and Lilla's letters bring
it all before us. Could anything be more dreadful – given
Aunt Kate! It is very touching what you say of her patience
and submission, for there is nothing she has ever dreaded so
as to survive her faculties. 'The family' are of course doing
what they can for her, but it does not lessen the grief and
regret of this member that she is as usual lying with folded
hands fostering her own aches and pains. It is hoped that the
trouble will advance rapidly for then she will lose the
consciousness of her condition.

Tell Alice with my love that the photos are lovely, the
baby charming, and Harry like a princeling, to match his
manners. The accounts of Bob and Ellen Emerson are too

---

[139] This addition is in Henry James's handwriting.

funny.[140] But what kind of Episcopacy can flourish in that arid soil? – from my point of view you may imagine how comic the combination of Concord and Celebration, Matins, Evensong, the Spirit in the shape of an intoxicating liquid, the Holy Ghost and the dear knows what! Tell Alice I have read some of Miss Wilkins' stories[141] and think them Zolaesque in their rendering of the New England nature, with its raw, formless, ugliness covering the ever-glowing moral intensity within such a contrast to the rustics here compact of beef and beer. This reminds me of the 'docu-ments!' What you say of my letters is quite just, don't fear to be florid or excessive, for like Dr Holmes I can never have enough, but I must confess to having rolled over in my bed with laughter at the suggestion of the collection of 'documents humains'. Imagine the millions of the Empire being labelled and pigeon-holed by a creature whose field of vision is densely populated by a landlady, a hospital nurse, and two Bath-chairmen, one perpetually drunk! Its too funny! It is all very well to say 'don't take on so about the Election', but I think if there were a little more 'taking on' things wouldn't be in their present state. It is a most hideous spectacle from here, when you have to send the *Nation* to an English friend, especially. I shall take on I think until I have drawn my last breath, that is, I hope so. I am sorry to have to tell you that you have again missed being released from me. Fate decreed that I should begin the year from the very bottom of my little hill and now Sisyphus-like I have begun the climb again. Henry was like an angel and watched beside my couch for a week, but a whirring heart and panting breath are such child's play compared to what might be. As the Prince de Ligne says after the death of his son, an absorbing sorrow shields one from all material woes, so does a supreme physical misery, nullify the

---

[140] Robertson James was at this time living in Concord. The reference is presumably to his encounters with Ellen, daughter of Ralph Waldo Emerson, and for Alice James, a representative of Concord values which she could never take completely seriously.

[141] Mary Eleanor Wilkins Freeman (1852–1930), writer, her stories had been gathered into a volume *A Humble Remonstrance*, which had been published in 1887.

distress of all other aches.[142] This peaceful and super-virtuous household we greatly fear, was the scene of a deed of darkness, we have no certainty, of course, but we know that a little human soul was left to die, a perfect and beautiful boy who lived for three hours and when its mother was asked whether she wanted to see him exclaimed 'Oh no, take the brat away!' and when told later that it was dead exclaimed that she was glad and hoped that the doctor would bring her waist into shape, for she had laced herself as tight as she could so as not to show her condition and 'Oh, where is my sealskin jacket!' If in some slum under a black archway a filthy mass of rags creeps in and lays herself down upon the reeking stones for her hour of agony and then kills the little diseased object she brings forth and thereby saves it from its hideous fate, penal servitude is meted out to her, when the possessor of a sealskin jacket and gold bracelets, with a sodden, sullen creature beside her with his pockets full of sovereigns, destroys her beautiful child she drives gaily off in her coach – and this is the 1889th year of Christianity! I was 'under' Dr Wilmot, as usual – fortunately he is a perfect skellington – being a lax fox hunter and the treasurer of the local Primrose League he cures me by local colour more than by his drugs.[143] He is a most perfect type and never had a theory or made a generalization in his life, as my symptoms decline and conversation revives I sicken him more and more and one day in the course of five minutes he flew back to the weather three times as a refuge from my 'very odd' questions. One day I said to him, 'My mind is simply cramped upon those people upstairs!' Then that delicious look of cessation came into his face and I said, 'I keep thinking about them all the time', then the mechanism started up again – 'Oh, I see!'

---

[142] Prince de Ligne (1735–1814), friend of Mme de Stael and Voltaire, whose miscellaneous prose work were published as *Melange militaires, litteraires, sentimentaires* (1795–1811); his letters were also published.

[143] The Primrose League was a Conservative association formed in 1883 in memory of Benjamin Disraeli and so named because of his fondness for the flower. By 1885 it had more than 1,000,000 members; it organized social activities as well as organizing political work.

He knew about the cramps in the stomach but one in the mind was without the range of his practice and as Henry said 'He knew there was no dose for it at the chemist'. This cessation is most curious and interesting to watch because it is absolute, something falls just without the cast-iron limits of their comprehension and they make no effort to get it inside, knowing their unexpandable quality they most wisely don't struggle and the muscles of reflection stop as visibly neatly and decently as the hands of a clock. This accounts no doubt for their handsome, firm and consistent features, for how can the poor Yankee who from the cradle is perpetually stretching himself out to reach what is beyond him, 'for whom', as Mrs Parkman said – 'there is always an alternative', have any thing but an accidental profile? But they are delightful creatures and one can but love 'em, especially as they titillate one's vanity by making one feel so exquisitely subtle and perceptive! – Henry told me some most amusing experiences of his en voyage and read me such a clever letter from a French woman, *a propos* of an article she had written on English fiction in which she said that, it would never have any substance or colour until 'Adultery' was made use of! Using it as a pigment, as Father said of Mrs Browning's use of the Deity. I have been 'taking in', *La Nouvelle Revue* lately, I would give all I possess to be inside of Mme. Juliette Adam for three months[144] – imagine yourself and Bismarck as the only known quantities, you having got him by the throat writhing in your grasp – what state could be more glorious! – Isn't Bismarck a spectacle for gods and men? Now that he has reduced himself to an object pour rire the more he does of it the better for humanity. But forgive my garrulous pen. Love to all and thank Alice for her letter with so much interesting news in it, which I will answer when you have had time to draw breath from this.

Always
Your loving
A. J.

[144] Juliette Adam (1836–1936), founder and editor of *La Nouvelle Revue*, through which she exercised considerable political influence.

To Frances Morse   [Harvard, MS 1516]

11 Hamilton Terrace
Leamington

25 February 1889

[DICTATED]

My dear Fanny

Thank you very much for two letters from you, one which came this morning, and another a few days ago. Thank you very much for your sympathy in my illness, which pulled me down very much. I am still kept very weak, owing to the extreme anxiety which we have been in for some months about our poor dear Aunt Kate, who was struck down last September apparently in the midst of her vigour. The first two months we had a ghastly fear that owing to her unusual physical strength that she might live for years with her mind gone. A happier fate however has been hers and ours, and now from day to day we expect to hear that her troubles are over.

I need hardly tell you what a sore trial it has been, to be so far and impotent to render any service to her who has done all her life so much for us. I am very sorry to hear that your mother has been so unwell, but I am glad she is somewhat better now. Please tell Lucy with my thanks that I got her letter and will answer it when nature allows, also give her my love and tell her that the thought of her happiness is a luminous spot on my somewhat clouded horizon.

Forgive this shabby note and with love to all of yours.

Believe me

Your loving A.

To *William James*   [Harvard, MS 1485]

11 Hamilton Terrace
Leamington

22 March 1889

My dearest William

I have been waiting to write until your letters giving definite details of dear Aunt Kate's end came, indulging in and expressing vague conjectures seems so futile.[145] Late yesterday came yours of the ninth from New York and one to Harry from Lilla dated the twelth which supplemented each other, and we now feel as if we knew all the outward details; as for the rest our ignorance, at 3000 miles distance, is no greater than yours close at hand, we were no more remote from her at the last moment than those by her bedside. What an inconceivable relief the rapidity of her illness was, in view of what the early months promised; the theory which Lilla repeats as having been the doctor's was most highly interesting to hear as the case seems to have been so different in its advance from that of usual creeping paralysis. Death at a distance from the scene is much more shocking and seems to emphasize the almost brutal aloofness in which we are from those to whom we owe the most, owing to the conditions of life and the unmodifiable nature of individual temperaments. This experience has given me a renewed sense of sorrow and regret that you and Harry were not spectators of the last hours of dear Mother and Father. Poor Aunt Kate's life on looking back to it with the new distinctness which the completion always gives, must seem to our point of view such a failure, a 'position' to have been so unable to have worked her way to them and instead to have voluntarily relegated herself to the contrary. But the truth was, as her long life showed, that she had but one motif, the intense longing to absorb herself in a few individuals, how she missed this and how much the individuals resisted her, was, thank Heaven! but faintly suspected by her. My failing her, after

---

[145] Catharine Walsh had died on 5 March 1889.

Mother and Father's death, must have seemed to her a great and ungrateful betrayal; my inability to explain myself and hers to understand, in any way, the situation made it all the sadder and more ugly. I am devoutly thankful that Lilla has been able to fill my place so fully. What an extraordinary gift for directness and distinctness Lilla has with her pen, giving her a positive distinction of style. I have no idea of Aunt Kate's will and am therefore greatly rejoiced to hear that you are to gain by it. All her silver, Grandmother Walsh's tea set, etc., which she lent to Mother, is in the silver box at the Safety Vaults, you will have to ask J. B. Warner for it and Alice will have to divide it as A. K. desires, there is a list of her articles in the box which constitute almost all the silver in the box. At Cousin Helen's death I asked her if she wanted it and she said no. The key of the box is in the box in the Vaults where J. B. W. keeps my papers, it is small, you will have to ask him to get it for you. The tin box is pretty worn out, if you think it best, buy a new box for what remains and charge it to J. B. W. There are lists I feel pretty sure in the box, perhaps at the very bottom.

I was greatly amused by hearing of my eloquence about my legs! on a postcard. Pray don't take them so hard and as if they were new and exciting, they are to me painfully humdrum and as if I had never know any others. It seems a long time since I have written and the 'situation' has been so tremendously exciting, but I can't say anything about it now, I will write in a few days. I think I wrote last to Alice about the bad people in the house, who didn't decapitate, but de-legged me. I'm glad that you are at length blazing upon the Irish question.

Henry is coming the first of the week. Give a heart-full or rather divide a heart-full of love between yourself and Alice.

Always
Your devoted sister
Alice

To *William James*   [Harvard, MS 1486]

11 Hamilton Terrace
Leamington

31 March 1889

My dear William

Many thanks for your letter telling me the contents of Aunt Kate's will. As my path is not entirely without its crumpled rose-leaves I am sure you will allow me my little joke, even tho' it be at your expense. I was greatly amused by some of your expressions, writing 'to put you out of suspense', 'going on to see about it', 'having no right to expect as much', your ease in your position as exceptional nephew, etc., showed an artless healthy-mindedness suggestive of primitive man and not attainable by, but very refreshing to, the more perverted. My amusement, let me hasten to add, didn't lessen my extreme satisfaction at your good fortune, the legacies too will give great pleasure – especially poor Carry's.*[146] Your postcards have also come. I had already been in correspondence with Helen Ripley and Lilla who are in the most cousin-like manner looking after my interests. I had given instruction to Lilla about the portrait, but, of course, if it has gone to Boston you will have to do what she was going to with it. I am in hopes my letter will get there in time to save the journey. I have absolutely declined to stretch out a skinny arm 3000 miles and grasp, with my bird-like claw, some objects out of that little house in which that kind, old man lies dying. Even were he not there I could never impose such a burden upon poor Lilla or Helen. There comes to me thro' a legacy to Mother from Cousin Helen the old blue china (which is worth its weight in gold here) a tray and some spoons and $500. I have asked that the tray and spoons should be sent to you for your use. I don't know what the tray may be, but, I suppose, the spoons are the pretty old shape and will be a pleasant reminder for you of

---

[146] Carry was Caroline Eames James, Wilky's widow. See also Alice James's footnote at end of letter.

the old days. The china is to be sent here for Harry, he clings so to the old things that I want him to have some of them, and before long I shall have sloughed off the old home-set upon you and Alice.** Harry also wants Grandmother Walsh's portrait and the old clock, will you therefore have them boxed and sent to the enclosed address by the agent whose name I send, as he is Sherlock's agent. The clock will be recognizable from its peculiar shape, I suppose. Now, dear Alice, I am going to ask a favour of you. In the cottage at Manchester, there is a very handsome old mahogany bureau and mirror with brass knobs, two tables, mahogany and four legs with claw-feet, not large, also a small fancy sort of stand with drawers and brass knobs, I want these to be taken from the cottage for your new house, and new, cheaper articles put in their place, as it seems absurd to have the pretty old things knocked about by tenants and they belong to Quincy St. – I forgot also the big press which stood in the hall at No. 20 for linen is there too, if you could find room for it and use for it, it seems unnecessary where it is and need not be replaced by anything. If you see any other old mahogany object which I have forgotten abstract that too. The way will be for you on some possible day to go to Manchester, where there is always a depot wagon and drive to F. W. Churchill, carpenter, who has the keys, and whom you can consult about moving the things for you. You had better ask Mr Warner about the keys first. It would doubtless be easier to do this in the autumn when your house is ready for the things, the only risk is the miracle happening of someone taking a lease of the cottage, but as I hear there is little hope of its renting at all this summer at any price, there will be little danger of that. I can warn Joseph to say that some of the furniture will be changed after the first year. If the wardrobe will be an elephant leave it alone. Take a candle as the house will probably be pitch dark owing to the boarded windows. You can make an appointment with F. W. C. so that he won't be off. Now, I give you these extra-ordinary valuable objects on one condition only, that you send the bill for the objects which you put in their place – and use your discretion about that if you think the house is furnished enough without them all – to me, or rather partner Joe!

I have a notion that one of the tables is the dining-table in which case the Quincy St. dining table might do as I think William said you were not using it. If this last is larger for your new house you could exchange it for the one you have now. Forgive what may seen an oppressive number of suggestions, but they are all made in the air for you to scoff at, or to follow, as may seem to you best. I think I have remembered everything and trust not to have to return any more to the odious topic of possessions. How ugly is life! I have much to say besides on 'general questions' but refrain as, 'I can no more' just now as I am extremely tired these days. I had a soul reviving day from Harry whose sympathy and understandingness and brotherly devotion are a treasure beyond price. I enclose an anti-fat recipe which he is trying with marked success in six weeks time. With much love to all.

Always yours
A. J.

P.S. I am so glad not to be the only heiress in the house. The slavey has come into a cream-coloured sunshade, 'all bugles at the top and lace at the bottom', thro' the death of a late mistress. She is, however, of so exalted an intelligence as to have preferred to have had a 'neat black one'.

A certain Miss Blanche Leppington, who writes in the *Contemporary*, etc. and who speaks as much like Miss Palfrey as a Briton possibly can, said to Nurse one day before my late illness, 'I was so glad to see Miss James looking better yesterday, there was much less of that going away of her face in weariness and pain!' Have William's and Bob's Beauty this vanishing quality? – The sister Leppington is more interesting, reads Father, etc, and has a pure New England strain totally different from any one I have seen here – a moral being in short. It doubtless comes from their Father having been a Wesleyan minister. She writes charming notes and has a noble countenance.

Here are a few names showing the pathetic efforts made by

this amiable race, so constantly, to mitigate the cruel fiat of Destiny as to their surnames.

Llewellyn Noott	Montague Crackanthorpe
Wellesley Tompkins	Percy Bunting
Percival Chubb	Edwin Tubb; ad infinitum

* 'Dim Carry' as Henry calls her.
** I don't mean through death, that would be too long a wait to inflict, but when I have more perfectly assimilated the fact that the lodging-house is my highest attainable abode – meanwhile the barrels of blue-china are my 'humble romance', their rings clasp not only precious memories, but my fancy plays about the soup-plates and the gravy boats as a nucleus of an impossible home. What an extraordinary luck that I fell ill in the only land where lodging houses exist, how could I have lived else?

To Sara (Sedgwick) Darwin   [Harvard, MS 1444]

11 Hamilton Terrace
Leamington

1 April 1889

My dear Sara

Although you only give me three days, I must send you a line to wish you *bon voyage*. I congratulate you upon the strength of back and limb which allows you to wander so frequently and far over the faces of the globe. I congratulate you also upon the subjection to which you have reduced your husband, please give him my condolences, although doubtless your system has been so perfect that he is unconscious of his wrongs.

To our unspeakable relief poor, dear Aunt Kate died on the 5th of March. It has been through the winter a long strain of anxiety, the first months haunted by a great dread, but fate has been kind to her and all her friends. It has been a sore-trial to Harry and me to have been so distant and helpless.

I was very ill this first of the year and am still far from having regained my starting point. Harry, who is a treasure beyond price, gave me a day last week and the faithful Annie comes tomorrow. Annie is such a comfort, as I feel in my helpless state as if I could call upon her for any friendly service. Why do you call this Parnell Commission unfortunate?[147] It strikes me as the most fortunate thing which ever took place, what else less grotesque could have emancipated the average Briton from his thraldom to that sacred entity *The Times?*

I also think that Messrs. Blaine and Wanamaker will advance matters at home, more than anything one could have hoped for.[148] What an old noodle Harrison must be, his *Inaugural* was enough to show that. Robert Lincoln I have never heard anything but good of.[149] He will babble less than his predecessors, which won't be a loss. Was there ever anything so absurd as the gush at the Phelps's dinner? No English minister at Washington and was insulting England on every possible occasion. How terrible about the Men of War. I never imagined we ever had *three.* The loss will cripple Mr Blaine in his crusade against the effete despotisms of Europe, it won't be so easy to wipe 'em out! Henry saw Herbert Bismark and says one glance at his back explains the whole situation.

Farewell – give my love to anyone who remembers my existence and also would not find the gift distasteful, this refers to the old folks at home, not to the native of Basset. Always affecty yours

Alice J.

---

[147] The Parnell Commission had discovered in February that the letters attributed to Parnell were forgeries. See note 73, *The English Letters*.

[148] John Wanamaker (1838–1922) helped in the election of Benjamin Harrison for which he was rewarded with the position of post-master general.

[149] Robert Lincoln (1843–1926) eldest and only surviving son of Abraham and Mary Lincoln; he was appointed British Ambassador in 1889.

To William James   [Harvard, MS 1487]

11 Hamilton Terrace
Leamington

7 April 1889

My dear William

A copy of Aunt Kate's will came to me last week, by which I see she has deemed it best to single me out from amidst all her heirs by simply leaving me a life-interest in the objects which she has bequeathed to me. As, if the silver should come to disaster through theft, fire or flood, I should be quite unable, out of my income, to make it good and I should be equally unwilling to burden my estate with the duty of replacing it – that is my other heirs, Harry and Bob, I have no choice except to now and forever renounce all claim to it and hand it over to you, declining further responsibility for it. This decision is irrevocable, will Alice therefore, kindly put the silver which came to me from Mother and Father* in a box of suitable size and send it to the vaults in Boston, giving the keys to Mr Warner. A life-interest in a shawl, with reversion to a male heir, is so extraordinary and ludicrous a bequest that I can hardly think it could have been seriously meant, my desire would of course, naturally be to renounce my passing claim to that also, as I can hardly conceive of myself under any conditions as so abject as to grasp at a life-interest in a shawl! I, however, refrain from doing so fearing to be ungracious to you and propose this solving of the problem – viz., that you, your heirs and assigns should give me the shawl, renouncing their rights of reversion in it, and making me its absolute possessor. I may, or I may not, leave it to you in my will, but if I should, it will be entirely a voluntary action on my part and in that way you must look upon it and accept it with any ravages which moth and rust may have brought about. I might make a condition of doing so, that you should drape your manly person in it at my funeral – or, better still, wrap it about you to protect you from the breezes on the wharf when you perform that unaesthetic duty, which may some days be yours, of passing my

skin and bones thro' the Custom House. Owing to my
unbaptized and ecclesiastically detached condition, I could
hardly find burial here – and then what a cruel sell for the
British worm, who must, in the frequency of sudden death,
have such succulent morsels to feast upon!

Your enclosures from Kate Gourlay and 'Katharine'
Rodgers came this a.m.[150] I can hardly express to you my
surprise and annoyance that you should, in the presence of
Lilla and Helen Ripley, have mixed Katie up with any of my
affairs. I have been in constant correspondence with the
other two as to what I desired to have done with my things.
I had a most especial reason for no one touching the portrait
except Lilla. Besides the clock and portrait I desire that
Harry should have the picture of Venice and he has asked me
to send also for a little picture of Lizzie Boott's, a painting of
autumn woods.** If you will send the bill for packing to J.
B. W. he will pay it for me. I greatly regret that Aunt Kate,
didn't leave some small personal possession to Harry who is
always giving and never receiving.

When Alice has decided about the Manchester things, will
you please give the store-room keys to Mr Warner as I think
he will be more central to reach as I am likely to have a
chance of having some things brought to me this summer
when you will be in the country. Have you seen the attack in
the March *Universal Review* upon Harry by Buchanan?[151]
Harry says it is base and scurrilous so I have refrained from
reading. The Editor, Quilter,[152] wrote to H. apologizing for

[150] Kate Gourlay was a relative on her father's and Katharine (Katie)
Rodgers a relative on her mother's side.

[151] Robert Buchanan (1841–1901) had published 'The modern young man
as critic' in *Universal Review*, March 1889, in which he attacked Henry
James as a 'Superfine young man' who for all his 'cleverness' leaves a
'certain indescribable sense of vagueness, of superficiality, of indiffer-
entism; finally, if we must give the thing a name, a forlorn feeling of
vacuity, of silliness'. Buchanan was no stranger to controversy as a
critic; he had famously published 'The Fleshly School of Poetry' in the
Contemporary Review in 1871, attacking the Pre-Raphaelites.

[152] Harry Quilter (1851–1907) edited *Universal Review* 1888–1890; he had
previously worked as an art critic and journalist for the *Spectator* and
The Times.

it and offering money for an answer, but H. replied very good naturedly and declined of course to reply, which will disgust B. more than anything else. The necessity for writing it, is in itself a compliment to H. Did you write a notice of a book by Grant Allen recently in the *Nation*?[153] – if so I congratulate you, for never have I seen a book slain with a surer, lighter, more urbane, and gentlemanly touch. You ask in one of your letters for something typical of the Tories. They simply ring the changes on Lord Salisbury's cue, that the 'authenticity' of the letters not having been proved, does not prove them to have not been written by Mr Parnell. Balfour when asked questions in the House is unable to answer, because 'I have followed the evidence in the Commission with little interest or attention'. A member one night, I have forgotten who, was making a speech and whenever he referred to the letters as forgeries the Tories shouted out 'No, No, No!' and other forms of dissent, the speech over, Mr Parnell rose and challenged the gentleman opposite who had made these disclaimers, 'to, by word of mouth, by any faintest sign, or motion of dissent', to deny that the letters hadn't been proved to be forgeries and not one of the cowards dared even to wink, let alone utter an inarticulate sound! Of course the Tories' position is easily to be understood and they could, given what they are, naturally take no other, but the incredible baseness of the Liberal Unionists is what makes one sick for our common humanity. They regret the 'folly' of *The Times* – 'Too bad the poor *Times* was so taken in, etc, etc.' When you consider that these men are not the discredited, mushroom politician of the hour, known to us, but the heirs of centuries of education, of noble traditions and honourable birth, with responsibilities, not only to the present and the far-reaching future, but to the historic past, what an ignoble picture do they present! Apart from its political bearings the Piggott episode, or rather tragedy, has been one of the most instructive revelations of the depravity latent in human nature, the temptation once

---

[153] Grant Allen (1848–1899) had just published *Force and Energy: A Theory of Dynamics*; he was best known for his novel *The Woman Who Did* (1895).

given.[154] The spectacle of each of those dishonest wretches fighting for his own hand, bent only, upon casting off and driving to his death that poor, abject, scum of the human race, upon whom they have been living and growing rich for two years, is surely degradation unequaled in history. But eno' of Piggott and me.

With love to all
yours affectly
Alice.

I saw the name of Budd Stubbs, the other day!

* which is all marked.
** I send the addresses again.

To Alice H. James   [Harvard, MS 1458]

Leamington

5 May 1889

My dear Alice

I have two delightful letters to thank you for. The one you deprecate as 'unworthy' was very interesting and entertaining, gossip being the salt of life. Your regrets about it give me a shuddery feeling that even before moving into Kirkland St. you have fallen under the shadow of that deadly, baleful influence that infects the atmosphere thereabouts. Poor Theodora wrote me the other day a letter all about the effect of Coquelius upon her mind! The lingo pure Nortonese. As glad as I was about your having a permanent house, it was almost neutralized by hearing of its miasmatic placement. The idea seems to be that the *sevenths* of A. Kate's property will be less than William supposed, if in

[154] Richard Piggott (1828?–1889) had forged the Parnell Letters and broke down under cross-examination by the Commission in February 1889; he fled to Madrid where he committed suicide.

consequence he should have to raise money, for Heaven's sake don't involve yourself with Chas N. in any business way. *Strictly between ourselves* I know that he isn't on the square on all occasions, then it is disastrous to have business relations with *friends*!! You can get money so easily other wise. What you tell me of Grace Norton's doings, shocking as they are, are in noways worse than what I've *known* of her doing before. I long ago became aware of what vulgar texture was her soul! Why try and like her because William does? – if he is a less highly organized being than you, why deny the most sacred instincts of your nature to fit a lower form? Every woman, wife or maid, knows that her fellow man, is to *flattery* as blotting paper to ink, he soaks in it, in no matter how crude a form or how wreathed about in mouthing inepitudes, with endless ecstasy! What you tell me about the medium is curious but makes no impression on me, somehow.[155] Telling of A. K.'s death was singular, she may have known about my being ill from William being rather known in her circle but how odious that 'fortitude' clap-trap! What you predict of Bob's longevity is rather alarming. As I'm never to die, a *sedentary* Jew, a picture presents itself to my mind of surviving alone in the world with Bob, all my natural protectors in the way of you, William, and Harry gone. (Let us pray that the Episcopal Church with the 'majesty of its fictions' will not have been diluted out of existence, it may prevent him from having a bit of me.)

One must allow, however, something fine in Bob's attitude, (his detachment from material affairs, his fitting his needs to the supply and refusing to descend to toil and soil in the grubbing crowd) if one could only *read* about it! I am rather amused at your speaking of 'that foreign world against you', the foreign world as far as the mild and placid Britain is concerned is a most manageable quantity and I feel in complete command of the situation, the only demons I have to fear are those of my stomachic economy. *A propos* of demons how demoniac Elly Temple sounds. How terrible to

---

[155] The medium was presumably Mrs William Piper. See note 22, *The English Letters.*

be within her orbit, but how much more terrible to be within herself. But why when a person is insane, or simply silly, from self-love and vanity, sacrifice another wretched being to her! Isn't her husband, her four daughters, and poor Dick Emmet enough of a holocaust to her pretty face? I am delighted to hear of the Gurney books. Mrs Mason having told H. that Sturgis Bigelow had sent the book to her as from Mary Tappan was what made me suppose 'the Humble Romance' was written by her. Tell the Putnams to be sure and tell the authoress that I(!) admire the stories very much and have lent it with great success to several Britons. How pathetic about the poor monk, how raw he must be with east wind shiver in all that his senses touch upon! Chocurua with your soft manipulation, can't fail to be restorative and soothing. The fluid Yankee, with the *absolute* undreamed of, must horribly exasperate the creature stiff with a thousand traditional, unconscious rigidities; his contentment in the *à peu près*, from the non-arrival of a steam-boat to Mr Wanamaker's balance-sheet – the Captain did his best and the dishonest one was as honest as he could be, poor fellow. Fines to the all of a piece Briton, fatally naked and defenceless before the unexpected, be it only in the turn of a phrase, he must be especially loathsome. I am so deeply glad that you have the Chocurua home for the children, think of the delight in the future for 'em to have the memory of all their little emotional epochs associated with the scent of hay and breath of cows, but for them it will rather be the sighing pines and lapping lake! Mine have a background of French cupboards, the smell of them I mean, and a certain blue camel's hair shawl worn by a lady in the Champs Elysees when in the golden summer sunshine! My soul was in a moment flooded by a sense of the throbbing union, the mystery and the pain of which has never since been silenced. Give loads of love to all.

Always your loving A.

Lilla writes that she has two teaspoons of A. K.'s if you have enough for Louisa Walsh she can send them to her.

H. has seen Mr Parnell in the box, 'sweetness' and a 'lovely

smile' the prominent impression, and a far away reminder of
Shyler van Renzedas. In the evening he met A. J. Balfour at
dinner!! He also *very sweet* in private, in strong contrast to
his public impertinence.

To Mrs Francis Morse   [Harvard, MS 1428]

11 Hamilton Terrace
Leamington

9 June [1889]

My dear Mrs Morse

I am long in answering your pleasant letter which you were
so kindly inspired as to write to me on your sixty-third
birthday – my congratulations however upon that fortunate
event are none the less sincere. Since your letter came I have
not been well. This has not been a happy winter and I am
always at the mercy of what are called the events of life –
what to the active and busy would be an imperceptible breeze
is to me a devastating hurricane – so I am sure you will
forgive my shortcomings. Pray give Fanny a thousand thanks
for all the good letters she has sent to me, for which I shall
shortly punish her by several prosey sheets.

I suppose you are quite settled in Beverly by now having
already had a little summer. How trying such a jump into
hot weather always is. Here it has been what the natives call
intensely 'ot, 78°! a moment upon which I seized for getting
out wrapped in a fur coat from my ears to my feet. Never
has there been such a beautiful spring, too green, absurd as it
may sound – stupidly green, as the French say. I have got a
Chairman now who has all the beer of Leamington in his
cheeks and I am sure there can be none left for this legs, so he
won't betray me as the man last summer did. Nurse has
great plans for getting me into some lanes that she knows of
but I'm afraid they are all in Spain. There is a sweet little bit
which I can get to, when I am at my best, where the trees

meet over head and where stands a manor house an over-grown farm house, a delicious little church in its graveyard – a microcosm of England in short. It rejoices also in the name of Lillington. I am very glad to hear that Mary and her doctor are having a holiday.[156] I am afraid that they will have too many more interesting objects to contemplate than Warwick Castle and Me, I bearing the same relation, please observe, to other creatures as Warwick Castle to the ordinary human habitation.

Do you remember about a certain clericule, of whom I told you, who burst, or rather aspired to burst, into my room in the middle of the night? He has just been taken to London by a certain Miss Owen and married, to secure permanent possession of the rare and precious creature she employed five clergy men and four yards of train, I myself think that this plethora of satin and ecclesiastics was to divert attention from the exiguity of husband. He is thirty-three years old and she forty-eight! It was quite a horrible shock to me for Miss Owen I had seen a good deal of as she had been very kind in coming to see me and she is altogether the most amusing and intelligent person in Leamington, being the first English woman I have seen with a humourous turn. But she has behaved so treacherously that the poor animalcule seems like an angel beside her. The desirability of a husband I suppose cannot be grasped by a Western woman, so we must have charity!

What a change Mr Higginson's death will bring to you, but after such long good lives isn't it good to have them gain their rest? There seems nothing to say about the Pennsylvania floods, we exhaust our adjectives so upon the trifles that take place that we have none left for the appalling. How delightful it is to hear of dear Lucy's happiness, one that seems, to our limited vision, secure too, may it only be so!

There is a young couple who have lately come to the next house, who are simply bubbling over with youth, health, and

---

[156] Mary Morse, Fanny's sister, had married a Dr John Elliot. Alice also recorded their visit to her in her *Diary* on 12 June: 'what a joy to see anyone from home! Two such nice creatures especially' (p. 29). See also the next letter.

happiness, giving one infinite satisfaction simply to know that they exist. They are from twenty to twenty-five and have recently acquired a baby whose acquaintance we have made on the balcony. I hope dear Mrs Morse that you will have a better summer than you have had winter. Give my love to Mr Morse and Fanny and thank the last for the pretty little photograph she sent and give my congratulations to the Aurist on his charming daughter.[157] Farewell and believe me.

As always. Affectly yours
Alice James

To Frances Morse   [Harvard, MS 1517]

11 Hamilton Terrace
Leamington

15 July 1889

My dear Fanny

You may have perceived, doubtless with relief, that I haven't overwhelmed you with letters of late or thanked you for all your goodness in writing last winter. Although my affairs are of a microscopic nature they involved this spring an endless number of long letters about trifles, and friendship, as it always does, went to the wall. Just after I wrote to your mother my joy was great upon the rise of Mary and her Doctor above the horizon. They made what was to me a delightful call, though sadly short, for their native aroma supplemented by their individual *parfum* made a combination I would fain have clung to. Mary looked very well, but they were both tired by London, they said. It was very interesting to see Mary's sweet face grown firmer with the added experience of five years – she touched my heart by her friendly inclination me-wards. Dr Elliot, whom I had but just

---

[157] Possibly a reference to Fanny's brother Henry.

seen before, I liked greatly, he is so manly and frank.

Your letters were a great comfort and I thank you very much for 'em. I was rather crushed by the way you received my political jeremiads, but continue to feel that my hysterics are much the higher state than your apparent laxity! Please also tell me if there is any pamphlet on the workings of the Associated Charities which gives an idea of the *system*.

This is simply a perfect summer here, although the native is, of course, collapsing as usual; anywhere between 60° and 75° standing for the tropics! The rain has come now just to renew the greenery as it was getting a little parched. I have been out already fifteen times and feel like a vagrant, as if all the bloom of modesty and retirement had vanished from my elderly cheek. Within my little world serenity reigns – it all sounds chaotic and topsy-turvy outside. The Parnell Commission has been dying so long that when the moment comes of absolute extinction it won't make any difference. The verdict of the Judges has been discounted by Parnell being made one of the Commission on *Royal Grants*, while he is undergoing a State Trial as accessory to Murder! Could humbug further go! They have the patent for it in this land. The poor Liberals are in a sad way, so split up. Then these absurd Radicals who are forcing the pace, about 50 years in advance of the needs of the people, handicap them so. Meanwhile the *American Girl* is at the core as usual. Mr Chamberlain ruling the Unionists, the Tories at the mercy of these last, Mrs Chamberlain having complete dominion over the Chamberlain family from Joseph, the despot down, it follows that the little girl from Salem, un *petit trou*, as some Frenchman called it, is virtually the ruler of Great Britain.[158] Meanwhile 'our Princesses' are refused by Dukes and taking up with Earls with two divorced sisters! Its curious that the Queen through her sons-in-law should be brought so near her *bête noir* the Divorce Court. Its rather pretty to have the

---

[158] Joseph Chamberlain (1836–1914), radical politician who held office under Gladstone but who had resigned in 1886 on the introduction of the Home Rule Bill which he consistently opposed, helped to foster fragmentation amongst the Liberals. His third wife was Mary Endicott, whom he had married in 1888; she was the daughter of W. C. Endicott, secretary for War in Cleveland's first administration.

Duke of Portland decline three princesses and marry a Squire's daughter.[159] The three princesses were to be had in succession, you'll understand! We've not got any further than that yet.

I am so glad to hear you say that Mr Boott seems well and cheerful. He has the good fortune, for himself of wearing all his complexities upon the surface. Altho' so simple when you come to think of it his life has the elements of tragedy, his whole existence having gone in being an appendage to failures, only the more striking from his own choice of the function. The early death of his wife, the disproportion of Lizzie's achievement to his labour, the transference now of his devotion to Duvenick whose genius I believe, grows not and his own long unremunerative soux-production. How curious to see how the Chapman Timmins wealth works. Poor Mrs Lodge how sorry I am for her. If you ever see her be sure to give her my love. With unlimited measure of the same article to your Father and Mother.

Believe me
Your loving A. J.

To William James   [Ms, Harvard 1488]

11 Hamilton Terrace
Leamington

25 November 1889

My dear William

I am long in answering your pleasant letter telling of your happy return and imbedment once more in the soft domestic bosom, but whilst Katharine was here my tongue babbled so constantly that my pen was perforce silent with small loss, surely, to its victims. I look back upon all the incidents of the

[159] The sixth Duke of Portland had married Winifred Dallas-Yorke, June 1889.

summer with great delight and have laid up a store of transatlantic 'freshness' which will carry me well through the
winter.[160]   K. P. L. was as convenient and stretchable a
Yankee as ever, did all the odd jobs in the house which had
hopelessly been waiting for the last two years and explained
me to the native and the native to me by revealing the extraordinary interpretations they put upon my most commonplace remarks, so that when she went we all agreed with old
Mrs Clarke who boomed out with her bassoon-like voice on
the stairs – 'I oughtn't to be saying it to your face but just as
you are going away there never wasn't anybody like you'.

I had to my surprise a week ago a call from Mrs Lucian
Carr who was as dropping of eyelid and pallid of face and
manner as ever, she, in truth, made me rather sick and
lessened somewhat that protesting patriotism which is so
ardent with me. This wasn't brought about by her physical
anaemia, but her mental, as shown in her talk about the
Mind Cure by which hundreds of her friends, she herself
among 'em, have been cured. She cures herself now, altho'
her health is perfect, whenever the necessity occurs having
listened! to a course of twelve lectures by her prophetess each
two hours long. When I asked her what the attitude of mind
was that she assumed in her wrestle with fate the poor lady
could not make an articulate sound notwithstanding her
thirty hours of instruction, she finally murmured that it was
'to lose oneself in the Infinite, which process seems to bring
one rather successfully to the surface in the finite as the Curer
says her power is the same as Christ's only less perfect'. You
will be amused at my pouring all this out apparently as news!
but it was new to me and Miss Clarke and Nurse were inadequate to responding; and it came as a shock as revealing the
passion women have for rushing into any distasteful
imbecility which may arise. Why can't they go and be cured
by the creature's 'magnetism' or what not, if they can be,

---

[160] William James had come to Europe in the summer of 1889, a trip
financed by Aunt Kate's legacy to him. Alice recorded in her *Diary*: 'He
doesn't look (much) older for the five years, and all that there is to be said
of him, of course, is that he is simply himself, a creature who speaks in
another language, as Harry says, from the rest of mankind and who
would lend life and charm to a treadmill.' (*Diary*, p. 51)

without degrading their minds by assuming that it is an intellectual process. From a religious point of view it's revolting too for losing oneself in the Infinite is to accept illness or health without a struggle, surely. But a truce to such 'vital' questions. We all go on here as usual and are all sealed down for the winter, and the weeks and days fly by like magic. I had an immense excitement recently, I saw and talked with a man – so good for the man!

Harry is still in Paris but he promises to make his appearance next week, which will be a great pleasure as I haven't seen him since you and he were here on August 14th. He is busy translating Daudet, a hard job to turn Tartarinese into English.[161] A *propos* of the Braz. Rev. he writes – 'The Orleanists (their Comte d'Eu etc.) seem really to excite the sense of humour of Providence – which shows, I fear, that Providence isn't after all English!'

We are all on a 'Merry-go-rond' here, 'honest John',[162] Lord Roseberry, etc. etc. have plunged in. Since the immortal Docker's Strike the face of Labour has been transformed, such a shaking up and 'awakening' of humanity was never before seen, all brought about by the most peaceful and absolutely legitimate means and organization.[163] Did you see that 200 trades in London had gained a 10% increase of wages in consequence, the masters caving in to keep the men from going on strike. Lord Roseberry and Sir Chas. Russell[164] taking the Chair at three a.m. at great meetings of the tram and omnibusmen. How ignoble Godkin would be on the subject were he not so ludicrously and naively ignorant.

[161] Henry James's translation of Alphonse Daudet's *Port Tarascon: The Last Adventures of the Illustrious Tartarin* was published in 1890. Henry wrote that he had undertaken the task of translation 'for the bribe of large lucre'. (*Letters*, vol. 3, p. 264)

[162] Honest John was John Morley (1838–1923), one of the most popular Liberal public orators who denounced coercion in Ireland and supported Home Rule.

[163] The strike by the Dockers was successful in securing them a minimum wage of sixpence an hour.

[164] Lord Russell of Killowen (1832–1900), former Attorney-General and from 1894 Lord Chief Justice.

The Parnell Commission has been flickering on Sir Henry James gesticulating to empty benches.[165] Did you see the neat shuffle he executed about Pigott? On Saturday it came to its death. There are all sorts of stories to the effect that they have P.'s diary and it is to be brought out in the House etc., but that remains to be seen. Meanwhile you are more interested in seeing the end of this, forgive such a dull scribble of time worn stuff. Give my love to Alice who is I suppose up to her ears in business.

Always your affectionate sister
Alice

To Sara (Sedgwick) Darwin   [Harvard, MS 1445]

11 Hamilton Terrace
Leamington

29 November 1889

My dear Sara

The lovely chrysanthemums have faded, but not the memory thereof! They lasted many days and greatly beautified my humble lodgment. My flowers of rhetoric, the only kind I grow, are a very inadequate return. My dear friend left me a fortnight ago and her visit now seems like a happy dream. We are shut in and sealed down for the winter and one week differs from another only in the more or less intensity of the various episodes of head and stomach which though they lend quite a sufficient excitement to my personal experience, your refined mind will agree with my baser one, in thinking it unfit for ladylike correspondence. What therefore can I tell you? William of course, after five years was a draught of champagne. He was very entertaining after Paris which

[165] Sir Henry James (1828–1911), Liberal Unionist, was Solicitor-General under Gladstone. He appeared for *The Times* in front of the Parnell Commission.

seemed to have been an immense success and pleasure. What is the meaning of the psychic compliment of Mrs Myers, 'Oh, Mr James, we are so glad that you are *as* you are!'[166] It is a good remark to remember, so entirely uncompromising, and can be taken anyway you choose. Katharine probed the bosom of a bewildered old maid here and found that she was cherishing the idea that I was an illegitimate flower of my sex. Something I had said had forced the conviction upon her. The first time she saw me she said to herself – 'They say that there is no rank in America, it's not so, *this is Rank!*' Imagine the subsequent conflict in her virgin mind when she had to reconcile these two extremes – I suppose I came out to her florid imagination as a sort of Royal Bastard. What a cruel blow to find that my progenitors were not only 'umble but 'umdrum, and all the delightfully wrong and compromising swept from her calls! N.b. I stand for *rank* in the abstract, a height to which you never will attain, although you have got legs to stand upon!

29 November: What a horror the *fires* at home! A letter this a.m the first Kath. wired since she landed. She sat next to Mrs Sally Norton in the car going home. Monsignor Doane was on board, he had a very handsome ruby ring which he was taking home for Mrs Cleveland to give to Mary Perkins as a wedding present.[167] Kath. and her friends were very curious to know what he would do with it at the Custom House. He came up from the ordeal in the cabin smiling and said that the paper specified only objects in ones *trunks*, 'Now I have the ring in my *pocket* so I have passed it with a perfectly clear conscience'.

Henry is in Paris but comes home tomorrow. He is very busy translating Daudet's story which is said to be deliciously funny. He sends the following which as it has not in its adventures lost any of its native flavour I send along. A young man takes his young woman to a restaurant and after

---

[166] Mrs Frederic Myers was Eveleen Tennant of Glamorganshire.

[167] William Croswell Doane (1832–1913), first bishop of the Protestant Episcopal diocese of Albany. Presumably he had been to England as spokesman at the Lambeth Conference for the American Episcopate.

ordering dinner asks what she would like to drink. 'I guess I'll have a bottle of Champagne.' 'Guess again!' saith he.

Forgive my general, not to say particular, frivolity of tone and believe me.

As ever affectly yours

Alice J.

P.S. Have you read Motley's *letters?*[168] How the second volume revives all the old emotions, the protesting patriotism, and all the rest of it. He seems to have had a charming nature but was evidently not given to subtle analysis. What a pity he did not instruct 'dearest Lily' in the use of the handkerchief, which is so eminently desirable.

'Fancy!' as they say here, I have lately seen and talked with a man, so good for the man!

To Frances Morse   [Harvard, MS 1518]

11 Hamilton Terrace
Leamington

7 December 1889

My dear Fanny

Your letter of November 11th gave me both pain and pleasure; pained by the naughtiness by which it was somewhat flavoured, but this was so voluntary that pleasure in the unconscious virtue revealed soon wiped the impression away.

You ask if leaves were then falling, they had all gone long before and the trees before my windows, all that are within my ken were quite bare. The English elm as grown at home

---

[168] John Lothrop Motley (1814–1877), American historian and diplomat. His *Correspondence* (2 volumes) had been published in 1889. Lily was presumably one of his daughters, all of whom had settled in England.

is such a different, graceful stripling as compared to the parent – blowsy dowager! – that its habits may well be different too. I wish you could see my room now its so different from the bare barn it was when you were here three years ago – no, I've made a mistake, two years. It has been gradually improving itself, but Katharine quite transformed it while she was here. I take great delight in some American photos. I have, a glance at which seems to carry me back in a second to where I shall never be again. I have a delightful one of the dear State house. I don't know how to approach your various calamities in the way of fires. If one says what one feels it seems hysterical, and fond relations invite one not to 'take on', and after all the writing out of a succession of adjectives doesn't seem to be an intelligent contribution to the occasion, so I will confine myself to hoping that you are not actively suffering, which after all is not often the worst fate. I have often thought of Sara's friend who pictured America to herself always as a vast wind swept plain. One can do little else here, for the few lines in the papers devoted to the vast Continent relate simply to various convulsions in the way of disasters, and when there are no disasters there is nothing at all. Harry told me that a lady asked him about some *dear* Americans whom she had met, if he knew anything about them. She being so anxious 'because it must be so unsafe for them'. That is much the way I am getting to feel myself. Thank you for the 'Associated Charities'. But why your surprise? I have the human instincts common to my kind. I had been told that the Boston plan was different from that here in vogue so I thought I should like to see an account of it. The two articles you mark are very good but seem as if addressed to the infancy of the race, that is in tone – but I suppose that is inevitable. *A propos* of infancy I am horrified at your *selfish profligacy*! no other word for it. As quantity is all you desiderate in your offspring it's a pity you are not in this seething land where you would have satisfaction doubtless in gazing at the offspring of what they call the three c's – 'cockroaches, criminals, and clergymen!' I read the other day of seven of these last individuals who had fifty children between them and an average income of £130, as

they 'had had no luck with the burying', as the slum-ites say, they were advertising their children for adoption! You may think this unrefined but you brought it upon yourself, please remember. Give your dear parents and Mary much love. I suppose poor Mr Lodge is still living. Farewell.
Yours as ever
Affectly

A. J.

I was delighted to hear of Lucy's prospects. Pray Heaven that all may go well with her.

To Alice H. James   [Harvard, MS 1460]

11 Hamilton Terrace
Leamington

9 January 1890

My dear Alice

Your delightful and charming letter of 1 December would have been answered immediately had I followed the inward promptings, but some minute Xmas complications and a sense of humanity arrested the performance. But pray never feel that I have to be answered, for that would double my susceptible quality with an oppressive sense of quantity. You have such a grace with your pen and such sympathetic feminine perceptions that I am greatly amused to find that you have a Censor – a male too! If he ever rears his head again send him about his business. I would fain not be a creature who has to be kept under glass – and such very thin glass too as my friends find to their tribulation – but Fate seems to have decreed it so and I must submit and the friends endure, I suppose; theirs is the hardest share, for I have the measure of my quiverings, whilst their imagination roams at large. I was deeply sorry to hear of poor Mary's loss.[169]

---

[169] Mary was Mary (Gibbens) Salter, Alice H. James's sister.

The wrench of the maternal bowels is the one experience that cannot be entered into from the outside, but there is surely hope that another may come, not to take this one's place, but to fill her empty heart and arms. Pray give her my deepest love and sympathy when you write to her.

I have many things to say, but I must begin with the furniture. Don't try to spare it with a view to my wanting it. Should I be strong eno' in five or six years to go home, I never could stay there, as lodgings are not possible and I never could afford to keep house; this is the place for me (I mean Europe) during Harry's life, at any rate. So use the things just as you need them, carpets and all – they are all left to you in my Will. What a marvel that green carpet, it descends from the Thies days![170] Thank you for the offer of Father's portrait. I should be sorry to have it knocked about with the journey and as I live it would be so much of an incumbrance as to greatly lessen the pleasure. In many lodgings you can't put anything on the walls and have to mind your p's and q's at every turn, or you are turned out at a week's warning. Invalids and Nurses are greatly objected to so I feel as if this was a haven of refuge. I am rejoiced to hear that the house is so comfortable and delightful but can easily picture the strain upon your domestic sinews and consequent sinking of your heart at its size.[171] You will get used to that. Tell William not to complain of his Irish servants, whatever their vices they are creatures with whom it isn't a degradation to live, not polishing machines with the spiritual substance of a dead life which crumbles to dust at the first human contact. Also remember that on the score of wages things are pretty well made up, for Mr and Mrs Smith would have to be multiplied by three, at least, to do the work of your house and family, they would have to have five meals a day and beer ad libitum. Towards the end of my stay I had to suspend intercourse with Mrs Smith she affected me

---

[170] Alice and her father had rented 20 Quincy Street from Louis Thies, who was a Curator of Engravings at Harvard; his daughter, Clara Crowinshield Thies had been a member of Alice James's sewing Bee.

[171] William and Alice had moved recently to a larger house, 95 Irving Street, Cambridge.

morally just as a black-beetle does bodily, she has, by the-
way, just the furtive manners and scuttling motion of that
interesting native.[172] Had you heard her rushing along the
corridor in a fury of rage at Nurse who had picked up, or laid
down a book, it being Smith's function to perform said
ceremony, you would have thanked Heaven that your lot
was not cast with 'Upper Servants', or any Servants. Their
function is abject and they must be abject. Never lisp a word
to Harry.

Since I began this a letter of a pleasing nature has come
from William. I am sorry you are down with the influenza –
five out of seven in this household have had it. As it is
supposed to attack chiefly the 'general strength', I, having no
more of that useful quantity than wet blotting paper, present
an invulnerable front to the enemy. I hope it will go lightly
with you all and not lead to suicide, which the papers say is
the American form.

The photos of the house are charming, many thanks for
'em and for the burial suggestion, it is a good idea to preserve
my beauty for coming generations instead of surrendering it
to the envious flame to lap up. In view of the congruous and
picturesque what a pity Sarah Bernhardt wasn't burnt at the
stake![173] Chance lost in this wasteful world. One grieves for
the Lodge! How incongruous that that flow of human health
and jollity should have been arrested by that peculiarly
morbid, unholy disease. I am thankful that she suffered no
pain at the last. I heard something of Mrs Bell that I liked
not much, the other day. I sent *The Speaker* and shall
continue to do so unless you tell me to stop. It promises to be
solid and good and it is a great relief to have a decent Liberal
paper at last, after five years of the Standard and shrieking
Radical sheets. We are over our heads in scandals. No hope
for Parnell this time I believe but Irish Home Rule, like
Emancipation, is one of the immutable moralities sure of

---

[172] Alice had been staying at Henry James's flat, 34 De Vere Gardens.

[173] Sarah Bernhadt (1844–1923), the French actress, had appeared in a
drama as Jeanne d'Arc in 1890. 'How revolting Sarah Bernhadt acting in
a Passion play!', Alice James recorded in her *Diary*. (p. 101)

triumph in spite of all set backs.[174]   The whole thing brings back the old ups and downs of the War days.   If you can remember tell me sometime if any tree or planted thing has ever grown and come to anything at the cemetery.   I fear I shall strike a very jangling note when I say that I am not sorry to be out of range of Bob's exaltation.   His luminosity and enthusiasm on the subject of humanity always strikes me as having as little body as 'a dancing ray of sunlight reflected from a mirror', as was said once of the eloquence of another. The chance of his being likened to Father makes me shiver, which I am doubtless making you do at the present moment, but the protest will have its own way.   You must have heard me shouting over your account of Grace Norton's dissolute pruderies.   A being writing about the nieces of Mazarin whose chaste lips cannot emit the word 'mistress', the sticky *Montaigne* and the condition of poor Mable Quincy's fingers as she turns the glued leaves, which I do her the justice of thinking she immediately applied to the spout of the tea-kettle – is the ludicrous carried to the sublime and a rare treat to hear of![175]   Oh Lord, how thankful I am I didn't take to refined spinsterhood, to be able, if only once in one's life, to call a spade a spade is more productive of labial and mental health and decency than all the prunes and prisms and prudish evasions of a lifetime.   But, my dear Alice, how can you steam your clear vision to make out the blurred outlines thro' Grace's polysyllabic fog? – Isn't her clumsy handling of creatures whose raison d'être was the graceful and the light and sure of touch, most irritating? – But I must hold up. Give my love to all and the young ones especially and tell them I hope they will have fun with their skates.   Tell Marg. I hope she hasn't any more Professors to put to bed and give

---

[174]   Parnell had been cited as correspondent by Captain William Henry O'Shea in a divorce case against his wife Katharine.

[175]   In her *Diary* Alice had commented on Grace Norton's interest in 'French ladies of the 18th century': 'Her clumsy and blundering handling of creatures whose whole raison d'etre was the graceful and the light and sure of touch, must be truly painful.'   She also noted that 'Grace gave Mabel Quincy, as a wedding present, a copy of *Montaigne* with the "naughty" pages gummed together, could there be anything more deliciously droll!'. (p. 67)

a warm bath to.

Always
Your loving sister
A. J.

Tell William that I am much pleased to hear such good accounts of the children, but that I hope Marg. Mary will not attain 'sister Alice's elevation' thro' so much prostration.

To Alice H. James   [Harvard, MS 1461]

11 Hamilton Terrace
Leamington

5 February 1890

My dear Alice

You will fear that the mantel of 'communication', which has been wrenched so cruelly away from poor, tragic Cousin Henry Wyckoff, has descended upon my shoulders, but I only have a word to say. Spinster-like I am driven to re-enforce your maternal wisdom with advice about the babes. Bend all your energies to instill in them the most conservative habits with regard to their family letters, their own, as well as the rest, they will have priceless value in time. This has been brought home to me by the arrival of dear old Davenport about a fortnight ago, in it were father's and mother's old letters, I fell upon them and wallowed for two days in the strangest and most vivid experience. I had to tear myself away for pathologic causes and I do not dare return yet, but they are perpetually soliciting me; like living things sucking me back into the succulent past out of this anomalous death in life – an existence as juicy as that of a dried cod-fish! They both exist so in their letters! The rich robustness of Father's texture is simply overpowering when you have been divorced from it for a little and I hadn't looked into the *Lit. Rem.* for a good while.[176] What 'fun' it must have been to roll out his adjectives. And the curious thing is that notwithstanding the broad swing and sweeping volume of the current, his style never mastered him and degenerated into 'manner', but in the least little note springs as from a living fountain, as unconscious as a singing bird.

How inestimable this too from the blessed Mother, written to me in '66 when I was spending the winter at Dr Taylor's in New York at my life-long occupation of 'improving',[177] – 'I am so sorry to hear that round waists are coming in, they are so unbecoming to my figure and Miss Marchington has just made my new rep. with very long points!' – giving instantly, that which the wisdom of the sages is inadequate for, body to her ghost! For doesn't your feminine soul immediately picture to itself your 'new rep.' coming home, at this long-drawn-out, pancake moment, with a huge Bustle? Such are the real tragedies of life! Tell William that I find from one of the letters that I am neck and neck with him in the race for Beauty. Remind him of his 'having dropped teeth into the consciousness of a Mrs Smith' in days gone by, it turns out that at some unknown moment, that I too dropped a feature – nose probably or beetling brow – into the consciousness of Prof. Lovering of all people in the world! Does his half-baked family, by the-way, of the boarding house pie complexion, still indigest and remain indigestible?

A post card from William just arrived. I shall send regularly *The Speaker*. Did you discover Henry in Westminster Abbey?[178] Wemyss Reid, the editor,[179] told him he had had many letters about it, 'the last from William

---

[176] William James (ed.), *The Literary Remains of the Late Henry James* (Boston: Houghton Miflin, 1884).

[177] In November 1866 Alice had visited Dr Charles Fayette Taylor (1827–1899) who was an orthopaedic surgeon who believed there was a link between orthopaedics and nervous diseases in women. He published *Theory and Practice of the Movement Cure* in 1866.

[178] A reference to Henry James's anonymous obituary of Robert Browning. 'Browning in Westminster Abbey' published in *The Speaker*, it was reprinted in *Essays in London*, 1893.

[179] Sir Thomas Wemyss Reid (1842–1905) founded *The Speaker* in 1890.

Minto, Professor at Aberdeen declaring that it must have been written by George Meredith, or the Devil'. I thought it quite beautiful. I am very sorry to hear that Billy is ill but hope 'tis o'er by now. A good letter has come from Mary Tappan, what a curious product of that fantastic pair, embodying as she does the unexcessive – altho' of course from here, enthusiasm over lectures upon Kant seems sadly morbid. If the Miss Ashburners die I suppose Theodora and Charles will permanently intertwine and have done with 'loungun 'roun 'en suffer'n' from wet feet!' How dangerous for a man of his age. How old it makes one feel that there should be only three of the old men left at Harvard. I have received a most remarkable letter from Wilkie's Alice, as if it were written by a woman of 30.

Did Kath. tell you of the old maid here whose bosom was fluttering over the hope that I was an irregular growth? What Sarah Bernhardt calls 'un petit accident', not however, a fleur du mal in any way, but only an efflorescence of dislocated virtue, from that land whence all things are possible and acceptable. Can't you see Father's expression at this view of his cherished daughter? – It comes over me sometimes as I lie here among this baser sort with the breath of scandal in the air, that I may be 'broadening' too much and that to your New English snowdrop souls I may seem to be developing a Rabelaisian strain. I haven't read the *Master*, but get the chaste Grace to send me over a gummed copy. What a talent for expurgation the family have, when you think of Charles's Froude. Have you seen Father's wonderful letter to Mr Emerson about Hawthorne and Charles's 'spectral smiles'? Mary was inspired enough to send me a copy. Think of all that substance hidden away from the world, as packed with meat as a nut. But as H. says it all belongs to us, which is best. Loads of love and apologies for my length.

Your affect.
A. J.

To William James   [Harvard, MS 1490]

11 Hamilton Terrace
Leamington

16 March 1890

My dear William

Thank you very much for sending Lilla's letters. I have heard as yet nothing myself, for she will naturally wait until she can tell me a little more than the mere facts. It is indeed a relief that the poor dear man has emerged into day out of the night of his long bondage.[180] Seen in his entirety what a curiously impressive and melancholy figure he is! And what marvellous docility and self-control thro' those fifty years that he was entombed in that moral dungeon as effectively as Bonnivard in Chillon with the benignant Cousin Helen for inexorable turn-key! It seems to be a favourite joke of Providence to give us these surprises, to take us down a bit by showing us what powerful agents those whom we have been in the habit of complacently considering the simple and the impotent, are in the human drama. But what an interesting moment it is, when the familiar figures recede one by one and are seen in the right perspective and live at last. I am entirely overcome by that inspired document his will, the embodiment of 'sweet reasonableness' – what jury could, or would break it? I should like to have the money in order to 'cut up' better for my heirs, but the twenty-thousand which I have inherited from C. Helen and A. K. since I have been in England has caused my income to be much less than it was the first three years that I was here. I mention this, *not as a lament*, but as a very droll illustration of the vanity of inheritances. I am rolling in money, not-withstanding, and no Rothschild *feels* as rich as I do, I sound too like a bloated capitalist which is

---

[180] Alice is referring to Henry Wyckoff, brother of 'Cousin Helen'. He was 'simple-minded', and was looked after by cousin Helen. Henry James in 'A Small Boy and Others' drew an analogy with *David Copperfield*: 'Cousin Henry was more or less another Mr Dick, just as cousin Helen was in her relation to him more or less another Miss Trotwood'. *Henry James: Autobiography*, p. 84.

always entertaining.

I was greatly distressed to hear of the children's illnesses. What a curious attack of Billy's, poor little man I hope it hasn't left him head-achy. It has been a wretchedly sick winter here not only the grippe but illness of all kinds so that the doctors are almost dead, altho' there are forty of 'em. We have got off well in this house, Nurse alone having a very mild attack. Alice must be well-nigh spent, give her my loving sympathy. Also thank her for the *Ethical Review* and congratulations on her brother-in-law.[181] I feel a reflected glory in being even so distantly connected with a man whose writings are forbidden in Russia! If my brain allowed of the consumption of any other pabulum than three volume novels, I should ask to have the book sent, but don't do so it would simply be a waste. Tell A. that the name Davidson made me 'vision' a waistcoat made out of a bath-towel surmounted by a face with a space between the eyes which it seemed, by some freak of nature, an impropriety to look at, which ornamented a party one evening at our house. I never saw the creature but once or twice but that space survives. Harry came on the 10th and spent the day. He looked and seemed very well and cheerful. He is going to the Continent for the 'season'. He has 'lent' me his flat so probably Nurse and I will go up for the third Drawing Room. He is much and superfluously distressed over my reclusion for it must be confessed that I have no power to seduce the Midland mind and my minute circle is dwindling and dwindling so as to be almost imperceptible. I go for three and four weeks often without speaking to a soul but Nurse and Clarkey, and then mayhap will come a half hour of tabley talk. I ought to have been started by Barnum. I am perfectly cheerful and content myself but you will admit that when there is naught but material suggestion 'tis dreary to suspend oneself and remain alone in the empyrean, so that I shall become more and more rudimentary and tax your indulgence further and further. This however has been a very gay week, for Mrs William

[181] Alice's brother-in-law was William Mackintire Saltre (1853–1931), who taught at the University of Chicago and published on Ethics and Religion.

Sidgwick came over from Rugby to tea one afternoon.[182]
She is very anxious that I should let her bring the Henry S.'s
who are coming to her at Easter, the inspiring motive to give
me a hearing of *his* 'flow' – 'the most *flowing* talker in
England, etc.' The dear beings have no hyperaesthetic, but if
Providence doesn't rescue me from that stammer by a
whacking sick-headache I shall become a confirmed Atheist
on the spot.

Revive Alice, who lately feared the infants were not preco-
cious, by telling her that Father announces, in one of his
early letters that none of the children 'save William' show any
intellectual taste. 'Just fancy that now!' and *Me* among the
group – who all unconscious, sometimes gives birth to the
profoundest subtleties and am so *very* clever. If you could
only hear what small coin produces that desirable result
amidst this grateful public you *would* laugh.   One's head
would be turned by having one's commonplaces so
applauded if it were not neutralized by the perfect failure of
all flights of fancy. Is it not a despairing moment when your
lyrical gymnastics fall flat; it seems to permeate with collapse,
as if the bones had all become gelatinous, suddenly. Arm
yourself against my dawn, which may at any moment cast
you and Henry into obscurity, and take a hint from this
'repartie qui annonce de l'apropos et de la bonhomie...'.
Comment, Monsieur; s'ecria l'un d'eux, tout eboli 'vous êtes
le frère de M'me la Marquise du Chatelet? Vous appartenez,
Monsieur, a cette femme se spirituelle so digne de tout éloge?'
'Oui Mons' respondit l'Abbi de Breteuil, '*j'ai cet esprit*'.[183]
The other day a Miss Leppington who is the only bookish
person I see, brought me back Ms Jewitt's pretty story 'Betty
Leicester', saying she saw a great difference in the life at
home but she insisted that it contained only elements that

---

[182] Henry Sidgwick (1838–1900) was Professor of Moral Philosophy at
Cambridge.

[183] 'Take a hint from this response, both relevant and friendly...'. Well sir,
credit one of them, quite crushed, 'you are the brother of Mme la
Marquise du Chatelet? You are linked, Sir, with this woman so witty and
worthy of praise?' 'Yes sir', answered the Abbot of Breteuil, '*I have the
same wit*'.

were suppressed in the Briton but nothing different in kind.[184]
This you may imagine was too much for me to remain
passive under, so I insinuated that there was a flexibility in
the Yankee of which there was no germ in the English mind,
which *couldn't* play with anything that had been taken
solemnly for a year or two. She pondered for a bit and
resisted and the dear lady fell into the trap, turning herself
into a document in the most obliging manner by naively
asking 'Do *you* think it is possible to take what is serious
lightly?' She has a sister by the way who has as much
grammar and as many syllables in her sentences, or rather
paragraphs, as the Norton and Palfrey families rolled into
one.[185] I wonder if it does not come from a Wesleyan descent
keeping her remote from 'good form' which pens them in a
dozen monosyllabic locutions articulated as imperfectly as
possible. But let me stop for Heaven's sake if not for yours.
My letters added to your work will bring you down with
brain fag. Love of the best to all.

Your loving sister
A. J.

I meant to say how glad I was of your legacy but it all seems
so in the blue. I only wish our plans were reversed if the will
stands. I was very grateful for the 'griminess' of Father's style
the 'raciness' which 'belittles' while it 'individualizes' shows
genius. What started up the chirrup at this date?

---

[184] *Betty Leicester* had been published in 1889.

[185] John Gorham Palfrey (1796–1886) was a clergyman and historian. He
wrote *The History of New England* (4 volumes, 1858–75).

To Sara Sedgwick [Harvard, MS 1446]

11 Hamilton Terrace
Leamington

17 March 1890

My dear Sara

You must be wondering why I have not acknowledged the flowers – but the truth is that I must reveal the melancholy fact that none have as yet arrived. Your note came by noon on Friday and I waited in eager and grateful expectation for the box but all in vain! It has gone on a little excursion somewhere I suppose, isn't it too bad that they should have perished suffocated in a box? I am just as grateful for your kind thought in sending them, however. Would it seem grasping, à la lady Shrewsbury, should I insinuate, 'try again?'

I have been meaning to write for some time, but my lazy life involves a certain amount of busy-ness, and in my stagnant career between Nurse and Clarkey what have I to relate?

I am very grieved to hear that your dear Aunt is still so ill. What a wonderful constitution she has, she can hardly after such an illness recover sufficient strength to have much comfort I should fear. Henry tells me that a recent telegram, private, doesn't give much hope of Mr Lowell's recovery. Did you know that the Lincoln son was very brilliant in his scientific promise? It seems almost a personal loss to have the name die out, doesn't it?

To our immense relief poor Cousin Henry Wyckoff, who has been lying paralysed, motionless and speechless for more than a year, died three weeks ago. He had a large amount of accumulated income which he has willed in an admirable way, your humble servant coming in for a small amount, but we are in fear that the nephew, or rather his depraved wife will make a rumpus and go to law. As she will now be in possession of $1,500,000 this is hard to swallow. She spends all her time betting on race-courses. Henry came on the 10th. He seems well and cheerful and has lent me his flat for the season and is going on the Continent himself. Nurse and I will probably go up for the third Drawing Room. I should like to have you present me so prepare your train and feathers, to say nothing of the spine of your back!

Two mild and ancient ladies were calling on Mrs Kemble who proposed that their niece should bring her banjo, fiddle or some instrument of torture and play to her, whereupon Mrs K (Mrs Kemble) with much emphasis said that her health would not permit of her listening, when one of the ill-starred pair said, 'oh, but she would have no objection to come on the chance of your being well enough to hear her'. 'The objection would not be *Hers* but *Mine!*' Complete prostration of mild and ancient ladies.

What a curious story of Captain Beaumont's origin. Given the Buen's 'tis rather virtuous in them to have allowed the fair Mary to marry him.

But I must cease, believe me, dear Sara, as ever.

Yours affectionately
A. J.

To Edwin Godkin   [Harvard, MS 1449]

11 Hamilton Terrace
Leamington

20 June 1890

My dear Mr Godkin

You made me very happy yesterday. When I looked at the address on the book I thought it looked very much like your hand-writing and later your kind note confirmed my hopes most agreeably. Thank you greatly for your good thought in sending it to me, I had meant to get it from Mudie but now the reading of it will be doubled in interest and value. I am indeed a strong Home Ruler – how could I be anything else under your enlightened leading? – the *Nation* is my weekly safety-valve for seeing only that hybrid creature, the virtuous(!) Unionist, I go through much internal anguish, my politics being strictly feminine and emotional.

Thank you most warmly for proposing to spare me some of your precious hours, but I could not put such a tax upon your philanthropy. I am too uncertain a creature to be able to count upon myself from day to day and happinesses are even more destructive to my old bones than griefs, and surely seeing you would be a great happiness in this alive land, for truly, how unspeakably the lengthening of memories in common endears our old friends.

Harry *is* good! *bon comme le pain* (not, however, as they knead it in Britain) and the staff, of course, of my life. He writes that he is enjoying your 'impressions' greatly and I am sure that having you with him is a great pleasure.

Hoping that the sun, which you must have brought over in your portmanteau, will continue to shine upon you and grow any *à l'Anglaise*, believe me with all good wishes

Very gratefully and sincerely yours

A. J.

To Edwin Lawrence Godkin   [Harvard, MS 1450]

11 Hamilton Terrace
Leamington

4 July 1890

Dear Mr Godkin

Should it seem the duty of a true patriot to print the enclosed in the *Nation*, please do so, if, on the contrary, 'tis too frivolous for that valuable weekly, please tear it up!–: confident, in either case, of the unalterable friendship of

Yours very sincerely

Alice James
True Considerateness.

TO THE EDITOR OF THE NATION:

Sir: For several years past I have lived in provincial England. Although so far from home, every now and then a transatlantic blast, pure and undefiled, fans to a white heat the fervour of my patriotism.

This morning, most appropriately to the day, a lady from one of our Eastern cities applied to my landlady for apartments. In the process of telling her that she had no rooms to let, the landlady said that there was an invalid in the house, whereupon the lady exclaimed: 'In that case perhaps it is just as well that you cannot take us in, for my little girl, who is thirteen, likes to have plenty of liberty and to scream through the house.'

Yours very truly,
Invalid.
England, 4 July 1890[186]

To Frances Morse   [Harvard, MS 1520]

South Kensington Hotel
Queen's Gate Terrace
London S.W.

24 November 1890

My dearest Fanny

Katharine got back from Rugby the day before yesterday and told me of the great event that had taken place in your household. I must send you a line to try and tell you how my heart goes out to you in tenderest love and sympathy. We know none of the details but I am anxiously hoping that the change came easily for him and that you have not had the impotent watching of suffering added to the wrench of loss. How I wish that I could see you, if only for a moment and

[186] Alice's letter was published in *The Nation*, 17 July 1990.

learn at a glance how it has come to you, whether the shock and surprise obscure all else, or whether its blessed naturalness and simplicity encase you about with strength to see its true proportions. I cannot say anything that will help or comfort you, but you know all that my heart holds of affection. I am very anxious to hear how your poor, dear Mother bears the shock, I am afraid the strain will be very hard for her. If you think she would like to read the enclosed please give it to her. Give dear Mary and Harry warmest love and most sympathetic greetings.

I am ashamed of sending such dry husks but you will understand darling Fanny, how juicy they would be could we speak spiritually.

Your grieving and loving
Alice J.

To Alice H. James [Harvard, MS 1464]

South Kensington Hotel
Queen's Gate Terrace
London S.W.

26 November 1890

DICTATED TO EMILY ANN BRADFIELD

Dear Alice

I am going to ask of you a sisterly favour, that you should tell us of any favourable notices there may be of William's book, as we are quite out of the way of getting any here.[187] Our absorbing interest just now is of course Harry's dramatic debut at the end of next month, which I suppose you have heard of by now. In case you have not, I will say that it is 'The American' dramatized, to be brought out by the Compton's at Stockport, which is the Brighton of Liverpool,

[187] William's *Principles of Psychology* had been published in 1890.

and their best provincial audience. It is commercially most important that this should not be spoken of before its production.[188]

I have been on tenterhooks about it for a year and a half now. If it succeeds at all, it will be a very brilliant success, and a very interesting illustration of the law that you can't hasten the moment, in any development.

In first reading the play, the impression of the perfection of its stage mechanism is quite overwhelming, and astonishing as a first effort, every word seems to act itself. The movement is very rapid and direct, the dialogue very 'bright', and emanating from the whole a subtle human beauty. The public density is of course an immeasurable quantity so we must not let our hopes run too high.

How Harry, Katharine, and I are to live through the first night I have no idea. There is little change in my state, the only variety in the day being the varying degrees of discomfort, and I find much entertainment therein. I am working away as hard as I can to get dead as soon as possible, so as to release Katharine; but this play of Harry's makes a sad complication, as I don't want to immerse him in a deathbed scene on his 'first night', too much of an aesthetic incongruity! The trouble seems to be there isn't anything to die of, but there are a good many jokes left still, and that's the main thing after all.

Love to all,
Your affectionate sister
A. J.
(E. A. B.)

---

[188] Edward Compton's production of Henry James's dramatization of *The American* for Compton Comedy Company.

From Katharine Loring   [Harvard, MS 1492]
To William James

London

30 July 1891

Dear William

Alice tried to write to you for three days, but had finally to take refuge in dictation.

Since I wrote to you, Dr Baldwin made another inspiring visit with no new result – Alice discussed her case and her demise with him as if she were talking about Queen Elizabeth, and he as well as Sir Andrew must have thought 'preparation' unnecessary.[189]

Dr Baldwin is convinced that the potent cancer is in the liver; a pain under the point of A.'s right shoulder blade strengthens his belief. Although the pain is intermittent – he judged of the case very much by Alice's appearance – an 'earthy hue' in the complexion, which is really quite marked – sometimes more, sometimes less; when more I had supposed – to her biliousness. He said this cancer of the liver is as a rule painless.

The pain in the breasts which was so bad is mitigated greatly by the morphine which is acting well – the sore ache cannot be much helped, but Alice begs me to remember to tell you that she does not suffer all the time and I assure you that we have much joking; as her letter to you proves.

Harry seems to be extraordinarily content at Kingstown.

Give my love to Alice and believe me,

Always most sincerely
Katharine P. Loring

---

[189] Alice James had been diagnosed as having breast cancer. She wrote in her *Diary*: 'To him who waits, all things come! My aspirations may have been eccentric, but I cannot complain now that they have not been brilliantly fulfilled. Ever since I have been ill, I have longed and longed for some palpable disease.' (p. 206)

To William James   [Harvard, MS 1492]

41 Argyll Road
Kensington, W.

30 July 1891

DICTATED TO KATHARINE LORING

My dearest William

A thousand thanks for your beautiful and fraternal letter, which came, I know not when, owing to Katharine's iron despotism. Of course I could have wanted nothing else, and should have felt, notwithstanding my 'unsentimentality' very much wounded and incomprise, had you walked round and not up to my demise.

It is the most supremely interesting moment in life, the only one in fact, when living seems life, and I count it as the greatest good fortune to have these few months so full of interest and instruction in the knowledge of my approaching death. It is as simple in one's own person as any fact of nature, the fall of a leaf or the blooming of a rose, and I have a delicious consciousness, ever present, of wide spaces close at hand, and whisperings of release in the air.

Your philosophy of the transition is entirely mine and at this remoteness I will venture upon the impertinence of congratulating you upon having arrived 'at nearly fifty' at the point at which I started at fifteen! – 'Twas always thus of old, but in time, you usually, as now, caught up.

But you must believe that you greatly exaggerate the tragic element in my commonplace little journey; and so far from ever having thought that 'my frustrations were more flagrant than the rule', I have always simmered complacently in my complete immunity there from. As from early days the elusive nature of concrete hopes shone forth, I always rejoiced that my temperament had set for my task the attainment of the simplest rudimentary ideal, which I could carry about in my pocket and work away upon equally in shower as in sunshine, in complete security from the grotesque obstructions supposed to be life, which have indeed, only strengthened the sinews to whatever imperfect accomplishment I may have attained.

You must also remember that a woman, by nature, needs much less to feed upon than a man, a few emotions and she is satisfied: so when I am gone, pray don't think of me simply as a creature who might have been something else had neurotic science been born; notwithstanding the poverty of my outside experience I have always had a significance for myself, and every chance to stumble along my straight and narrow little path, and to worship at the feet of my Deity, and what more can a human soul ask for?

This year has been one of the happiest I have ever known, surrounded by such affection and devotion, but I won't enter into details, as I see the blush mantle the elderly cheek of my scribe, already. – We are smothered in flowers from kind friends: Annie Richards has been perfect in her constant and considerate friendship, that you must remember in the years to come, her atrophied cousin of Basset is incroyable![190]

You can't imagine the inspiring effect of Baldwin, from amid your surroundings.[191]   Ansoni, Conn., pur sang! emitting a theory about you from every pore, grasping you as a whole, instead of as a stomach or a dislocated elbow, after the fashion of the comatose creature sicklied o'er with bed-side manner, manufactured by the wholesale here.   The soothing nature of his imaginative manipulations after the succession of bruises administered by the anchylosed joints to which I have been exposed of late years, has been most restorative.

Give much love to Alice and to all the household, great and small.

Be sure, please, to give my love to Henrietta Child and to thank her for her sweet and pretty letter, and my love to Mrs Child, too.

---

[190] Sara Sedgwick Darwin.

[191] Dr William Wilberforce Baldwin (1850–1910) was an American expatriate physician who practised in Florence and was a friend of Henry James.

Your always loving and grateful sister

Alice James

P.S. I have many excellent and kind letters, but the universal tendency 'to be reconciled' to my passing to the summer land, might cause confusion in the mind of the uninitiated![192]

To Frances Morse   [Harvard, MS 1521]

41 Argyll Road,
Kensington, W.

5 August 1891

DICATED TO KATHARINE LORING

My dearest Fanny

I have been trying for the last weeks to be able to write to you with my own goose-quill, but I have now left such hopes behind: you will, however, be able to hear through the hand of Katharine the quavering chirp of Alice. I send a thousand thanks for your lovely letters, all your expressions of affection deeply touched my heart although I felt that they reflected the generous subject much more than they were deserved by the unworthy object. But we are both of us sure that all that is best in our long and happy friendship will never perish.

I feel selfish in rejoicing over my easier lot, leaving all you good people to struggle under the dreary burdens and illusive pleasures. Thank you very much for the kind thought of sending me Mary's sketch, I think there is great delicacy and refinement in the expression and it gives me great pleasure to have it.

I want you to know, directly from us, just what my condition is: Sir Andrew Clark, when he examined me, beside

---

[192] The summer land was a term used for the afterlife by members of the Society for Psychical Research.

the trouble in my heart, said that a lump, that we had felt in my breast, since February, was a tumour, about which he could then give no decided opinion.[193] A little while ago, Dr Baldwin of Florence, told us that it is unmistakeably a cancer, which explains very satisfactorily to us, my long, slow decline, and, at times, extreme distress – for which, however, he has given us many alleviations, in true Yankee fashion, and has changed our outlook for the next few months.

We have not spoken about it before, because one dreads imposing the details of one's degenerate state on such sympathetic hearts; I now inflict it only on you and two or three others, one shrinks so from parsimonious gossip, but I hated the thought that you might hear it accidentally, for you must know that it sounds so much worse than it is. I have every alleviation, blessing, and consolation.

Tell your mother that we are enjoying the garden immensely, and it does Katharine the greatest credit; for she has worked it all herself, having had a man, only to cut the grass; our poppies are exquisite.

Give a great deal of love to Lucy when you write, and tell her I am so glad of her happy future, but abnormal as it will seem to her, I think I have the better lot: the Spouse is, of course, included in this message.

With loads of love to your mother and thanks for her letters and to the sweet Mary and her husband, believe me, as always, your loving

Alice James

---

[193] Sir Andrew Clark (1847–1913), cancer specialist. Alice wrote in her *Diary*: 'Sir Andrew is doubtless good and kind at bottom, but they are all terrible, with that globular manner, talking by the hour without saying anything.' (p. 226)

To William James   [Harvard, MS 1493]

41 Argyll Road
Kensington, W.

2 December 1891

DICTATED TO EMILY ANN BRADFIELD

Dear William

Supposing that your being is vibrating with more or less curiosity about the great hypnotic experiment on Camden Hill, I report progress.[194] As far as pain goes the result is nil, save on four occasions the violent resuscitation of a dormant toothache, a wretched dying nerve which demands an agony of its own, impatient of waiting for, or too vain to lose itself in the grand mortuary moment so near at hand. What I do experience, is a calming of my nerves and a quiescent passive state, during which I fall asleep, without the sensation of terror which have accompanied that process for so many years, and I sleep for five or six hours, uninterruptedly. But then, I slept like a dormouse all last year before taking morphia. Katharine has very much better results than 'Tuckums',* that is as long as she remains silent and operates only by the gesture; but when she with solemn majesty addresses herself to the digestive Boreas and with persuasive accents suggest calmness and serenity of demeanour, cachinnation is the sole resource.

We were fortunate in our ignorance, to have fallen upon an experienced doctor as well as a hypnotist. He seems to be much penetrated with my abnormal susceptibility and says that to put me actually to sleep would be a very risky experiment. He seems to look upon the reckless use of it as

---

[194] Camden Hill in Kensington was where Alice and Katharine were living. William had suggested Alice consult the hypnotist Dr Charles Lloyd Tuckey, author of *Psych-Therapeutics: or Treatment by Hypnotism and Suggestion*. Alice wrote in her *Diary*: 'this vast field of therapeutic possibilities is opened up to me, just at the moment when I have passed far beyond the workings of their beneficent laws.' (p. 222)

absolutely criminal. He is only coming once this week and then he will die, of course, a natural death. My pains are too much a part of my substance to have any modifications before the spirit and the flesh fall asunder. But I feel as if I had gained something in the way of a nerve pacifier and one of the most intense intellectual experiences of my life. Too tired for another word – Love to all.

Alice
P.S. Tuckey is a white soul and sheds a gentle social radiance which has made grateful the various occasions.

* meaning Lloyd Tuckey her hypnotizer. W. J. [in W. J.'s hand].

To Frances Morse   [Harvard, MS 1522]

41 Argyll Road,
Kensington, W.

5 December [1891]

DICTATED TO EMILY ANN BRADFIELD

My dearest Fanny

I sent Mary a little while ago, a line *a propos* of the son, whom you so kindly told me had just taken upon himself the burden of existence – how interesting to compare with him the point of view, and how should we wish for an exchange of generations! But you have been in my mind as the person chiefly concerned, for doesn't the Aunt bear the heat and brunt of the battle and where is the Aunt-essence so perfectly embodied as in thee, my beloved spinster?

I send thanks from my heart for all the loving words and memories which you have addressed to my unworthiness and I should return them multiplied a hundredfold, were I not a paralysed dictator. Don't let the 'sound' of us reverberate within your imagination. The echo of our ills as it is tossed from billow to billow on its long journey must fall with the most exaggerated magnitude upon your too sympathetic ear. It is also natural and simple and nothing comes to which we are not adequate, save when morphia destroying pain tilts us from the philosophic attitude all too suddenly; but under the hypnotic suggestion, or rather pawings of an amiable necromancer I have regained all my native dignity. You will be glad to hear that Katharine grows fat under all her harassments, and keeps us constantly jovial by her relations with the outside world, which however, are sadly curtailed by my unbridled demands upon her. Best love to your mother, Mary, and Harry, and all the good.

How I should like a look at you, although I am sure that this even could not add to the sense of unity and understanding, an understanding to grow even more perfect as the mists vanish before the glories so close about us, my long and always to be loved friend.

Farewell and God bless you
Alice

To William James   CABLE[195]

London

5 March 1892

Tenderest love to all farewell am going soon.

Alice

---

[195] Alice died in the afternoon of 6 March. Katharine took her ashes back to Cambridge where she is buried in Cambridge cementery beside the graves of her parents.

ALSO AVAILABLE FROM THOEMMES PRESS

Her Write His Name

This series makes available the forgotten works of neglected women writers whose literary contributions have been overshadowed by those of a more famous male relative. These diverse and intriguing authors can now be valued in their own right and not for the insight they give to the work of men whose name they share.

New introductions provide the social context for these writings and explain why these authors should now be allowed to shine in their own right.

Old Kensington *and* The Story of Elizabeth
Anne Isabella Thackeray
With a new introduction by Esther Schwartz-McKinzie
ISBN 1 85506 388 3 : 496pp : 1873 & 1876 editions : £17.75

Shells from the Sands of Time
Rosina Bulwer Lytton
With a new introduction by Marie Mulvey Roberts
ISBN 1 85506 386 7 : 272pp : 1876 edition : £14.75

Platonics
Ethel Arnold
With a new introduction by Phyllis Wachter
ISBN 1 85506 389 1 : 160pp : 1894 edition : £13.75

The Continental Journals 1798-1820
Dorothy Wordsworth
Edited with a new introduction by Helen Boden
ISBN 1 85506 385 9 : 472pp : New edition : £17.75

Her Life in Letters
Alice James
Edited with a new introduction by Linda Anderson
ISBN 1 85506 387 5 : 320pp : New : £15.75

Also available as a 5 volume set : ISBN 1 8556 384 0
Special set price : £70.00

For Her Own Good – A Series of Conduct Books

Cœlebs in Search of a Wife
Hannah More
With a new introduction by Mary Waldron
ISBN 1 85506 383 2 : 288pp : 1808–9 edition : £14.75

Female Replies to Swetnam the Woman-Hater
Various
With a new introduction by Charles Butler
ISBN 1 85506 379 4 : 336pp : 1615–20 edition : £15.75

A Complete Collection of Genteel and Ingenious Conversation
Jonathan Swift
With a new introduction by the Rt Hon. Michael Foot
ISBN 1 85506 380 8 : 224pp : 1755 edition : £13.75

Thoughts on the Education of Daughters
Mary Wollstonecraft
With a new introduction by Janet Todd
ISBN 1 85506 381 6 : 192pp : 1787 edition : £13.75

The Young Lady's Pocket Library, or Parental Monitor
Various
With a new introduction by Vivien Jones
ISBN 1 85506 382 4 : 352pp : 1790 edition : £15.75

Also available as a 5 volume set : ISBN 1 85506 378 6
Special Set Price: £65.00

Subversive Women

The Art of Ingeniously Tormenting
Jane Collier
With a new introduction by Judith Hawley
ISBN 1 8556 246 1 : 292pp : 1757 edition : £14.75

Appeal of One Half the Human Race, Women, Against the Pretensions of the Other Half, Men, to Retain them in Political, and thence in Civil and Domestic, Slavery
William Thompson and Anna Wheeler
With a new introduction by the Rt Hon. Michael Foot and Marie Mulvey Roberts
ISBN 1 85506 247 X : 256pp : 1825 edition : £14.75

A Blighted Life: A True Story
Rosina Bulwer Lytton
With a new introduction by Marie Mulvey Roberts
ISBN 1 85506 248 8 : 178pp : 1880 edition : £10.75

The Beth Book
Sarah Grand
With a new introduction by Sally Mitchell
ISBN 1 85506 249 6 : 560pp : 1897 edition : £18.75

The Journal of a Feminist
Elsie Clews Parsons
With a new introduction and notes by Margaret C. Jones
ISBN 1 85506 250 X : 142pp : New edition : £12.75

Also available as a 5 volume set : ISBN 1 85506 261 5
Special set price : £65.00

LINDA ANDERSON
is a Senior Lecturer in the Department of English,
Literary, and Linguistic Studies at the University of
Newcastle, England. She is the author of *Bennett,
Wells and Conrad* (1988), *Plotting Change* (1990),
and *Remembered Futures: Women and Autobiography
in the Twentieth Century* (1995). She is also one of
the editors of *Writing Women*, a creative writing
magazine and her own poetry is included in *Flambard
Introductions 2* (1995).

COVER ILLUSTRATION
Alice James at Newport, 1862
Cover designed by Dan Broughton